Chi Chi's GOLF GAMES *You Gotta Play*

Chi Chi Rodriguez
and
John Anderson

Human Kinetics

Library of Congress Cataloging-in-Publication Data

Rodriguez, Chi Chi, 1936-
[Golf games you gotta play]
Chi Chi's golf games you gotta play / Chi Chi Rodriguez and John Anderson.
p. cm.
ISBN 0-7360-4631-3 (pbk.)
1. Golf. 2. Golf—Betting. I. Anderson, John, 1965- II. Anderson, John. III. Title.
GV965 .R569 2003
796.352—dc21 2002014982

ISBN: 0-7360-4631-3

Acquisitions Editor: Martin Barnard; **Developmental Editor:** Leigh LaHood; **Copyeditor:** Erin Cler; **Proofreader:** Sue Fetters; **Indexer:** Betty Frizzéll; **Graphic Designer:** Robert Reuther; **Graphic Artist:** Sandra Meier; **Cover Designer:** Keith Blomberg; **Photographer (cover):** Mike Powell/Getty Images; **Art Manager:** Dan Wendt; **Illustrator:** Matthew Liam Brady; **Printer:** Versa Press

Human Kinetics books are available at special discounts for bulk purchase. Special editions or book excerpts can also be created to specification. For details, contact the Special Sales Manager at Human Kinetics.

Printed in the United States of America

10 9 8 7 6 5 4 3 2 1

Human Kinetics
Web site: www.HumanKinetics.com

United States: Human Kinetics
P.O. Box 5076
Champaign, IL 61825-5076
800-747-4457
e-mail: humank@hkusa.com

Canada: Human Kinetics
475 Devonshire Road Unit 100
Windsor, ON N8Y 2L5
800-465-7301 (in Canada only)
e-mail: orders@hkcanada.com

Europe: Human Kinetics
107 Bradford Road
Stanningley
Leeds LS28 6AT, United Kingdom
+44 (0) 113 255 5665
e-mail: hk@hkeurope.com

Australia: Human Kinetics
57A Price Avenue
Lower Mitcham, South Australia 5062
08 8277 1555
e-mail: liahka@senet.com.au

New Zealand: Human Kinetics
P.O. Box 105-231, Auckland Central
09-523-3462
e-mail: hkp@ihug.co.nz

Contents

Chapter 4 Singles 63

Chapter 5 Tournaments 77

Chapter 6 Side Bets 99

PART II Games for Stroke Improvement 115

Chapter 7 Fundamentals 121

Chapter 8 Off the Tee 143

Foreword

When you think of fun . . . and games on the golf course, there's really only one player that comes to mind, and that player is Chi Chi Rodriguez. Never in the history of the game has any player done more for golfers on or off the course than Chi Chi Rodriguez. From charitable contributions to hilarious clinics, Chi Chi has helped to put smiles and laughs into the game of golf like no other. He has been an inspiration to millions—from his humble beginnings to a PGA Tour champion. Chi Chi knows how to please, and he knows how to entertain.

But don't be fooled by Chi Chi's antics on the golf course. To this day, he is considered to be one of the greatest ball strikers of all time—crafting shots of all shapes and sizes. Having had the pleasure of playing with Chi Chi in many PGA Tour events, I can attest to not only his wit and humor, but also his incredible ability to make the golf ball do anything humanly imaginable.

In *Chi Chi's Golf Games You Gotta Play,* we get to peek inside the creative world of golf that is Chi Chi's.

In his book, Chi Chi brings us a game of golf that is fun, challenging, and more interesting than you've ever played before. From competitive games and side bets to simple and easy-to-understand instruction, we get to see a whole new side to the world's national pastime.

For me personally, Chi Chi has not only been a friend but a mentor, as well. He is a true gentleman in the game of life, as well as the game of golf. I can only hope that golf's future superstars appreciate the style, class, and humor of this original superstar and strive to continue Chi Chi's legacy of fun and games and—most importantly—giving.

Peter Jacobsen
Six-time PGA Tour winner
Member of Jake Trout and The Flounders
Host of The Golf Channel's
Peter Jacobsen Plugged In

"Every golfer can learn two things
from my friend Chi Chi—
how to play better golf and
how to have fun on the golf course.
Chi Chi's among the best at both of them!"

Lee Trevino

"Golf, Chi Chi, money, and you—what a foursome.
Chi Chi's Golf Games You Gotta Play
is not only good for your game
but it also gives terrific insight
into what makes Chi Chi
one of the greatest and
most loved golfers
of all time."

Dan Patrick, ESPN

"My friend Chi Chi has the greatest imagination on the golf course
that I have ever seen and now delivers a book
that will appeal to readers of all skill levels.
Enjoy Chi Chi at his best!"

John Daly

Acknowledgments

To my wife, Tamara, now that I'm done typing I can come to bed before 4:30 A.M. Thank you for your love and patience. To Collin, now that Daddy's done writing we can go play. To my dad, thanks for taking me golfing for the first time when I was 12 years old, and to my mom for loaning me her clubs. To The Doj, Lucky Dog, Higgo, Stroh, Audrey, and Cross, perhaps we'll find a course that allows a sevensome. A 635-yard par-5 thank you to the Chi Chi Rodriguez Management Group and Human Kinetics Publishing for taking a flyer on a talking head. Thanks to ESPN Inc. for allowing me to work on a project outside of television. And, finally, unrepayable gratitude to Chi Chi Rodriguez, a man and a golfer I am proud to know and whose life story inspired me every time I thought I was working too long or too hard—I wasn't—and whose golf tips I plan to put into practice immediately upon the completion of this sentence.

—John Anderson

Introduction

You're trembling. Chilled, too. It's a beautiful sun-washed summer morning, and you can't get your teeth to stop chattering. You've never played golf before, or perhaps you're a scratch player—it doesn't matter.

Standing on the lush, level, emerald-green back tee box of the first hole at The Royal and Right Old Hazeltroon Hunt, Fish, Skeet and Golf Club, you and your partners have agreed to play, just to spice things up, a two-dollar Nassau, automatic two-down press, greenies on par 3s, sandies from anywhere, birdies pay double, the snake is loose, first guy to Geiberger owes everybody an extra five bucks, and dropping golf bags in mid-backswing is not only acceptable but also encouraged.

This is fun? *you think to yourself.* Cotton-mouth pressure and I haven't even pulled a club.

You have the honors. Play away.

Relax. Forget the complicated accounting and possible loss of lunch money, and look down. As you grip and waggle your new state-of-the-art, "guaranteed to go 10 yards farther," titanium-steel-kryptonite blend driver, be thankful you are not standing over a crunched-up tin can and holding, in your still shaking hands, a golf club fashioned from the branch of a guava tree. *You* are lucky. You are, in fact, an 813-yard par-6 ahead of how Chi Chi Rodriguez started in golf.

In a game that dates back more than 600 years, Chi Chi Rodriguez is one of the most popular and colorful golfers of any generation. Known worldwide for his skill and showmanship, he's so famous that he's recognized by people who don't generally follow the sport and couldn't tell persimmon woods from metal woods from Tiger Woods. And if you want to truly enjoy 18 holes of golf, you want Chi Chi in your group.

But Chi Chi Rodriguez is not just a panama hat and a putter waiting for a sword fight; he is a Hall of Fame golfer, his 1 iron every bit the equal of his one-liners. After trading in the guava branch and tin can for more traditional clubs and balls, Rodriguez went on to win eight PGA Tour titles and claim first-place trophies in 22 more tournaments on the Senior Tour. "When I was seven years old, I saw everything through golf that I have in life," Rodriguez says. He may be no bigger than a golf pencil, standing just five feet, seven inches and weighing a mere 130 pounds, but the man can flat-out play.

In this book, he's going to teach you how to play and teach you how to improve your golf game, from tee to green. And, perhaps more important, he'll teach you how to enjoy the game of golf, from the start house to the clubhouse. Golf should be fun and can be even more fun if you have a buck or two riding on it.

But the main purpose of this book is not to turn you into Johnny Highroller or turn your Saturday mornings into a four-hour trip to the ATM. The hope is simply to end the monotony of hit it, chase it, find it, count-'em-up golf.

One way to spice up your round is to play games within the game. A second way is to just play better. Chi Chi Rodriguez will help you with both. His expertise and experience, embellished with anecdotes from the dusty streets of Puerto Rico to the finely mown fairways of Augusta National and encompassing more than 50 years in golf, will serve to amuse, enrich, and inspire golfers of all handicaps.

Horace Hutchinson, the first great Englishman in golf, believed that "you cannot learn golf from a book." Nonetheless, Hutchinson wrote a book on how to play golf, *Hints on Golf,* which was published in 1886. Authors and pros alike have been penning books about the small, dimpled ball, and how best to move it from here to there, ever since. Jones, Hogan, Nicklaus, Leadbetter, Haney, Harmon, and so on . . . it's a lot to remember.

Strange as it may sound, we want to encourage you to read less and play more. Replace studying with swinging. Make your muscles remember the moves and not rely on your brain to remember what it's read. Golf is best learned through practice and repetition. Of course, practice and repetition are boring, which is why Chi Chi has tried to replace dull drills with fun games that can accomplish the same results—*better golf.* If it's fun, it can't be practice, right? And it most certainly can't be work.

Because life is not all fun and games, this book also includes some basic instruction. Indeed, much of the second section is devoted to it. Although nearly every bad golfer wants to improve, it is impossible to do so if the bad golfer begins in a position or has rudimentary flaws that allow him or her to do nothing but play bad golf. However, even this instruction we've tried to make light-hearted and tolerable. A spoonful of sugar to make the mechanical medicine go down, so to speak.

Some of what follows may seem simple and no more than common sense. That's because for most golfers "simple" and "common sense" are the first things abandoned when a round starts to go badly; ironically, they seem to disappear even more quickly when a round starts to go exceedingly well. Try doubly hard to remember these truisms, lest you're forced to have them written out and pinned to your collared and well-pressed polo shirt before teeing off.

Above all else, golf is a community game. There's friendship in foursomes. It's strangers on the first tee and pals planting the pin on the 18th green. The games and side bets listed in this book are intended to add life to your round and your group. They provide the opportunity to pair up and work together as a team or, perhaps, to bail out a partner and then needle him or her about how bad your back hurts from carrying him or her, to mesh your driver with your pard's putter, to try a dangerous and heroic shot or settle for the smart and safe one, to succeed under pressure or fail, to be able to say something more at the end of the day than just, "I shot 83."

And just as Rogers and Hammerstein suggested in a song that "the farmer and the cowman should be friends," so, too, may we suggest that the scratch golfer and the plus-36 hacker play in harmony. They both, after all, are pasture games. Funny how often the fine player admires the jovial temperament of his struggling partner, while the struggling partner envies the fine player's game and can't figure out why he or she is so angry about being one over par at the turn.

Fine player: "I'd be even if not for that stupid @#$^★ putt back on number six."

Struggling partner: "Wow! I only lost three balls and almost broke 50. How great is that?"

We hope this book helps you both. And whichever one you are . . . *you have the honors. Play away.*

PART I

Games and Side Bets

"You should never play a round of golf for nothing."

Chi Chi Rodriguez has a theory as to why golf spoiled Mark Twain's good walk—he didn't have a game. He was, literally, just walkin', swinging a club now and again, but mostly just walkin'. The game had no action, no juice, nothing to be won or lost. If Twain had been paired with Chi Chi Rodriguez, guaranteed, the golf world would have been deprived of one its greatest quotes because Chi Chi would have had the author playing for something—money, a drink, tees, cigars or pipe tobacco, a signed copy of *The Adventures of Tom Sawyer*, perhaps. To play a round of golf for nothing is just that—nothing.

According to Rodriguez, "The greatest exercise in golf is a right-handed man reaching around to pick his wallet out of his left back pocket." Do it enough and a man either goes broke or gets better. Chi Chi Rodriguez learned to make a golf ball dance and the dollars followed.

Growing up poor in Puerto Rico made money a great motivator in Rodriguez's early golf games. "The pressure to win some when you have none to pay if you lose," says Rodriguez. And when Chi Chi began teeing it up as a kid he had none, though you couldn't tell by listening. He used to put pieces of broken glass in his pocket and then jingle the shards to make it sound as if he at least had some spare change to wager.

He definitely had no spare change at home. His father, who was raising six children on $18 a week, certainly didn't have any pay left over to stake on his son's hope of becoming the next Ben Hogan. Likewise, his son couldn't exactly build a hustler's bankroll earning the princely sum of 25 cents a bag carrying clubs at the local course. The exception came one summer day when the 12-year-old Rodriguez made the windfall sum of $1.70 for making a single loop in the morning round, followed by 18 holes in the afternoon, lugging *three bags.*

What caddying did do for the young Juan Rodriguez, however, was give him access to the course. One day a week caddies were granted playing privileges (the rest of the week he and his friends had to sneak on the course after hours), and Rodriguez competed fiercely. "Every golf shot I hit I thought about how much I wanted to eat," he says. He dreamed just as aggressively and told his friends that one day he would play with, and beat, the likes of his heroes Hogan and Sam Snead. "They told me I was a stray dog dreaming about pork chops," says Chi Chi. "Even my own father nicknamed me 'El Millonario' because of my dreams. But my father, he did not understand golf. When I was 16 and he found out I had broken the course record at Berwind Country Club where I caddied, he said, 'Well, he better fix it because I don't have money to buy another one.'"

The stakes in his early golf games seem laughably insignificant now, but those nickel-a-hole bets (the price of a loaf of bread at the time) eventually allowed Chi Chi to play his way out of the caddie yard and the sugarcane fields, and eventually onto the PGA Tour. From Poor Street to Wall Street is how the former caddie describes his ascent from poverty to prosperity.

Having grown up in poverty, Chi Chi Rodriguez has no desire to see any golfer lose ground and make his trip in reverse—from prosperity to poverty. Playing for something is great; leaving with nothing is not. Winning is what everyone aims to do during any round, but set a limit on what you might be willing to lose, just in case. Do it in the locker room or the driving range or on the first tee, but don't hit a ball until the bet and any possible debt are settled.

USGA Policy on Gambling According to *The Rules of Golf*, 2002-2003 Edition

The USGA does not object to informal wagering among individual golfers or teams of golfers when the players in general know each other, participation in the wagering is optional and limited to the players, the sole source of the money won by the players is advanced by the players on themselves and their own teams, and the amount of money involved is such that the primary purpose is the playing of the game for enjoyment.

As printed in *The Rules of Golf*, as approved by the United States Golf Association and the Royal and Ancient Golf Club of St. Andrews, Scotland.

The stakes can be anything from pennies to dimes to dollars. Play for a round of drinks or dinner after the round. Bet for bragging rights or barroom beers. Ante up a shirt from the pro shop or simply a sleeve of balls. Just never gamble beyond your comfort zone, and don't gamble to the point of hurting the other person(s). Golf is equal parts athletic event and social event—don't ruin the mood by bankrupting opponents or harassing them when they're down on their luck. Golfers playing poorly feel bad enough about their game and wallet without the other side having to remind and rib them about it. Win graciously.

Likewise, losers should take it well and pay up as soon as possible. It's the polite and sporting thing to do. Golfers remember good partners. After a while, Bobby Look-How-Bad-I'm-Beating-You, Nicky Needler, Johnny I'll-Owe-Ya, and Paul Pay-Ya-Later run out of friends and games. Don't join their foursome. Hustlers and sandbaggers are both poor sports and poor partners.

Nobody's quite sure why golf seems to lend itself to betting. Is it the pace of the game? The routine? The amount of time it takes up? I'm sure an occasional wager is made at the bowling alley, softball diamond, or gym but certainly not with the prevalence you find at the local club or muni. People can get fresh air and fresh-cut grass mowing their lawn, but they don't gamble on it, although my father used to have quite a competition going with our neighbor across the street to see who could grow the thickest and greenest Kentucky bluegrass in all of northeast Wisconsin. Pity the poor 10-year-old John Kenneth Anderson who took a divot out of *that* lawn with his mother's Spalding Lady Classics. No, most likely golf and gambling are agreeable because it's a game without much action, so action needs to be introduced. I read somewhere (three pages back, maybe?) that if you're not wagering you're just walkin'.

The first part of the book lists and explains some of Chi Chi's favorite golf games. Some are famous and familiar. Others are obscure and a little odd. Try them one at a time. Combine a couple of them for more complicated fun. Try 'em all eventually.

And, if you're looking for the secret to finding a guy you might be able to beat, don't look for a bad swing or bad slacks. "Look for the guy with a new grip on his ball retriever," says Chi Chi, "or head covers on his irons."

chapter **1**

The Classics

You've probably heard of them all and played in most—that's why they're considered the Classics. Their names are known at courses in every country and golf clubs on every continent. They have a language all their own and are understood in all corners, a universal system of mathematics and accounting that requires only a three-inch-long pencil and scorecard. These games can forge friendships among strangers and ruin relationships made in childhood.

Because most of these games require a partner, Chi Chi Rodriguez suggests teaming with someone who can "drive the ball long and straight, hit lots of greens, and putt like butter." In the event the Tour pro or a scratch-shooting neighbor described isn't handy, then "find a guy who can make a 15-footer every time," says Rodriguez. "Dropping putts cures everything. It gives your team confidence, and it wounds the other guys. Putters can play with anybody." It also helps to get a partner with good vision, "'cause sometimes it's easier to look for lost balls with two sets of eyes," says Chi Chi. In team games, one is not half of two—two are halves of one. Get a good partner and a Classic game, and make your four- or five-hour round worth the walk or ride.

Nassau

Golf's classic and most popular bet. A Nassau is really three wagers in one. The front 9 holes make up the first bet, the back 9 the second, and the 18-hole total makes up the third. The point or dollar value for each bet is generally equal and set before the round. A two-dollar Nassau is $2 to the winner of the front 9, $2 to the winner of the back 9, and $2 to the winner of the overall match. This bet is generally offered on the first tee with a player merely asking "Two, two, and two?" of his opponents. The round is scored at match play, with the better of the partners' two scores counting for the team. If team A wins the front 9 holes 3 and 2 and team B wins the back 9 holes 1 up, team A wins the third bet, 2 and 1.

Then it gets complicated. The bet has many variations and expansions. Most often a player or team falling behind can "press" the bet, meaning a new (fourth) bet begins at that point. The other team or player isn't obligated to accept the press, but not to do so is the sportsmanship equivalent of bringing a bouquet of dandelions to the Rose Bowl. In many cases, the bet is pressed automatically when one side is down two holes. An "automatic" two-down press can lead to scorekeeping that only an accountant can love as the presses and bets mount throughout the round. Be sure to have somebody in the group or the clubhouse who can work the math at the end of the match.

Rumor has it that the back nine didn't exist until Mary, Queen of Scots lost eight pounds sterling off a double press one Saturday morning at St. Andrews

Hole	1	2	3	4	5	6	7	8	9	
Gold	400	426	450	383	183	393	550	190	590	
Hdcp	13	7	1	17	15	9	5	11	3	
Par	4	4	4	4	3	4	5	3	5	
Team A - Player 1 Hdcp (2)	4	4	5/4.	3	3	4	5	3	5	
Player 2 (15)	5/4.	5/4.	6/5.	4	5/4.	4/3.	7/6.	4/3.	6/5.	
Team B - Player 3 (0)	4	3	5	4	4	3	5	2	4	
Player 4 (9)	6	4/3.	4/3.	4	5	4/3.	5/4.	3	6/5.	
Team A								P		
Team B	AS	1 up	2 up	1 up	AS	AS	1 up	2 up	3 up 1 up	

El Legado Golf Resort
Home of Chi Chi Rodriguez

Team B wins 2 bets on the front side.
The 9 = 3 up; the press = 1 up.
Team B also leads the 18 at the turn 3 up.

Date ____________

Scorer ____________ Attest ____________

continued ☞

and immediately demanded that the Royal Surveyor lay out a second nine holes so that she could attempt to win her money back.

Despite what appears to be a small sum of money wagered in a $2 Nassau on the first tee, a total of $6, when pressed and repressed and double pressed, can quickly become a big hit. The $2 pressed once makes $4 and, pressed again, adds a third $2 bet to the front 9 for $6. Press the entire side, and it becomes a $12 wager before a player's even gotten to the 10th tee. If the back side goes as poorly, that's another $12, for a total of $24; and if you get bold and press the entire match on 18 and lose, that's pretty much a $50 shot ($48) right there. Again, it's a good idea to set a limit on total loses before the match starts.

"On one occasion Doug Sanders and I, at Augusta, won $400 on a $2 Nassau. Sanders wanted to play these two fellas a thousand-dollar Nassau at Augusta, but they wouldn't bite. Doug told me before we started it felt like [he could shoot] a 63. He made a triple bogey on number 12 and still shot 63, by himself. I made birdie, best ball we shot—58.

"Doug Sanders was the best money player I ever saw. A great player. He could drive it straighter than I putted it. People talk all about the putt he missed at the British Open, but that was for a trophy. If he had needed to make that putt for $5,000, he would've knocked it straight in the cup. He was a better golfer playing with his money than playing with other people's money." [In 1970, Sanders missed a short par putt on the 72nd hole to win the Open championship at St. Andrews. The resulting bogey dropped him into a tie with Jack Nicklaus, who won an 18-hole play-off the following day with an even par 72 to Sanders' 1-over-par 73.]

The Nassau is a great game for players of all skill levels, but only if handicaps are applied. Getting strokes on a hole helps keep the high handicapper involved in the action. Knowing that his or her gross 7/net 5 is as good as the opposition's straight 5 can add some confidence and extra concentration to the game. Generally, playing a Nassau doesn't add any extra time to a foursome's round, although it could potentially take a while to add it all up once the group is back at the clubhouse.

Handicaps

A handicap is the best way to level the playing field, although for a small wager some golfers will forgo giving strokes and offer to play left-handed, one-handed, or from their knees. If you don't have a handicap, work with your club, public or private, to establish one. Handicaps are essential because they make it possible for all players to compete equally on any course from any tees.

If you have to make an estimate, take your average score and subtract par for the course. Check the course rating from the tees you'll be playing, and give yourself another stroke for every rating point over par. As an example, a golfer who typically shoots 90 plays to roughly an 18 on a par 72 course (90 – 72 = 18). If it's a tougher course with a rating of, say 74.1, add two more strokes, for a handicap estimate of 20.

A 20-handicapper will get 20 strokes during a round—one stroke on all 18 holes and a second stroke on the two hardest holes. A 7-handicap gets seven strokes on the seven toughest holes, three on one side and four on the other. Each hole's difficulty is ranked along the handicap line on the scorecard (so that's what those arbitrary numbers are!).

Groups of players can play their handicaps off scratch or off the best player in the group. Scratch means all golfers play to their full handicap index. To adjust off the best player in the group, take the low handicap and make it zero; subtract that handicap from all other players. In a group made up of a 4, 12, 7, and 19, the adjusted handicaps would be 0, 8, 3, and 15.

Medal Play Games

Hit 'em and add 'em up. Medal, or stroke, play is how we all learned to play golf—18 individual hole scores and one grand total at the end of the round. It's the game you and your golfing friends probably still play every time you tee it up. It's the one on your television set almost every week. It's the way they keep score at the Masters, the U.S. Open, the British Open, and the PGA Championship. It's also a major bore! The quickest way to liven up a medal-play round is to add a few of the side bets listed in chapter 6 (sandies, greenies, putts), but a more creative way is to make each shot count for cash.

As in a Nassau, players can make a simple bet on total strokes on the front side, the back side, and the 18. Golfers can also steal an idea from the card sharks and put a value, say a nickel, on each stroke. My 87 to Chi Chi's 70 has me out $.85 (17 × .5 = .85).

Because golfers always seem to be obsessed with breaking some barrier—100, 90, 80, or 70—choose your goal and play your partner in an Over/Under. I'll bet you I can break 80. You pay me a buck for every stroke I'm under 80. I'll give you a quarter for every shot over 80. This is an ideal way for golfers of all handicaps to play together. No pressure to try to beat the other person, just the golfer, the course, and a number.

"Only fools live in the past. In medal, a golfer has to learn to immediately forget the last shot, good or bad, and move on to the next one. Compliment yourself on a ball well hit or scold yourself for a poor shot, but then move on quickly. You've got to get out of the past. Put a price on each swing, and you'll learn to concentrate and scramble around a golf course to save every shot. Even on a bad day, it's better to lose only a little money, and every stroke you save is change that stays in your pocket. Play every shot as if it is important, because it is."

Chi Chi Rodriguez's Career PGA Tour Wins

1963—Denver Open
1964—Lucky International
1964—Western Open
1967—Texas Open
1968—Sahara Invitational
1972—Byron Nelson Classic
1973—Greater Greensboro Open
1979—Tallahassee Open

Skins

Playing for skins is not a new concept, but the game exploded in popularity about 20 years ago when some television executive was looking to fill airtime opposite football on Thanksgiving weekend. Voilà! What was simple counter-football filler became a full-blown hit. The format and big-name foursomes soon had everybody at every club seeing that golf beauty is indeed only skin deep.

In Skins, each of the 18 holes is assigned a value. The value can be the same for all 18 or can escalate every three or six holes. As an example, a foursome can play all 18 holes for a dollar, or they can play the first six holes for a buck, holes 7 through 12 for 2 bucks, and the 13th through 18th holes for 3 bucks apiece.

Scoring is simple—the player with the lowest score wins the skin. If two or more players share the lowest score, the skin carries over, and the value of the next hole increases by that amount. Holes continue to carry over until a player wins a hole outright. If 18 is a carryover, players can either play another hole or, in a more practical and time-saving solution, chip closest to the pin or putt for the final skin.

Skins should be played with full handicaps to give all players involved a fair shot at the pot. Those faint of heart can forgo carryovers and merely let holes that are tied and their dollar amounts go unclaimed.

Here are some variations to the standard Skins game. Good players may require a par or birdie to win a skin. Bogeys or worse force a carryover. Other groups insist on a "validation" of a skin, meaning the player who wins a skin must either win or tie the next hole to claim his or her prize. This variation makes for some big money late on the back nine but can make the round stale for most of the day.

You might be surprised to know that despite all his appearances in the Senior Skins Game; his two wins in the event; his knack for entertaining a crowd; and his ability to hit a low, screeching 4-iron hook 200 yards around a saguaro cactus and between Jack, Arnie, and Gary all while wearing a wireless microphone, Chi Chi Rodriguez is not a big fan of Skins games.

"On the TV it's hard 'cause I think it's a little better if everybody wins something. So, maybe you feel some compassion and try more to play to entertain than to win," Chi Chi says. "The money we play for is not ours. It comes from the networks or the sponsors, so there's not so much pressure. Now if it's for my money, or yours, I will play very hard."

Foursomes

A staple on the first two days of the Ryder Cup, Foursomes, or Alternate Shot as it is also known, is about the only way golf is played in most clubs in Great Britain. Aha! The secret to playing a round in three hours and being back in the men's grill or pub by noon revealed—share the workload, hit only half the shots.

Foursomes is the ultimate team game in golf. One player tees off, and shots are alternated until the ball is holed. Players also alternate tee shots, with one person hitting first on the odd holes and the partner doing the chores on the evens. The game is scored at match play, and the bet can be played either straight, with the team ahead after the entire round winning, or played as a Nassau, with bets on the front 9, back 9, and the 18. Press as your prospects, confidence, and pockets allow.

Be sure to make a careful check of the scorecard before determining who hits first, you or your partner, in the rotation. If the layout of holes falls so that your big hitter can tee off on the majority of the par 5s, alter your order to account for that on the first tee. If it's not possible to get home in two on the long holes, take a look at the short ones. Are they short par 3s or longish? Do they have water or another type of forced carry? How well is the green protected?

Most often it's best to let the weaker player handle first-swing duties on the par 3s because they're more reliable with a shorter, more lofted club. But if the par 3s are tougher than a 10-penny nail, it might be better to let the A player have a go. One penalty stroke on a par 3 is much harder to erase than a poor drive, a second, or even third shot on a par 5. It seems like a simple tip, but it can save strokes. Check the card and see where your games best fit in on the course.

Golfers also must be careful in choosing a partner because Foursomes can test a friendship. Bad shots happen, and sometimes you'll be forced to hit from a bad lie, the wrong side of the fairway, or putt from above the hole. Worse yet, your ex–best buddy, so called pard'ner, fool is more like it, might leave you in the bunker, the trees, behind the port-o-let on the 6th, or with one foot in the retention pond on 13. Remember, most often your partner is as upset as you are over his bad shot, probably worse because he hit it. Keep in mind that both of you would do better if you could. Nobody goes out and deliberately tries to screw the other person.

Put the team and making the best possible score first. Don't allow your opponents the psychological luxury of hearing you bicker about how bad your back hurts from carrying your partner. Save the fighting or, hopefully,

In the 1973 Ryder Cup at Muirfield, Chi Chi Rodriguez and Lou Graham partnered in two Foursomes matches as the U.S. easily won the first matches ever played in Scotland.

good-natured barbs for after the round. "You call that a golf shot? My cat can throw up a hair ball and get it closer to the pin from 50 yards off the green."

A final note on Foursomes strategy—*always* keep an eye on your opponents' situation. In this game, you're playing them more than the course. If the opposing team plays itself into trouble, make the safe shot and force them to play heroically out of trouble, which can often lead to even more trouble. Be aware of their circumstances at all times. If they rinse an approach going for a par 5 in two, that's your cue to lay up. Take advantage if you're given an advantage. Getting handed a hole counts just the same as winning it outright. Now go out and start "ham and egging" it!

Greensomes

A modified Foursomes game, Greensomes doesn't take the driver out of a player's hands for half the round. In Greensomes, both players on a team tee off. They select the better of the two drives and then alternate shots the rest of the hole, as in Foursomes, until the ball is holed out.

Because each player gets to hit a drive, this game eliminates the preround planning of who should tee off on even holes and who should handle the odd jobs. Essentially, though, the strategy is the same as in Foursomes, and you should look for the same skills in a partner.

Despite the extra tee ball, this game should move at a fairly brisk pace, and the scores should be slightly lower because most often the second shot will be hit from a good position.

Gruesomes

This game is the less attractive, frequently Phyllis-Diller ugly, version of Greensomes. Again, both partners on a team tee off, but after both players drive, the *opponents* choose which ball has to be played for the second shot. You probably guessed this, but they generally select the poorer of the two. For that reason, it's important for both players to make a smart choice off the tee. Hit with the driver if you're feeling confident and can back it up; if not, a 3 wood or good solid 3 iron stinger off the box is a wise decision. If you're in a particularly good twosome, then both players can fire away, figuring even the second-best shot will be in a decent enough position to reach the green. As in Foursomes, after a drive is chosen, players alternate shots until the ball is holed out. Play Gruesomes and prepare yourself for high scores and long hours—this game can take some time to finish.

Four Ball

Often confused with Foursomes, a match of Four Ball features two teams of two players each playing their own ball the entire hole. Basically, everybody's just playing golf. At the end of each hole, the team score is the better of the two scores. Simple. The bet can be a Nassau or total strokes. Extra juice, or value, can be added to the game by putting a price on each swing, as explained in the medal play section earlier in this chapter. Handicaps should be applied, or twosomes can agree on the number of strokes given before the round starts. Score the game at match or medal play.

Simple strategies can help in Four Ball. Let the weaker player tee off first. Then, depending on the outcome of the shot, the stronger player can decide whether to play his tee ball safe or be more aggressive. This will also have a relaxing effect on the weaker player, knowing he has a steady ball behind him as insurance.

Play a team game on the greens, too. Players on the team don't have to putt in the normal order of farthest out to closest. The "team" is either closest or farthest away based on the closest ball to the hole. If the player closer to the hole putting for bogey can give his or her partner a "read" on a par or birdie roll, go ahead and putt in reverse order. Similarly, hole out one ball before playing the other. Knowing what score you have booked will help to determine whether the second player should charge the hole because he or she can do no worse or just get it close to make sure he or she scores better.

The game should last no longer than an ordinary round. Make sure it doesn't. Too often Seymour Shank is plumb bobbing an 18-inch putt while the group behind him is rotting on the tee or back in the fairway. If a putt's inside the leather or it's a short one for triple bogey after a hole is already won, go ahead and let 'em pick it up. Be aware of pace of play. Don't just stay up; stay ahead.

Round Robin

This modified version of Four Ball is especially fun for good friends or, better yet, complete strangers. Because three combinations of players in any foursome can be made in Round Robin, it allows all the players in the group to partner with every other player for six holes. Mingle and make money at the same time—a brilliant concept. Round Robin is a great way for players of mixed abilities to spend an afternoon. A weak player has a chance to win a bet or two, and no one player feels that he or she has to carry the day.

Picking opening partners can be done voluntarily or by tossing balls. Take each player's ball and toss it in the air. Balls landing closest to each other are partners for the first six holes. Rotate teams on the 7th tee and again on number 13. As in Four Ball, the better score in the twosome is the team score. Winning partners each receive a point. At the end of the round, add up each player's points from all 18 holes.

Hole	1	2	3	4	5	6	7	8	9	10	11	12	13	14	15	16	17	18	In	Tot	Hcp	Net
Gold	400	426	450	383	183	393	550	190	590	420	173	449	599	426	155	376	400	600				
Hdcp	13	7	1	17	15	9	5	11	3	12	14	4	10	8	18	16	6	2				
Par	4	4	4	4	3	4	5	3	5	4	3	4	5	4	3	4	4	5				
Player A	4	4	(4/3.)	4	3	5	5	(3)	(4/3.)	(4)	3	5	5	(4)	3	4	5	5/4.	38	74	3	71
Player B	(4/3.)	6/5.	6/5.	5	4/3.	(4/3.)	7/6.	5/4.	6/5.	6/5.	4/3.	6/5.	6/5.	6/5.	3	4	5/4.	6/5.	46	93	15	78
Player C	4	5/4.	5/4.	6	3	5	6/5.	3	5/4.	4	3	(4/3.)	6	5	(2)	5	6/5.	6/5.	41	83	7	76
Player D	4	4	5/4.	(3)	3	4	5	4	5	5	3	4	5	4	3	(3)	4	(4/3.)	35	72	2	70
	Teams		A &	B vs.	C &	D	Teams		A &	C vs.	B &	D	Teams		A &	D vs.	B &	C				
Scores	A&B	—	A&B	C&D	—	A&B	—	A&C	A&C	A&C	—	A&C	—	A&D	B&C	A&D	—	A&D				

Player A - 10 bets
Player B - 4 bets
Player C - 6 bets
Player D - 4 bets

El Legado Golf Resort
Home of Chi Chi Rodriguez

Date ____________ Scorer ________________ Attest ________________

If the bet is a dollar a hole and player A has 10 points; player B, 4; player C, 6; and player D, 4, then player D owes player A $6 (10 – 4) and player C $2 (6 – 4). Player B's payout is identical to player D's, and player C is out $4 to player A (10 – 6).

Best Ball

Everybody's heard of a scramble. This is it. Most often used for tournaments or golf outings, Best Ball can also be used in a foursome or a threesome. Played in teams of two or two against one in threesomes, it's like getting a team mulligan on every shot.

Partners tee off and then identify the best of the two drives and play their second shots from within a club length of the best ball. This process is repeated until the ball is holed. In Best Ball, bogeys are high crimes, and failing to birdie a par 5 is almost as sinful.

When partnering up for Best Ball, try to match a solid ball striker with a solid short-game player, or pair up a big hitter with a good putter. Try to put together an all-around golf game by combining the individual strengths of the partners. Although teaming a high handicapper with a low one might seem like a good strategy to make things even on all sides, it's really not the best plan. Invariably the double- or triple-bogey shooter gets tired of never getting to use his or her shot, especially if it's one of his or her better ones. No experience is worse than feeling that you spent all day hitting for nothing. Everybody wants more than an occasional putt to count toward helping the team. Conversely, two average or below-average players can have a ball and really challenge a better player if they go two on one in a threesome.

Best Ball can make a round considerably shorter (if two good players make a lot of birdies) or interminably longer (if two bad players are chasing balls all over the lot), so make sure to budget the extra time and keep an eye on the group behind you to make sure you're not slowing up their day.

Stableford

Popularized by the pro golfers when they began playing the modified Stableford scoring system at the PGA Tour's International Tournament in Castle Pines, Colorado, this game was originally designed for players with middle to high handicaps—in *1898!* More on that date in a minute.

The rules of the game were originally written, before the Tour "modified" them, so that bogey was the baseline score. The inventor of the system, Dr. Frank Stableford, believed that too many golfers were having too little fun and tossing away their scorecards after a few bad holes early in the round. He saw a lot of angry hackers tearing up their cards and trying to stab themselves in the neck with golf pencils, and wanted to do something to help them. He was, after all, a doctor. The point system he devised to make life easier on the links is as follows:

Eagle = 4 points
Birdie = 3 points
Par = 2 points
Bogey = 1 point
Double or worse = 0 points

The beauty here is that the worst a player can card on any given day is a big fat zero, which is far better than two big fat zeros with a one in front of them. The game really does help the average and below-average golfer enjoy a round

Hole	1	2	3	4	5	6	7	8	9	
Gold	400	426	450	383	183	393	550	190	590	
Hdcp	13	7	1	17	15	9	5	11	3	
Par	4	4	4	4	3	4	5	3	5	
Player 1 Hdcp (12)	4	5	6	5	3	4	6	4	5	42
Stableford score	+2	+1	0	+1	+2	+2	+1	+1	+2	12
with handicap	+2	+2.	+1.	+1	+2	+4.	+2.	+2.	+4.	20
Player 2 (12)	4	5	6	5	3	4	6	4	5	42
Modified Stableford	0	–1	–3	–1	0	0	–1	–1	0	–7
with handicap	0	0.	–1.	–1	0	+2.	0.	0.	+2.	2

El Legado Golf Resort
Home of Chi Chi Rodriguez

Date ______________

Scorer ____________________ Attest ____________________

because he or she can stop counting and pick up once he or she hits the double-bogey mark, one or two bad holes don't ruin an entire day, and the joy of actually making par is well rewarded.

But who was this Dr. Frank Stableford fellow, you ask? Well, until 1990 it was believed that Stableford invented his game while he was a member at the Wallasey and Royal Liverpool Golf Clubs in 1931 and that the first tournament using the doc's system was played in May 1932. But in 1990, a London journalist discovered that a Dr. F. Stableford had been a member in good standing at the Glamorganshire Golf Club in south Wales way back in 1898. And an article in the *South Wales Daily News* in September of that year reported the following at Glamorganshire's first fall meeting:

> *A special prize was given by Dr. Stableford in connection with the foregoing event, the method of scoring as follows: Each competitor plays against bogey level. If the hole is lost by one stroke only, the player scores one; if it is halved, the player scores two; if it is won by one stroke, the player scores three; if by two strokes, the player scores four. To the score thus made, one-third of the player's medal handicap is added. . . .*

After years of bickering, the fine members at Glamorganshire and Wallasey now jointly celebrate the doctor's contribution to golf. As for Stableford, he was born in 1870, began his medical career as an army surgeon in the Boer Wars, and played to as low as a 3-handicap while a member at Wallasey. Told he was going blind, and with his health failing, he committed suicide in 1959. He was 89.

The Stableford scoring system encourages risk taking because pars and birdies pay well and the cost of bogeys or worse is minimal. Grip it and rip it. Shoot for the pin. And, if you want to play it as the pros at Castle Pines do, it's 8 for a double eagle, 5 for eagle, 2 for birdie, 0 for par, –1 for bogey, and –3 for a double bogey or worse. Looking for a score to shoot at? The winner of the inaugural Stableford tournament in 1898 was W. Hastings Watson with 42 points. The winner in the 2002 International? Rich Beem with a four-round tally of 44 points.

Wolf

Here's howl to play Wolf . . . and aren't you glad your golf game is better than my pun, which was awolful?! Please, stop, the laughter's hurting my side.

Wolf is a classic four-player game that creates a different team on every hole or a gutsy one-on-three situation. An order one through four is established on the first tee and will continue to roll over through the entire round. The first player in the rotation tees off first on number 1, followed by players two, three, and four. On number 2, the second player in the rotation has honors, followed by players three, four, and one. The third player has the box on the number 3, followed by players four, one, and two. And player four leads off on hole number 4, followed by players one, two, and three. The wheel then repeats, starting with player one on the 5th hole and continues to turn over through the entire 18 holes. How the order is picked doesn't matter—by height, alphabetically, shoe size, or show of hands.

The player teeing off first on a hole is the wolf (my, what sharp teeth you have). As the wolf watches (my, what big eyes you have) the other players in the group tee off, he has the option to pick one of them as a partner on the hole, the rub being that the wolf must choose the player immediately after his tee ball. No waiting to see how all the players fare off the box before choosing. If the wolf chooses to partner with the second player, he must announce his intentions before the third player tees off. If the wolf passes on number two, he can tab player three but only before the last player hits. The same goes for the third player. If the wolf decides none of the shots are to his liking, he may go the hole alone and play against the other three.

To win a hole, the wolf and his partner, or the wolf alone, must combine to make a better ball score lower than the opposing team. A tie is a wash. A higher score, and the bet is won by the hunting team. A wolf playing alone receives double the bet if he wins and pays double *to each of the other three players* if he loses.

A brave variation of the game is to play Lone Wolf in which the first golfer on the tee announces he will play the hole solo immediately after his drive and without seeing any of the other tee shots. In Lone Wolf, the winnings are tripled, but so are losses, and again it's triple to all other players in the group. For those truly wild animals who would keep Marlin Perkins safely above in his helicopter while Jim Fowler runs through the burning forest floor, the Lone Wolf may declare his intentions to go it alone before ever putting his tee in the ground. In this case, all bets are quadrupled. Happy hunting.

All bets on tied holes may be carried over but most often are erased and started new on the next tee. Because the 17th and 18th holes are left over after four turns of the rotation, the player in last place is generally given the courtesy of teeing off first and being the wolf on the final two holes.

Wolf strategy is as much about self-confidence as it is about faith in a partner. A good player will go it alone as often as possible, especially on par 3s and 5s. Because this is a game played to full handicaps (3/4s or 2/3s for complete strangers), it helps to check to see who may be getting a stroke on the hole. Partners can be picked either to help win a hole or just to share losses, depending on your own tee ball. Hit it and howl golfers.

"I played the Wolf several times with Fuzzy [Fuzzy Zoeller's Wolf Challenge at Covered Bridge Golf Club in Sellersburg, Indiana, just outside Louisville, Kentucky]. In fact one time, due to a cancellation, Fuzzy called me while I was in midair on my way to another tournament in California. I like the Wolf event and playing with Fuzzy so much that I had my pilot make a U-turn. It was a good decision, too, because I shot 65 that day. I was so hot that on the back nine Hal Sutton would call for me as a partner before we even teed off.

"I also once had to sub for John Daly in California, and still another time a player got sick and I went to Hawaii to take his place. So now I tell tournament organizers that if they ever get into a bind they should just make a Nine Juan Juan call and I'll come to the rescue."

High–Low–Total

High–Low–Total is a bookkeeping game that is actually three matches in one on every hole. All four players in the group play their own ball at medal. The first match is between the low ball on each team, with a point going to the lower of the two scores net. The second match is between the high ball on each team, with the point, again, going to the lower of the two scores. The third match is the team total of both balls on each hole, with the lower combined score earning the point.

Any ties are split and worth one-half point or, better yet, ignored. The team with the most points at the end of the round wins the match and collects on the difference in points. Fifty-four points are available during any 18-hole match; so if team A finished with 34 points (including ties) and team B notched 20, and points are worth 50 cents apiece, each player on team B would owe \$7 (34 – 20 × .50 = 7.00).

High–Low–Total is one of the best ways to play matches when partners have a broad range of abilities. The format allows each player to focus on his or her ball and play a normal un-gimmicked round of golf, while the handicaps keep the match competitive.

Mentally, High–Low–Total can be exhausting on players because there is no letup during the round; every shot is worth something. The person playing the low ball has a fairly easy time of it, but the high-ball player must really grind not only to try to win his or her part of the match but every extra shot puts the third, or total, bet in jeopardy. Both partners must stay committed to the game and encourage each other throughout, or else valuable points will slip away.

Hole		1	2	3	4	5	6	7	8	9	
Gold		400	426	450	383	183	393	550	190	590	
Hdcp		13	7	1	17	15	9	5	11	3	
Par		4	4	4	4	3	4	5	3	5	
Player 1	Hdcp (5)	4	4	5/4.	5	5	5	4/3.	4	5/4.	
Player 2	(14)	5/4.	5/4.	5/4.	5	4	5/4.	6/5.	3/2.	5/4.	
(Team A)		H+T	—				—	L+T	L+T	H+T	⑦
Player 3	(10)	5	5/4.	5/4.	5	3	5/4.	5/4.	4	6/5.	
Player 4	(1)	4	4	4/3.	3	3	5	5	4	4	
(Team B)			—	L+T	L+T	H+L+T	—				⑦

El Legado Golf Resort
Home of Chi Chi Rodriguez

H - High: Lower of each team's high ball
L - Low: Lower of each team's best ball
T - Total: Lowest total of team's two balls

Team A = 7 points
Team B = 7 points

Date __________

Scorer __________ Attest __________

Aggregate

Aggregate is playing only the total part of a High–Low–Total game. Again, every shot can be a difference maker, so don't give up on the hole. It sounds corny, but it is true: A 9 is better than a 10, and an 8 is better than a 9, and so on. Birdies and pars are great, but most Aggregate bets are won on the high end because far more players shoot 90 than 70. Keep working the entire round—the one seemingly meaningless shot you make may save or win an entire hole.

Best Ball/Aggregate

A combination of the previous games, Best Ball/Aggregate is a two-part bet on every hole. One point is awarded to the low ball, and a second to the low-team total. Essentially all you're doing is dropping the high from High–Low–Total. Do we need to stress again the importance of every shot? Let's hope not.

The game is slightly better for high handicappers because they only have to worry about winning or losing one point. Because they rarely will be in contention for the low ball, they can focus solely on playing well for the team score. In High–Low–Total, the weaker player has to worry not only about the team but also about his or her quasi-individual match. It can be a little too much. Use full or nearly full (three-quarter) handicaps, and this game is tremendous for teams of mixed abilities.

Las Vegas

True to its name, Las Vegas is a game for high rollers, as money can switch hands in large quantities and in fast fashion. Las Vegas matches two twosomes, and the team score is a combination, not total, of each player's score. On each hole, the low ball of the team is joined with the high ball. If player A makes a four and his or her partner (player B) makes a six, the team score is 46. If the opposing team makes a pair of fives on the hole, their score is 55, and they would lose the hole by nine. Las Vegas is usually played for a dollar a point so that's $9 changing hands on a single hole. And it can get much, much worse. What if everybody made six except for player A, who managed to scramble and make that four? Now the payout is 46 to 66, and it's a $20 hit.

Adding to the pain is "flipping the bird." In this variation, a team making a birdie flips the other team's scores. So, on a par 3, if team A makes a birdie for two and a bogey for four, making a score of "24," and team B makes par and bogey, instead of a "34," team B's score is reversed to a "43," and a $10 payout is nearly doubled to $19.

Some mercy does exist in Las Vegas, and that occurs when a player makes a 10 or worse. Then the higher score gets to go up front. The easiest way to remember Las Vegas scoring is to always make the lowest possible number with the two scores. So, if your partner makes 6 and you cough up a 10, the team total is a 106 and not 610—both are pricey losses, but one borders on bankruptcy.

Hole		1	2	3	4	5	6	7	8	9	
Gold		400	426	450	383	183	393	550	190	590	
Hdcp		13	7	1	17	15	9	5	11	3	
Par		4	4	4	4	3	4	5	3	5	
Player 1	Hdcp (13)	4/3.	4/3.	5/4.	5	4	4/3.	7/6.	5/4.	6/5.	
Player 2	(6)	4	4	5/4.	4	3	5	6/5.	3	5/4.	
Team A		34✓	34✓	44	45	34	35✓	56	34	45	
Player 3	(20)	6/5.	6/5.	8/6.	6/5.	4/3.	7/6.	7/6.	4/3.	5/4.	
Player 4	(2)	4	3	4/3.	4	3	5	5	4	5	
Team B		45	35	36✓	45	33✓	56	56	34	45	
		−11	−1	+8	—	+1	−21	—	—	—	−24

+ & − figured in relation to team B

Total on front 9 = −24 points

El Legado Golf Resort
Home of Chi Chi Rodriguez

Date ______________

Scorer ______________ Attest ______________

For that reason, novice golfers and anything less than a good golfer should stay away from shaking hands on a Las Vegas bet. Even playing with full handicaps, the money can get out of hand in a hurry if you or a partner is having an off day. And good players may want to avoid this bet if they have a tendency to get loose and make a big number once in a while. A player making nothing but yawn-inducing fours and fives has a better chance than the player carding all fives and occasional threes but then tosses in an eight or nine.

You'll be able to tell a group in front of you playing Las Vegas because you'll see great outbursts of emotion, both joyful and despondent. Also, long waits will be the norm as players hole out everything and grind over putts of a foot or less. With so much at stake, every swing can mean $10 or more, and thus the pace of play tends to drag.

To play Las Vegas, a golfer needs not only the game for it but also the wallet and the stomach. In the event you have neither, go ahead and try the game, playing for a penny or dime a point. You don't necessarily have to be a Rockefeller or Vanderbilt to play Las Vegas, though it's generally a high roller's game.

Daytona

Daytona is the nasty cousin of Las Vegas. Where the method of scoring in Las Vegas is to always arrange the scores to come up with the lowest possible number, in Daytona the final number is determined in relation to par.

If one player on the team makes a par or better on the hole, then the team score is the lower combined number. If both players play bogey or worse, the scores are combined to form the highest possible number. Yikes!

As an example, on a par 4, team A makes a four and a six for a total of 46. Team B makes a five and a six for a total of 65 and a loss of $19. The result is a payout $9 more punishing than a Las Vegas, where the sums would be 46 and 56 for a $10 loss for team B.

It gets even worse if one of those awful 10s gets in the mix. If, on a par 5, team A makes a 6 and a 10, the total is a whopping 610. If team B is just one stroke better each player and makes 5 and 9, its total is a measly 59. The difference is an inheritance-killing $551. Even playing a poor man's version for a penny, a 551 difference equals $5.51, and at a nickel the figure jumps to $27.55. For that reason, as in Las Vegas, Daytona is not only for good golfers but ones with deep pockets. Both places are great vacation spots—just be careful not to finance someone else's trip!

Head Games: Picking a Partner—Temper or Talent?

Stay away from hot-tempered and ill-mannered partners. Emotional players tend to have erratic swings in both moods and scores, and their bad behavior will eventually wear you out, too. Players that curse, throw clubs, and stomp will pout before they grind it out. They may have a streak of brilliant golf in them, but eventually they'll implode and take the team down with them. People who get so involved in their own anger will forget they're supposed to be helping you.

On top of that, after a couple of outbursts, you'll be embarrassed for your partner, and you'll begin to feel bad that you and the other players are stuck with a jerk who seems to be ruining not only his or her day but everyone's. And don't think opposing teams won't pick up on a weakness of temper and turn on the heat even more. A well-timed "there's finally a good shot" or "we might be able to find that" will just help nudge Harry Hothead over the edge. Tempers can get costly when uncontrolled. Everybody gets frustrated at some point during a round, and a little mild scolding of oneself is to be expected and can even help. But don't get to the point where you boil over or play with someone who does.

chapter **2**

Groups

At 19, Chi Chi Rodriguez left Puerto Rico and joined the army. "I signed up because I knew, as a golfer, I could get special detail and continue to play," says Rodriguez. And so it was that Juan Rodriguez (the service doesn't stamp nicknames on dog tags) ended up marching in formation at Ft. Sill in Lawton, Oklahoma. Truth is, Rodriguez spent more time carrying a 3 iron than he did a rifle, and soon the best players in the area found themselves handing money over to the little brown wisp of a man with the fast swing and an even quicker wit. Somewhere in a Lawton clubhouse is a scorecard with a remarkable, and extremely profitable, course record 58 scrawled on it.

But Chi Chi never went out and worked a dishonest game in his life. Never hustled anyone, unless they were foolish enough to believe Chi Chi's claim, "I was so skinny the army used me to clean the howitzers." He let his partners know up front he was a player, and it was usually his opponents' own hubris that ended up hurting them in the wallet. "I never got a stroke in my life," says Chi Chi. "The macho man in me wouldn't let me take *no* strokes from *nobody*. I played everybody even or gave. I never took."

"I was so skinny the army used me to clean the howitzers."

Golf games are great, but don't ever overreach. Greed pays—the other guy. At the many corporate outings he does every year, Chi Chi imparts this cautionary tale about his gambling experience with good friend, blind golfer Charlie Boswell. "Charlie says he'd like to play me for a thousand dollars," Chi Chi tells the group. "I said, 'Name the time and the place.' And Charlie said, 'Midnight, at my club.'" As with everything else in life, enjoy these games in moderation.

Rabbit

Shhhhhhhhhhhh. We're hunting wabbits.

All right, here's the game, Elmer Fudd. Players put a price on the rabbit's head before the match, maybe a $1 or $5 for conservative types, $50, $100, or even $1,000 for the well heeled and wagering hardened.

Bugs is turned loose on the first tee, and the bunny continues to bound about the course property until a player wins a hole outright. At that point, the player is in possession of the rabbit and holds on to it until another player or players beat him on a hole. Then the rabbit is, again, set free and on the loose to be picked up by the winner of the next hole. The player holding the rabbit at the end of the round wins and is paid the predetermined bounty from each of the other players. In an effort to keep the game exciting on the back 9, the game is often played with a rabbit at stake on each side instead of the entire 18.

The "leg" is a valuable body part because, if the player already holding the rabbit wins another hole, he is then given a leg; to free the rabbit, his or her opponents must first free the leg before they can free the rabbit. While most rabbits have just four legs, the one in this game can have as many as a good player can win. A player with the rabbit and five legs is essentially six up on the competition because he or she would have to lose six holes before the beast would be off and running. When totaling up the damage after 18, the winning player is also paid for each leg, if any, he or she holds. That sum is often equal to the price of the rabbit but can also be a smaller side bet. If you find yourself in a game that

Hole	1	2	3	4	5	6	7	8	9	10	11	12	13	14	15	16	17	18	In	Tot	Hcp	Net
Gold	400	426	450	383	183	393	550	190	590	420	173	449	599	426	155	376	400	600				
Hdcp	13	7	1	17	15	9	5	11	3	12	14	4	10	8	18	16	6	2				
Par	4	4	4	4	3	4	5	3	5	4	3	4	5	4	3	4	4	5				
Player 1	5	4	4	5	3	5	4	4	5	4	2	4	6	5	3	4	4	5	37	76	3/0	73
Player 2	6/5.	6/5.	5/4.	5	4/3.	5/4.	7/6.	4/3.	6/5.	4/3.	4/3.	6/5.	6/5.	5/4.	4	6	5/4.	8/7.	48	96	18/15	78
Player 3	4	5/4.	6/5.	5	4	4	5	3	5/4.	5	4	4/3.	5	5	4	5	4	6/5.	42	83	7/4	76
Player 4	5	6/5.	6/5.	4	3	5	5/4.	4	6/5.	4	3	5/4.	5	6/5.	4	5	5/4.	6/5.	43	87	11/8	76
	Player			Player					Player	Player		Player			Player	Player		Player				
Rabbit	3	—	Loose	4	—	Loose	—	—	3	2	Loose	3	—	Loose	1	1+leg	—	1+leg				

El Legado Golf Resort
Home of Chi Chi Rodriguez

Player 3 wins front 9 & Rabbit
Player 1 wins back 9 Rabbit & One Leg

Playing off low handicap
Player 1 = 0
All other players less 3 strokes

Date ____________ Scorer ______________ Attest ______________

continued ☞

ends with a 17-legged rabbit, you have gotten in over your head, and you might want to negotiate a settlement or some sort of deferred payment plan.

Big-game hunters may wish to turn multiple rabbits loose (those varmints do have a reputation for reproducing quickly) in an effort to add lots of excitement to their morning or afternoon. In this variation, every time a rabbit is freed another rabbit joins in the race. A player capturing a rabbit and a leg in this version of the game generally bags the bunny for good, and a new rabbit starts hopping. It's possible, but highly unlikely, that as many as 10 rabbits can be on the run in the course of 18 holes. A rabbit's foot may be lucky, but in this game it pays better to get the entire leg and the whole animal.

Snake

Because, let's face it, putting just isn't hard enough under normal circumstances. I mean, really, why not take the most frustrating part of the game and double, redouble, redouble double, and quintuple the pressure?

Snake is a simple game with an oh-so-venomous bite. The bet starts small, say, a dime or a dollar (believe us, even a nickel is plenty rich to start for first timers). The first player in the group to three-putt is the not-so-proud owner of the snake. The bet on the line then doubles, and the next person to three-putt picks up the snake and doubles the bet again. The process continues for all 18 holes with the stakes mounting after each and every knee knocking; I hate this game; never could play this game; please somebody stab me in the neck with this Ping Anzer Two, Odyssey 988, Tear Drop 2000, White Hot mallet special, #%&*, three jack. The person holding the snake at the end of the round pays each of the other players the final total of the pot.

Just to show you how the bet can go from pennies to pocket change to painful, consider a dime bet, with all four players in the foursome three-putting once a side. Ten cents to start, then 20 cents after the second three-putt, 40 cents, 80 cents, $1.60, $3.20, $6.40, and $12.80 after the eighth and final three-stab. That's $12.80 times three, for a total of $38.40. Start the game at a dollar, and you're looking at a final payout of $128 per person. Hello! Now how comfortable are you over that two-footer on 17 or 18?

The key to Snake is obviously to two-putt, but if you find yourself down late and you don't care about your total score—and you probably won't if you're about to lose the Christmas Club account or the money you were going to spend on a present for your spouse's birthday—get that ball on the fringe and lag, lag, lag. If you can't mark it, pick it up and clean it; then it's not technically on the green. The fringe is your best friend late in a game of Snake. Hisssssssssssssss!

Zoo

Really, why limit yourself to just the reptile house when a whole zoo is available to golfers? Use the Snake format and play Frog for water balls, Camel for sand traps, Bear for balls in the woods, and Giraffe if you find yourself stretching your neck over a fence looking for a ball that's gone out of bounds.

Why so negative? Play positive animals. Double the bet and pay the last player to make birdie. Keep track and increase the stakes after every one putt; the mongoose is a snake's natural predator. In these positive bets, the animal owner at the end of the round should be paid off instead of having to pay out.

If the accounting becomes too much of a hassle in stepladder bets, just put a fixed price on each of the animals. And while it's fun to build the drama over the course of an entire round and declare the last person to make an

continued ☞

animal the winner or loser, consider adding some early excitement by wagering on the first person to hit in the sand, dunk a ball, birdie, or one-putt.

Chi Chi Rodriguez is clearly an animal lover—even the bull he slays after big putts he puts to rest with great care and style. His vocabulary, stories, and lifestyle are peppered by references to the animal kingdom, some of which follow:

- He eats meat because he's "never seen a sick-looking tiger."
- Walk, don't run, for exercise because "elephants are slow and they live to be 150 years old. Turtles are even slower, and they can live to be 375. Animals that run fast die young."
- He likes his baseball teams to play like hornets because "a hornet can sting a bear and nothing happens. But if the whole team, all the hornets, the whole hive gets on him and stings him, then they can put enough poison on him to kill him."
- Gary Player was such a tough competitor because he "had the guts of a rooster."
- When he's feeling sorry for himself, he goes to the beach and watches pelicans because "they have to eat their weight seven times a day. They dive from the sky for fish and crash into the ocean so hard their eyes eventually go bad; and when they can't see anymore, they can't fish any more and they die. I watch them and by comparison I feel a lot better."

Bingo, Bango, Bongo

"Sounds like salsa music," says Chi Chi. "And winning money is salsa music to my ears." Bingo, Bango, Bongo is a wonderful game for everybody, but it's especially good for groups filled with varying playing abilities. Tiger Woulds, Tiger Would-bes, and even Tiger Wouldn'ts can all play and excel in this multi-bet game.

Three points are available on each hole. Each point is worth [your wager here]; careful not to go too rich because 54 possible points are available during any round. The first point is awarded to the first golfer to get his or her ball on the green. The person closest to the hole once all balls are on the green earns the second point. The third point goes to the first player to hole out. Bingo, Bango, Bongo! Hallelujah high handicappers! The number of strokes involved is irrelevant. All that matters is being first.

If a hacker chops three shots and still hasn't reached the other players' drives, then catches it pure on his fourth and finds the putting surface, pay him the point. Big hitters may be playing shorter clubs into the green, but they're also hitting last, and the point may be lost before they ever make that second swing. A skilled short-game player may take eight shots to get on the green, but if that eighth shot cozies up to the pin, then all the birdie and par putts in the world can't take away the second point.

Likewise a six-inch putt, whether it's for 2 or 12, is worthless on the third point if somebody drains a snake from the fringe or no-brains a putt from 50 feet out. Points won don't have to be pretty. You don't have to draw them on the scorecard, just record them with a dot, slash, or check mark. One instance where making the best score on a hole is a benefit is on par 3s. Honors on the short holes give a golfer first shot at the first point.

Bingo, Bango, Bongo can also be made more challenging for golfers. The Tour version awards points for fewest strokes to reach the green, closest to the pin after all balls are on the green, and low score on the hole. Use handicaps in this variation of the game, and award half points for ties.

In any version of Bingo, Bango, Bongo, keep an eye on the clock. Possibly having to plumb bob and hole out every putt can be time consuming. Take care and concentrate on making any stroke, but remember you're playing for a little bit of green, not the Green Jacket.

Trifecta

No time to warm up on the practice tee? Skipped the putting clock and headed straight for the first hole? Tapped out after your wife sneaked that $20 bill from your wallet to buy an eyebrow pencil or your husband borrowed the cash to buy some newfangled gadget that he'll only use once, and now you can't afford a bucket of balls? Here's a game that lets you get loose before you have to loosen the purse strings.

Trifecta is another three-point game, but it doesn't start until the final three holes of each nine. Players, essentially, are given time to get in the groove while out on the course. The points involved in Trifecta are individual; the competition is not among players. Each golfer in the group can earn up to three points on every hole.

Hit it in the fairway off the tee, get a point. Hit the green in regulation, get a point. Hole out in two putts or less, get a point. Hit the trifecta and get a (fourth) bonus point! Add up each player's point total from holes 7 through 9 and 16 through 18, and pay the differences. A point can be worth whatever you, your friends, and your bankroll decide.

"Everybody should make enough time to hit balls before a round. Going to the first tee cold is a killer. But if there's not time to properly warm up, here's a quick 10-ball routine to get ready. Hit five pitching wedges or 9 irons. Follow it with three easy swings using a 5 or 6 iron. Use a driver or 3 wood on your final two balls, again taking the club back free and easy.

"If you don't have time to hit any balls or the practice tee is located too far from the first tee, get to the putting green and roll some putts. Getting the speed of the greens can be crucial, and a few putts will help you get a feel. Most golf shots are short ones. In a time crunch, get a feel for those first."

Embriago

How a golf game took the name of a Greek cheese made from goat's and sheep's milk I'm not sure. A more likely origin is that some poor golfer stumbled onto the word while trying his best to avoid cursing after his third provisional went ricocheting off an out-of-bounds stake.

Embriago is yet another game where a series of points, as many as four, are at stake on every hole. The match is for foursomes playing in teams of two. The lowest score on a hole is worth one point. The low total of each twosome's combined score is worth another point. Closest ball to the pin in regulation is worth a third point. And a fourth point is awarded if any player birdies. A team sweeping all four points on any given hole scores an "embriago," and the points are doubled from four to eight. That'll make the cheese a little more binding. Points are worth, as in all the point games described in this book, whatever the players in the game agree on when making the bet.

Because points are awarded for a series of good shots, rather than just one or two, Embriago is generally a game for better players, but it can work just as well in a mixed group playing to full handicaps. Picking a partner with a consistent game is key in Embriago because an erratic player can hurt the "low-total" point if he or she is throwing in a big number every other hole.

Nines

Play as you dress, to the nines. But bring some game. You don't want to be one of those sharp-dressed, no-playing people Chi Chi refers to as "big hat, no cattle." It's not hard to figure out where this game gets its name because nine points are available on every hole. Nines is a three- or four-person game, and points are earned in the following manner: winning score on the hole is worth five points, next high score is worth three, third high score gets one point, and the highest score is worth zero.

If players tie on a hole the points are split. For example, two people tying for low score on the hole receive four points. A four-way tie means one and a quarter points per person. Neat, a golf game where the biggest number added up at the end of the day is a good thing.

The strategy of Nines is pretty simple—play great golf. Shoot a scratch round, and you'll most likely come out ahead, way ahead. Threesomes playing Nines merely drop the fourth (zero point) score. The five, three, and one points stay the same. Nines can also be played in reverse, with the goal being to score the fewest points possible.

Marino

Named for Chi Chi's favorite quarterback on his favorite football team, Marino is a tribute to all of those 400-yard passing games in Dan Marino's surefire Hall of Fame career. Feel free to name the game after your favorite QB, or just call the game Yardages. Playing the game is as simple as a swing pass.

Each hole is worth its length in yards on the scorecard. Win the hole and pocket the yards and the payment. What's a yard worth? Well, in its cheapest form, a penny. A 525-yard par-5 pays $5.25. Golfers with the guts to go a dollar a yard are in Chi Chi's Senior Tour tax bracket. Call him "Ching Ching" Rodriguez.

"Sure I'm making a lot of money now. But years ago, the IRS would send me get-well cards. Before the Senior Tour, my banker used to call me Chi Chi. Now it's *Mr. Rodriguez.*"

The strategy in Marino is fairly straightforward: win the long holes. Par 3s are nice, but they just don't pay the same. It's the difference between shopping at Wal-Mart and Nordstroms. Players can carry over yardages on holes that are tied or just call the pass incomplete and move on to the next tee box. With golf courses playing anywhere from 5,500 yards to 7,200, plenty of money is out there to be captured from any tee box. If you're looking to set an NFL record, Marino holds the all-time mark for passing yards in a season with 5,084 yards.

Red, White, and Blue

Here's a patriotic game to be played on Memorial Day, the Fourth of July, or anytime a spell of national pride hits you on the first tee. Red, White, and Blue is a game based on the traditional colors of tee markers. Players play all the par 3s from the red tees, all the par 4s from the white tees, and all the par 5s from the blue tees.

No really good reason exists for switching tee boxes except to keep the game lively. It does make the game a tad easier because you hit from closer to the green on the short holes and not really much is lost on the long ones because most par 5s play as three shotters for the majority of golfers.

If the group wishes, it can rearrange the colors and the pars in any order. This is, after all, America—go ahead and make the par 5s red, the par 3s white, and the par 4s blue; it's your inalienable right as a golfer.

Chairman

The only thing better than being the king is being the chairman. In this game, the first player to win a hole earns the "chair." Every subsequent hole the chairman wins, his employees pay him one bet. The chairman keeps his title until he loses a hole. If he ties a hole, he keeps the chair and no money is won or lost. The chairman gets fired if one or more of his employees beat him on a hole, and the next player to win a hole outright fills the job. The new chairman then collects under the same rules until he is sent to the unemployment line.

This game should be played at full handicaps so that all players, regardless of ability, can enjoy the fun and power of being in charge of the group. It's an ideal game for threesomes and foursomes, and the bragging rights about being the big boss are often worth more than the amount of the bet.

Geiberger/59

With apologies to Chip Beck, David Duval, Notah Begay, Doug Dunakey, and Annika Sorenstam, this game is named in honor of the *first* player to ever shoot 59 in a PGA or LPGA Tour event, Al Geiberger. Geiberger's record round came at Colonial Country Club's South Course in the second round of the 1977 Danny Thomas–Memphis Classic, a tournament he won without shooting a single round in the 60s. His winning total of 273 was achieved with scores of 72, 59, 72, and 70.

Geiberger is a simple scorecard play where the first golfer to hit 59 pays everybody in the group $5—$50 if the parties involved are all well heeled. The game also can be played easily in reverse with everybody in the group paying the last golfer to reach 59 strokes.

And don't limit the fun to Al. Play other famous scores. Take a go at Johnny Miller's 63 in the final round of the 1973 U.S. Open at Oakmont. Target the Golden Bear's Sunday 66 at Augusta that won him a record sixth Masters Green Jacket in 1986. Go really old school, and play a 91 or 88—Tom Kidd's scores in winning the first British Open championship ever played at St. Andrews in 1873.

The best and worst rounds of Chi Chi Rodriguez's PGA career are perfect bookends to shoot at. For the scratch player it's a pair of 63s, one recorded at the '72 Walt Disney World Open and the other at the '74 Canadian Open. High handicappers take aim at the final-round 84 Rodriguez carded in the '77 U.S. Open at Southern Hills in Tulsa, Oklahoma. "I don't remember exactly what happened that day," Chi Chi says, "but I know a human being is a human being and some days we all just shoot a bad score. One time at Greensboro I shot 68 in the first round to take the lead and then shot 83 on Friday and missed the cut. That's why I love the phrase 'next time.' In golf there's always a next time, and I just tell myself I will do better the next time and move on happily."

Chi Chi's 58

Private Juan Rodriguez reported for duty at Ft. Sill in Lawton, Oklahoma, in 1954. When he wasn't drilling with his platoon, he was driving a golf ball. Time not spent in formation was spent in foursomes at the local municipal course. Despite being in Uncle Sam's service and under a sergeant's supervision, Rodriguez managed to make it to the course three times a week. He had a regular game on Monday with "seven other guys. Local pros and good players from the area."

On one particular Oklahoma morning, a calm day when the wind was not sweeping down the plain and neither the wheat nor flagsticks were waving, Chi Chi's game got hot, and he proceeded to blow through 18 holes in the remarkably small sum of just 58 strokes—an eagle, 11 birdies, 6 pars. That's a smooth little 13 under total on a par-71 layout—16 greens in regulation, 1 missed fairway, only 22 putts (he thinks). One pro was so humiliated by the beating he was taking from Chi Chi's clubs that he quit after 15 holes. Playing seven ways, a bet with the entire group, not just his foursome, Chi Chi pocketed the equivalent of "three month's pay for what I was doing in the army" and headed back to the barracks. Progress has asphalted over the track Chi Chi plowed under, but the number still stands—58.

Instant Replay

Tired of that one (two, three) golfer in the group who's always saying, "Oh, if I could just have that shot over"? Had enough of the player who hits a bad shot then pulls another ball out of his pocket and drops it before the first ball's even landed? And even though they're going to "play that first one," they hit a second one "just for practice." Instant Replay is a game to stop the whiners and put a plug in the pouters.

Each golfer plays to his or her full handicap; they are not adjusted to play of the best person in a group. Then instead of getting strokes on the scorecard, players get them on the course. If a player is a +17-handicap, he or she gets to hit 17 shots of his or her choosing over again. A 3-handicap gets three instant replays. A 10 can take 10 do-overs. It's a veritable cornucopia of mulligans. Take all your shots on one hole. Spread 'em out over 18. Use 'em to erase OB drives, chili-dipped wedges, fat sand shots, and yanked two-foot putts. Misclub an approach? No problem, grab the right stick and go at it again.

It's a fantastic way to get the woulda, shoulda, coulda out of a golfer's system, and at the end of the round you'll never have to hear "My game was great except for that 7 iron I shanked on 14. Boy, I wish I could have that shot back." Instant Replay puts an end to all the excuses! If Instant Replay sounds like your game, try to get out early ahead of other groups or tee off late in the day when the heavy course traffic is in front of you. All those extra swings and shagging the extra shots can increase the time of a round dramatically, and you don't want to back up play.

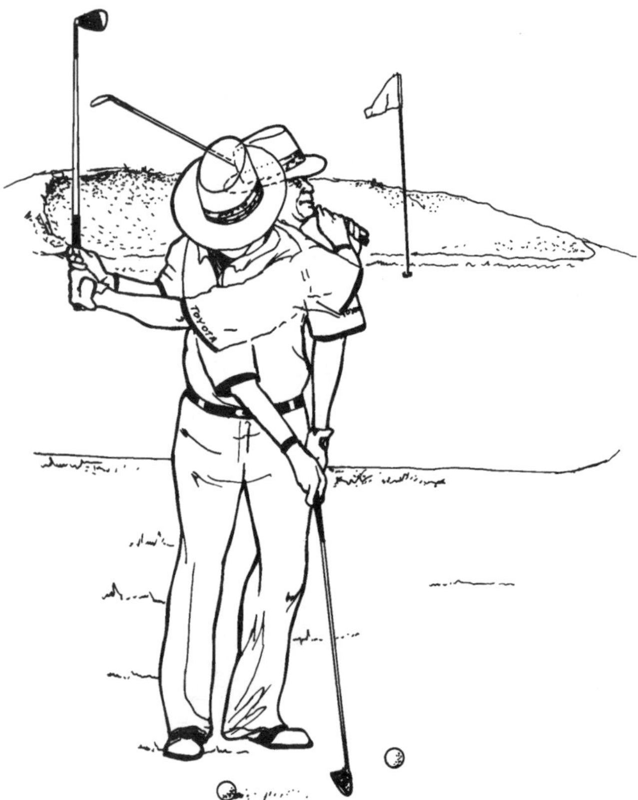

In a fun and unique twist on Instant Replay, spend one of your "shots" by demanding that your partner replay one of his or her good shots. If it's agreed on beforehand, it'll all add up the same. Nothing ruins the pure joy of a stiffed approach shot better than asking to see it twice. So ask.

Poker

The first in a series of card games you can play on the golf course, Poker is simply the best poker hand a player can make out of his or her scores on the front nine and the back nine. Two bets each for a set amount. Five of a kind, a full house, a straight, two pairs—high hand gets paid. The rub, of course, is that lower numbers are better than higher numbers. Sevens, 8s, 9s, and face cards (10s) are disasters. Fours, 3s, and 2s are terrific. And if you draw an ace, well, congratulations—and remember, the drinks are on you when you get back to the clubhouse. Tie hands go to the golfer whose five-card total score is closest to par.

Poker is a game for the masses and can be played with handicaps or without because winning doesn't really depend on having a traditionally good golf score. A player making three 3s, three 4s, and three 5s shot a terrific 36 for the side, but his or her hand's a loser to the hacker who made straight 7s for a 56.

Blackjack

Here's another card game and one that has absolutely nothing to do with golf acumen—the results are completely random. Bad players have just as good a shot at succeeding in Blackjack as Chi Chi Rodriguez.

Set a price on a blackjack, and then any stretch of the holes adding up to 21 pays. Four, 7, 5, 5 cashes. String together 3, 4, 5, 6, 3, pay me. Six, 5, 10, or 8, 6, 7, or 9, 2, 7, 3—money, money, money! If it equals 21, then a bet's won.

Hole	1	2	3	4	5	6	7	8	9	10	11	12	13	14	15	16	17	18	In	Tot	Hcp	Net
Gold	400	426	450	383	183	393	550	190	590	420	173	449	599	426	155	376	400	600				
Hdcp	13	7	1	17	15	9	5	11	3	12	14	4	10	8	18	16	6	2				
Par	4	4	4	4	3	4	5	3	5	4	3	4	5	4	3	4	4	5				
Player 1	4	5	5	5	3	5	5	4	5	5	2	4	7	5	3	7	6	8	47	88		
									21				21		21		21		4 x	21s		
Player 2	4	3	4	6	2	5	5	3	5	6	3	4	5	3	3	5	4	5	38	75		
						21					21	21							3 x	21s		
Player 3	5	5	3	6	4	5	5	3	4	5	3	4	5	4	3	5	5	5	39	79		
							21				21			21					3 x	21s		

Poker =	Player 1	Player 2	Player 3
Front =	Six 5s (win)	Straight 2-6	Four 5s
Back =	Straight 2-8	Full house 3s/4s	Five 5s (win)

Handicaps are not used!

El Legado Golf Resort
Home of Chi Chi Rodriguez

Date ____________ Scorer ________________ Attest ________________

Bridge

The card game, not the structure crossing Rae's Creek on the 12th at Augusta National dedicated to Ben Hogan or the small stone arch spanning Swilcan Burn on the home hole at St. Andrews. This bridge is a bid game for foursomes but differs from its playing-card cousin because it has no North, South, East, and West; Omar Sharif; or kicking your partner under the table and clutching your chest in mock pain to indicate a heart.

On each tee, one team "bids" on how many combined strokes it will take for them to play the hole. The bid can be made gross or net, and the bidding team alternates on every hole regardless of who wins the previous bid. A bid of 12 means the team thinks it can complete the hole in a total of a dozen strokes. If the hole at stake is a par 3, the opening bid may be seven. The bid can be passed, but that's soft. At least throw out a number, even if it's 20, so that the other team can make some sort of play. After the initial bid, the opposing team has three options:

1. Make a bid lower than the opening bid.
2. Call the bid.
3. Call the bid and *double* the bet. (If you really believe the other team couldn't make its number in a dream, prove it by doubling down.)

When the bidding is complete, the hole is played. The bet is won if the bid is met or bettered, lost if the bid number is exceeded. How much each hole is worth is strictly up to the group, but the bet typically (unlike Skins where it increases every so often) stays constant. Players wishing to add some extra spice to Bridge can add penalty or bonus points. The losing bidder is charged an extra fee for every stroke over the bid, while winners receive extra dough for each swing under the bid.

Misery

Golf is a game of companionship. Misery loves company. Here's a match made in heaven or Pinehurst, depending on where you'd rather play in the ever-after life. Misery is more of a mid- to high-handicap game that has nothing to do with total score and everything to do with avoiding trouble.

Hit a ball OB, that's a point. Dunk a ball in the drink, that's a point. Land in a bunker, point. Fail to get out of the bunker, two points. Leave it on the beach again, you're counting three. Three putt, that's a point. Four putts equals two points. Five putts . . . quit the game and take up woodworking. On second thought, don't—five-putters aren't good with their hands and might well cut off a finger.

"The worst trouble I ever saw a golfer get into was Homero Blancas," Chi Chi says, still giggling at the moment decades later. "Homero and I were at the Masters and playing the 18th hole at Augusta when he hit his drive way off line and into the crowd where it ended up landing in a lady's brassiere. So Homero asks me what he should do and I told him, 'Play it." I think he ended up taking a drop but I turned my back so I don't know if he retrieved the ball himself or if the lady gave it back to him. Homero and I laughed about this for many years, but I never did ask him how he got that ball back."

At the end of the day all those miserable points are added up, and players settle up the difference. Misery does reward good play. For every par and birdie on the scorecard, subtract one point. Point values are determined according to personal price range.

Caddy Shack

Just as loud and loony as the movie, Caddy Shack has just one rule—no touching the other player or his or her ball. Everything else goes. Talking during an opponent's backswing—legal but tame. Dropping a golf bag at impact—allowed. Shifting the golf cart into reverse so that piercing alarm sounds—clever. Driving that same golf cart directly at a player while he or she is teeing off—brilliant but, perhaps, a bit too bold.

Here's your chance to break every etiquette rule in the book and then make up some new ones and break those, too. Walk in the line of a putt. Put your shadow directly over another player's ball—then dance! Running low on rude ideas? Find a copy of legendary golf author Dan Jenkins's brilliant piece *The Glory Game at Goat Hills*. There's fun and then there's Jenkins's Ft. Worth, Texas, fun.

Play to full handicaps, and test the limits of your concentration. Yes, Judge Smales, there is gambling at Bushwood. And when your player's standing over a two-foot downhill slider for par, scream out, "Legog Ttam." That's "Matt Gogel" pronounced backwards. You could try "Zeugirdor Ihc Ihc," but saying "Chi Chi Rodriguez" in reverse is almost phonetically impossible. Finally, after sinking a crucial putt, don't forget this most famous phrase, "It's in the hole!"

Head Games: Betting Basket Cases

Bets make you nervous? Suffer from gambling-induced dehydration? The biggest reason most people are afraid to wager on a round of golf isn't that they're embarrassed by their playing ability—handicaps smooth over that obstacle. No, the simple and very valid reason golfers won't wager on the course is the fear of losing money. Here are some tips to overcome those fears:

1. Set a limit on losses before teeing off. If you're comfortable with the worst-case scenario, then you'll be comfortable with the game. Don't let your eyes get bigger than your billfold.
2. Don't think about the money. When great players are standing over a shot, all they're thinking about is the shot. Pros visualize ball flight, not a pile of money. Focus on your swing.
3. If you must think about money, concentrate on winning somebody else's; don't dwell on losing yours. Killer instinct is a good quality in gambling.
4. Don't constantly figure how far you're ahead or behind. Too much math too early in the round is a distraction. Take an accounting on 9 and 18. Otherwise, just play.
5. Play to win. As in football or basketball, playing not to lose is a surefire way to lose. The smart money is on smart play.

chapter **3**

Pairs and Couples

Squawk: "Up next, the Traprake twosome, joined by the twosome of Hither and Yon. Please pay in the pro shop and proceed to the first tee."

With an overmodulated blare, the loudspeaker hanging from the clubhouse patio announces that you and your best friend have just been paired with two golfers who might as well be from Pluto. Two things happen when unfamiliar golfers get thrown together: Anxiety heightens 10-fold hitting the first tee ball, for fear of embarrassment, and chances are you won't get a game.

Most people are shy when it comes to wagering with strangers. And rightly so. Are the outsiders slashers or sandbaggers, 2-handicaps or hacks? If you're uncomfortable in a foursome for any reason—shyness, unsure of the skill level, afraid to spend with strangers—then keep the game between yourselves. Two players can get involved in many of the games described in the previous two chapters or play any of the ones listed on the following pages. This chapter also includes games for players of widely differing abilities and coeds. Yes, boy/girl, husband/wife, man/woman, whatever the politically correct heading happens to be.

A hint for married golfers: Wives, you should never, never, ever, under any circumstance, listen to your husband about the golf swing unless he happens to be a touring or teaching pro. We men like to fix women's swings even if we're clueless. And usually it's a different tip after every shot. It's just our nature. Ladies, avoid the sure fights and frustration, and get a lesson from a good teacher.

One on One

On the basketball court, certainly, you'd put your money on Michael Jordan or Charles Barkley against Chi Chi Rodriguez. But on the golf course, put your money on the five-foot, seven-inch guy!

In One on One, the players, obviously, go head to head in a point game based on basketball scoring. Off the tee, it's one point for a drive exceeding 100 yards, drives 151 to 250 yards are worth two, and anything cranked 251 yards and over is worth three. Tee balls must be in the fairway to earn the points.

From the fairway, an approach shot hitting the green from more than 200 yards out is the trey. Two points are awarded for sticking it on the slick from between 200 and 100 yards. Any approach hit finding the putting surface from less than 100 yards is worth one point. We figure anything inside of 100 yards should be a free throw and is scored similarly. If you're missing the freebies, your wedge game needs work, and you may want to pay special attention to chapters 9 and 10 in the second part of this book. Approach-shot points do not have to hit the green in regulation to score, and it doesn't matter if they're hit from the fairway, rough, or a bunker. Good news—every golfer's going to score at least 18 points.

The final phase of One on One is all about putting. And if you play the shot with the putter, then it's considered a putt in this game. How many putts it takes to hole out doesn't matter. How far the last putt travels does. A putt made from inside the length of a standard putter, about three feet, is worth one point. Sorry—those long putters are fine to use for a stroke or to rest your chin on, but they go back in the bag when it comes to measuring putts. A two-point putt is anything drained from 20 feet to standard putter distance, and the trifecta is any putt buried from beyond 20 feet. Go ahead and one-putt or five-putt; all that matters in One on One is the final putt. If you have trouble figuring distances simply pace it off. A man's stride is about one yard. Add up the points at the end and pay out the difference. Handicaps are irrelevant because the number of strokes involved in the game is irrelevant.

Hammer

Hammer time! Looking for a two-person, turbocharged version of a Nassau? Get out the hammer, and pound away on every hole and, if one is so inclined, every shot. In Hammer, each hole starts with an assigned value, say a quarter, and a player holding the "hammer." The player holding the hammer has the right to nail his opponent and double the bet after any shot (his own or his partner's). The hammer then switches over to the other player who can, if he so chooses, hammer back after the next shot, thereby doubling the bet a second time. The hammer passes after every doubling of the bet until the hole is finished, with the winner of the hole pocketing the money. Hammering is only an option, and a player is not obligated to use it just because he is holding the tool.

As an example (starting at 25 cents), player A has the hammer and stripes his drive 275 yards down the middle of the fairway. He then hammers his opponent (doubling the bet to 50 cents), who hits his ball 200 yards into the woods. Player B then plays a remarkable recovery shot and gets his ball on the green 45 feet from the pin. He hammers back, raising the bet to $1. Player A then knocks his approach to 10 feet. Feeling confident, player A drops the hammer, and the bet is raised to $2. Lo and behold, player B sinks his no-brainer 45-footer and hammers again. The bet is now $4, and player A's 10-foot

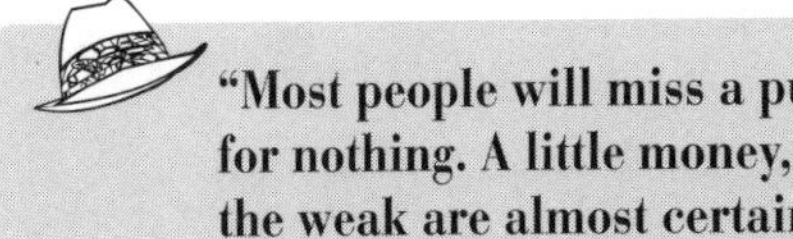

"Most people will miss a putt for nothing. A little money, and the weak are almost certain to miss."

birdie putt just got a whole lot longer. After gacking his putt left, player A taps in for par but is out $4 for losing the hole.

The amount of the bet stays the same at the start of each hole, and the hammer passes on each tee—essentially one player starts with the hammer on even holes and his or her opponent on the odd holes. In the event of halved holes, the final amount of the hole is carried over and added to the total of the next hole. A $4 hammer carried over doesn't double to $8, $16, $32, and so on.

Hammer is a game for players equal in talent (good or bad) because handicaps are nearly impossible to figure into the match. Strategy is required in knowing when to break out the hammer and conk the bet. Players in trouble early on are encouraged just to hold onto the hammer and limit losses; on the other hand, pulling great escapes or making unexpected putts are a great time to nail somebody. It also pays to hammer if you're the first player in and your opponent has a putt, no matter the length, to match the hole. Go ahead and squeeze a little.

Bisque

Yummy. If only it were the bisque served gratis to all those golf writers free-loading through the buffet line in the media tent. This Bisque is a British game that serves as a refreshing way to use handicap strokes. Instead of just giving "pops," as they are dictated by the scorecard, players can take their handicap strokes at any time. The only caveat is that the strokes must be offered up for use before a hole is played. Bisque can be used to liven up match play, stroke play, or Stableford events.

What's the advantage of letting players control their handicap strokes instead of just playing them as they fall on the card? Well, first of all, you can spend as many strokes as you want on a single hole. Second, a hole that may rate hard on the card may play easy for you, and why waste a stroke where you don't need it? Third, if a hole is too tough and you know you're going to lose it anyway, why not save the stroke and use it on a hole where it can work for you? Finally, by playing Bisque, a player gets all of his or her strokes instead of adjusting to the low handicap in the group. Just for fun, the next time you get ready for a game and you're figuring up handicaps, ask your partners, "Care to try the Bisque?"

Bag Raid

Rule 4-4a in *The Rules of Golf* reads: "The player shall start a stipulated round with not more than 14 clubs." However, the rule states nothing about how many clubs a person must be carrying when he or she *finishes* a stipulated round.

In Bag Raid, every time a player wins a hole he or she loses a club. The opponent has free license to simply stroll over and take away any club he or she wishes. Win another hole, say good-bye to another stick. The only caveat is that an opponent's putter can't be the first club to go and a golfer always has to have at least one club so that he or she can continue to play. Other than that, plunder away as your miserable golf game allows. Bag Raid can be played with full handicaps, but it's often far more fun without them. Let the loss of clubs even the playing field rather than giving strokes.

In a slight variation to the game, a player losing a hole can either choose to raid his or her opponent's bag for a club or get one of his or her own back. It's a twist but a boring one if players do nothing but exchange a 7 iron for 18 holes.

When raiding a bag, make sure to steal from an opponent's strength first. Most players rely on only about half of their clubs, so take care to choose wisely. Get woods and short irons out of the bag, then go after the putter. Good players can break 85 or 80 with no more than a 3 wood, 8 iron, and putter. When stealing, steal wisely.

Damaged Clubs

Did you know that according to USGA rules a club damaged during the normal course of play may be repaired or replaced during a round? You probably did. But what about a club damaged other than in the normal course of play? Ever gotten mad and thrown your putter against a tree? Slammed a club into a golf bag in anger? Well, if *you* damage the club to the point where it no longer conforms to the rules of golf, you must take it out of play. Bend a putter into a capital "C" but still use it and you're in violation of rule 4-3b. Smack a club so hard that the head loosens and then falls off while playing later in the round, you're also in breach of rule 4-3b. The penalty—disqualification. If you're going to damage a club, damage it well. Snap it so it's unusable, and you'll be obeying the rules.

Let It Ride

On a roll? Feel like pushing your luck? Have a hot run of holes going? Prove it! Let It Ride! In this game players accumulate points by going on runs. Full handicaps are used, and points are earned as follows: net bogey = 5 points; net par = 15 points; net birdie = 30 points; net eagle = 50 points; net albatross = 100 points.

After each hole, a player can "bank" his or her points or "let it ride." Points continue to add up until a player either banks the points or makes double bogey. If the double bogey comes prior to the bank, all the points on the run are lost. If the points are banked, a new streak can't start until a player makes *par*, so simply making a deposit doesn't solve all problems.

How gutsy are you about your game? Stringing together an opening five holes of bogey (5), par (15), par (15), bogey (5), birdie (30) is worth 70 points. Do you keep them in the bank or let it ride? Even the best golfers may not want to risk 13 or 14 holes of work; and yet, if a golfer ends a run, he or she has no guarantee that a new one can be started. Bogeys don't kill you in Let It Ride, but they can't jump start a run either.

What kills you in this game is making a double par. Make a six on a par 3, a snowman on a par 4, or double-digits on a par 5, and all points, banked ones included, are lost. Be smart, be bold, be conservative, just don't card a huge number.

Play for a dime or dollar a point, less if the budget's tight. Take on a surcharge if somebody tosses up a donut. Let It Ride is a gambling game not just with your opponent but also with your self-confidence.

Hole	1	2	3	4	5	6	7	8	9	10	11	12	13	14	15	16	17	18	In	Tot	Hcp	Net
Gold	400	426	450	383	183	393	550	190	590	420	173	449	599	426	155	376	400	600				
Hdcp	13	7	1	17	15	9	5	11	3	12	14	4	10	8	18	16	6	2				
Par	4	4	4	4	3	4	5	3	5	4	3	4	5	4	3	4	4	5				
Player A	5	4	4/3.	5	3	6	6/5.	4	5/4.	4	3	5/4.	4	4	4	4	4	5/4.	37	79	5	74
(Points)	5	15/20	30/50	5/55	15/(70)	—	15	5/20	30/(50)	15	15/30	15/45	30/75	15/90	5/95	15/(110)	15	30/(45)	155	pts =	275	pts
Player B	4	5/4.	7/6.	5	3	5/4.	5/4.	4	6/5.	4	4	3/2.	6/5.	5/4.	4	4	5/4.	6/5.	41	85	10	75
(Points)	15	15/30	–/0	–	15/30	15/30	30/(60)	–	15	15/(30)	–	(50)	15	15/30	5/35	15/50	15/65	15/(80)	160	pts =	220	pts
Player C	5/4.	5/4.	5/4.	5	5/4.	4/3.	5/4.	5/4.	7/6.	6/5.	6/5.	5/4.	5/4.	4/3.	3	4	5/4.	6/5.	42	88	15	73
(Points)	15	15/30	15/(45)	–	–	30	30/60	5/65	5/(70)	5	–/0	15	30/45	30/(75)	15	15/(30)	15	15/(30)	135	pts =	250	pts

Scoring: Net bogey = 5
Net par = 15
Net birdie = 30
Net eagle = 50
Net double eagle = 100

Hole points/run
◯ = points banked

El Legado Golf Resort
Home of Chi Chi Rodriguez

Date ____________ Scorer ________________ Attest ________________

No Putts

This game was inspired by Chi Chi Rodriguez's golfing idol, Ben Hogan.

"The first time I played with Ben Hogan—and this was after his car accident that nearly killed him—I asked him on the very first tee, 'Mr. Hogan, I know you have a bad leg that still hurts. Do you mind if I fix your ball marks?' He said, 'That's very nice of you to ask me. Yes, Chi Chi, you can do that.' He always liked me. He always talked to me and said hello. Bob Goalby once came and told me, 'Ben just made a comment about you that I've never heard him say about anybody.' So naturally I asked what he said. Ben had told him, 'That little man can really play some golf.' That was one of the greatest compliments I have ever received. Ben was such a great player—not only did he come back and play after his wreck but he won the U.S. Open again."

Hogan used to argue that golfing and putting were two entirely different games. Hogan didn't care for putting. Because he was Ben Hogan, he was right, so let's get rid of it. In the finest tradition of the four-time U.S. Open champion, count all your shots except the ones you take on the green. For a

golfer who usually shoots 95 with 34 putts, congratulations—you just carded a 61.

The flip side of No Putts is to play just Putts and count only the strokes a player takes on the green. Putts, however, is better played as a side bet because, although every shot counts the same, nobody really wants to take part in a five-hour putting contest. Why walk 6,000 yards to accomplish what can take place on the putting clock and within two minutes of the clubhouse bar?

Hogan

This is the highest form of No Putts, named for the Wee Iceman himself. To truly play as Hogan plays, keep track of fairway hits, greens in regulation, and closest to the pin. Players get a point for each accomplishment and settle up with each other over the difference.

This game puts a premium on accuracy. Bomb a drive 300 yards, but if it lands in the rough it's not as good as a 200-yard tee ball down the sprinkler line. Points go to those who play with precision.

Strategy and course management also become factors, as you may want to prudently choose that long iron for a tee shot to a narrow fairway instead of just banging the big dog and hoping for the best. If both players hit the fairway, then the points carry over to the next shot, with the player hitting the green in regulation getting two points. If both golfers hit the fairway and the green, the ball closer to the pin is worth three points.

Whether playing Hogan or any other game, a player should always keep track of fairways and greens hit during a round. A simple dot on the scorecard for each will do and will be a valuable help when trying to figure out why your round went so well or so poorly.

No fairway dots? Get to work on those tee shots. Finding the fairway but short on greens in regulation dots? Start practicing those approach shots. Also take note if you are dot deficient on longer or shorter holes to see if improvement needs to be made with longer or shorter irons. Want to play better golf? Connect the dots.

Birdies

A favorite of Chi Chi and his fellow pros is Birdies. It's an easy game to understand but a hard one to play because all that matters is making birdies. Put a price on each bird ($1, $5, $10, $25, $50), then get paid for each one you make during the round—provided you win the hole. If both players make birdie, the money goes on the line but carries over to the next birdie made in the game.

This game is popular on the Senior and PGA Tours during practice rounds because it's quick. Players can go about their business of preparing for the tournament and learning the course, wager a few bucks, but don't have to worry about spending time grinding over five-footers for par or bogey. Birdies is a better players' game because it pays on under-par holes, but the game can be easily adjusted for any talent level by making par or bogey the baseline bet.

Chi Chi, Jack, Trevino

"There is something amazing about golf that for some reason certain players do not ever match up well against other players. For some reason, whenever I played with Jack Nicklaus I never could beat him. And then, Jack never seemed to beat Lee Trevino head to head when they were playing. And Trevino hardly ever beats me when we play. So there is just something about something when you play against some people. Your games just don't fit right."

Switch

An excellent game for husbands and wives or for partners of widely differing capabilities on the course. Switch is actually a blatant violation of one of golf's most fundamental rules—golfers must play their own ball. This format calls for players to switch balls after the tee shot, then play out the remainder of the hole. Switch differs from Foursomes because shots aren't alternated the entire hole and because both balls are in play the entire hole.

The goal is to give the better player the more difficult shots, while the weaker player gets to hit shots he or she is more comfortable with and has a better chance of executing. It also allows both players to hit from places on the course they normally wouldn't see. The game can be an especially valuable tool for sharpening long- and middle-iron play among low handicappers who frequently go round after round hitting nothing but driver and wedge.

Chapman System

Very much like Switch, the Chapman System was the invention of Dick Chapman, one of the finest amateur players in the history of American golf. Chapman was a U.S. Amateur champion and played in the Masters 19 times as an amateur; he still holds the record for consecutive starts at Augusta by an amateur, with 17 in a row. It was while wintering and playing at Pinehurst that he came up with a format he hoped would make it easier for mixed teams with mixed abilities to compete in the game he loved.

The system works as follows: Two golfers on the same team each tee off, then play the other's ball. From there, the teams play out the best shot until the ball is holed. Basically, alternate shots for the first two shots, and then use a scramble Best Ball format until the hole is completed.

Although the system didn't catch on in the 1950s when Chapman worked with the USGA to invent the game, it has since grown in popularity as more women have taken up golf and accompany their husbands or boyfriends to the course.

Left/Right and Near/Far

For groups who can't seem to decide on teams, let your golf balls decide for you. All four players tee off, and in Left/Right the owners of the two balls farthest left partner and match up against the owners of the two balls farthest right.

The two teams then play the hole out with the low total winning the hole and a point. Left/Right can also be played as a Skins game with the low ball carrying the win for the entire team. A problem with the Skins version is that no provision is made to carry over halved holes, whereas the total strokes version tends to produce a winning team almost every time. Each point, or skin, is priced at a buck or five or whatever sum the partners agree on.

As in Wolf, the teams magically dissolve on their way from the green to the next tee and reset after the drives on every subsequent hole, although golfers who consistently hook the ball always seem to find themselves matched up against the players who are steady slicers.

Near/Far is the same game except the teams are made up of the shortest and farthest drives going against the two players in the middle. This version of the game is better when players in the group have varying talents. This allows the longer, generally better, player to help carry the shorter, usually weaker, player thereby leveling out the teams.

Long and Short

Another couples or partners game, Long and Short divides up the golfing chores by distance. One partner hits all shots from outside of 150 yards, and the other partner handles all work from inside of 150 yards. Once on the green, putts are alternated.

Long and Short is an excellent game for beginning golfers and the players trying to teach them. Rookies can learn the game from the green out and don't have to deal with the frustration of making a 9 or 10 on a 450-yard par 4. The game is also an excellent way to pair a young, strong player with an older golfer who may have lost a few yards off the tee but still has a splendid short game. Or maybe you just know a gorilla who can hit it a mile with his driver but couldn't hit a lob wedge or bunker shot to save his life—partner him with a touch player, and it's a team to be reckoned with on Saturday mornings. Team up to play Long and Short for fun and practice, or find another twosome or couple to play against for a few dollars.

Honey Dues

"I was giving a clinic in Ohio one time, and they gave away a very nice vacuum cleaner as a prize. The lady giving it away asked me, 'Chi Chi, are you the kind of man who likes to help out around the house—vacuuming, dusting, doing the dishes?' Well, I started to laugh because I said, 'No I am not. But neither is my wife.' "

This game is the ultimate in "significant other" golf bets! Honey Dues is a wager that, hopefully, brings couples together when the game of golf threatens to tear them apart.

In this wager, the nongolfing partner selects a hole on the front nine and the back nine, then bets a household chore, or CD, or dinner, or back rub that you, the playing partner, can't par the chosen hole. Par or better you win—bogey or worse, start shoveling or bagging the garbage or making reservations at Mondo's Casa de Red Meat. You lose! The game can be played net or gross depending on what agreement the two sides hammer out. The stakes can be graded so that par 5s pay better than par 3s.

As with any relationship, honesty is the key. Golf is a game of honor and integrity—don't cheat your significant other by bagging the results and altering the scorecard. The "playing partner" wins just by getting out of the house and onto the course; don't deprive your better half of a fair chance to win back his or her part of the bet.

The game also works for couples who do play golf together. Again, select a Honey Due hole, and the low score of the two wins, while the higher score just earned dish duty.

Out and Back

A man-on-man game that begins on the first tee and ends on the 18th green. Tee it up on number one, and play out to the farthest point away from the clubhouse. Then turn around and play back and hole out on the 18th green.

Surprisingly, par won't be as big a number as you might imagine, maybe 20 if you get a clear shot through some trees. To help the pace along and because not a wide variety of shots need to be played, the game is best played with one club—a long iron usually serving as the best and most versatile weapon.

Seeing as the director of golf, head pro, and course superintendent tend to frown on this sort of competition, Out and Back is strictly an early, early morning or a dusk, nightfall-is-closing-in-fast game. It's also easier to play at the country club where everybody knows who you are as opposed to the local muni where you'll likely get ratted out by strangers who think you're vandals.

If you find Out and Back does go over well at your club, try some more exotic adaptations of the game. Play from the parking lot to the swimming pool by way of the 5th green. Start in the locker room and play to the clubhouse bar by way of the 16th-hole ball washer. Out and Back is limited only by one's imagination.

"I don't know what the longest hole I ever played was, but the longest shot I ever made was going from poor in Puerto Rico to a millionaire on the Tour. When I was seven years old, my brother was pushing me in a cart down a big hill, and at the bottom of the hill they were playing golf. I didn't know what a caddie was, but I saw these guys carrying bags. I thought that sure looks easier than plowing a field, so I made a pest of myself until they let me forecaddie. That was my start in golf. And after I went out in the world, I also came back. I still have my home and live in Puerto Rico a majority of the year."

Head Games: Picking Tees— Give Yourself a Chance for Fun

Too often players get in their own way and ruin their entire day before they ever hit a ball. Playing from the wrong tees not only can be frustrating but also costly. Most scorecards suggest proper tees for specific handicaps. Follow the free advice. Play to your ability off the tee until you improve your game enough to move back; then move back.

It may sound macho to tell friends that you played a course from the tips, but they won't be impressed when you tell them you shot 129 and lost 13 balls. Playing well starts by giving yourself a chance to play well. A smooth 75, 80, 85, or even 90 from the white tees will be more fun and give you more confidence than puffing up your chest and shooting an outrageous number from the blues. Don't be color blind. If you get good enough, the very back tees will always be there waiting.

chapter **4**

Singles

One player. One club. One ball.

"The beauty of our game," says Chi Chi Rodriguez, "is that there is no one to blame. You mess up a golf shot, and you do not have to look far to find the culprit."

Ever since a bored shepherd accidently invented golf by flipping over his crook and beating rocks about the Scottish countryside to kill time, golf has been an individual game. Centuries later things haven't changed, only the grass has been mowed. Foursomes, partners, 150-player tournaments, caddies, scorers, markers, marshals, rules officials, galleries—none of them matter at the moment of impact. When it comes down to the actual defining moment of the sport, it's still just one player, one club, one ball. Every golfer is alone on the course when he or she swings.

As much as Chi Chi loves to entertain the crowds, promote his sport, and mix with his partners in pro-am events, he also enjoys an occasional round as a single. "I love being my own company sometimes," says Chi Chi. "When I was younger, I used to get up and get out to play before anybody else. I get lots of sleep—10 or 12 hours a night. I'm not out at bars and chasing bright lights. I go to bed early, and when the sun hits my window in the morning, I look forward to getting up and getting going."

Some days going solo is the only way to play; skip out of work early, and the starter fits you in as a single, a partner can't be found or calls in sick, or maybe, like Chi Chi, you just want to be alone. And then there are days when going alone is the best way to play. "The best practice rounds are the ones when you are by yourself and playing two or three balls at a time," according to Chi Chi the instructor.

And he adds, "People tend to play better alone for many reasons. There's no one else around to make them nervous, so they hit it freer, they are not so tense, and if they hit a bad shot they don't have to explain it to nobody. Also, they tend to think a little bit more about each shot and what it's going to require because they're not talking about the movies with their partner while they walk to the ball."

Technically, singles have no rights on a golf course. The pro shop should always try to pair you up, but if they can't, remember that groups ahead of you, no matter how large, are not obligated to let a single play through. If you're lucky enough to get out early and ahead of the field, consider yourself fortunate and don't take longer than three hours. (A player alone should really be able to finish in two or two and a half hours regardless of how many balls he or she is hitting.) If you get stuck behind traffic, take advantage of it—hit an extra shot here or roll another putt there to productively while away the spare time. The games in this chapter will help sharpen your skills and also prove that you don't always need a partner to find pleasure on the course.

Match Play Versus Mr. Par

Don't know if you've noticed, but there is an opponent waiting for a game on every scorecard in every pro shop, starter's shack, and first-tee mailbox in the world. If you're at a golf course, Mr. Par is always there, too, ready and willing to challenge you.

Perhaps the best of the solo games, Match Play Versus Mr. Par is you against each of the 18 holes. If you make birdie or better, you win the hole. Par, and the hole is halved. Bogey or worse loses the hole. Play the game to your full handicap, and see if you can put a four and two whipping or a one-up win on Mr. Par. For real fun give Mr. Par a name, and play your own personal Ryder Cup or President's Cup singles match against Sergio Garcia or Ernie Els.

Make sure when playing this game not to get lax. Don't give yourself any putts and don't rehit any shots. Play the game straight up as if you had a

continued ☞

partner there keeping an eye on you the entire match. Because money is useless against Mr. Par, play for a prize you'd like to have and would miss if you didn't win it: dessert, a beer, or a golf shirt from the shop. Work on your game and your willpower at the same time!

Hole	1	2	3	4	5	6	7	8	9	
Gold	400	426	450	383	183	393	550	190	590	
Hdcp	13	7	1	17	15	9	5	11	3	
Par	4	4	4	4	3	4	5	3	5	
Player 1 Hdcp (12)	5	5/4.	4/3.	4	4	6/5.	6/5.	4/3.	5/4.	43
	1 Dn	1 Dn	AS	AS	1 Dn	2 Dn	2 Dn	2 Dn	1 Dn	
AS = All square										
DN = Down										
UP = Up										

El Legado Golf Resort
Home of Chi Chi Rodriguez

Player 1 finished 1 down to Mr. Par

Date ______________

Scorer ____________________ Attest ____________________

Par for Me

"Par is what you're supposed to make; it's not what you have to make," says Chi Chi. "Par for me might be 72, but for you it might be 102." Realistically, not many of us are scratch golfers, so 70 or 72 is probably out of our reach, and in that case we can adjust par to our game. Earl Woods used to tell his son Tiger to ignore the scorecard and play to Tiger par. As he got older and better, the gap between Tiger par and regular par closed until, well, Tiger par is now about 68 from the tips.

You can do the same thing. Beginners may want to make par equal to a triple bogey on every hole, for a total of 126. Because par 3s are usually shorter and easier for first timers, par on the short holes may be just bogey. Take a look at the card and the yardages, and try to come up with a score you think you can make on every hole. Establish Par for Me, and then take a shot at breaking it.

Par for Me is more of a mental game than a physical one. If you decide bogey golf is the goal for you (breaking 90), really no difference exists between a 93 that's 3 over your par and a 93 that's 21 over regular par. The idea is to give a player something to shoot for during the round. Most golf barriers are far harder to break with your brain than your body. A putt on 18 for an even par 90 is a lot nervier than a three-footer for 18 or 19 over. It also takes away a lot of the negative feedback of always marking down a double or triple bogey.

Setting a par based on your ability is also a good way to gauge improvement. Break it a few times, and you can lower your goal or maybe move back a tee box. Par for Me is for middle to high handicappers, but it keeps a nice positive spin on the game and will keep players coming back.

"The funniest thing I ever heard about shooting par golf," says Chi Chi, "is when the country singer Willie Nelson bought a golf course and said par is whatever he decides he wants it to be. Willie Nelson, he says, 'This one here is a par 47, and yesterday I birdied that sucker.' I tell you what; I would like to play courses where the holes are par 47. I would win a lot of tournaments, I know that."

Two Ball

In another match play event, Two Ball pits your Titleist against your Precept. The Sabre in your bag takes on the Strata you found in the woods. Top Flite XL versus Nike Tour Accuracy is always a good battle.

Two Ball is, well, pretty self-explanatory and a great game for when you're stuck behind a foursome. Play two balls on each hole and record the score for each ball. Ideally, the two balls will mirror each other although you may end up seeing both sides of the course if you're struggling with your game or just starting out. Strive for consistency in your game.

And whatever you do, never make the same mistake twice. If the first ball duck hooks into the water off the tee, make sure the second one doesn't. If you're faced with similar approach shots and misclub on the first, be sure to grab the correct stick for the second swing. Two Ball is a competition for one, but a player should always learn from the preceding shot.

Two Ball is a good way to test if you're ready to move back a tee box. Play one ball from your normal tees and one from farther back, to see what kind of a difference it makes in your score. If you can handle the extra yardage, then you'll know your game is getting better.

Keep score at match play, but medal play works, too, or keep track of a mock-Nassau if you like. Play matches between your favorite golfers—Chi Chi Rodriguez versus Sam Snead, Tiger Woods versus Jack Nicklaus—or have your least favorites square off, such as Norm the Brother-in-Law Who Can't Count versus Billy the Cheating Neighbor. The key is to play just as you would if you were in a real match. Play smart when you have an advantage on a hole. Be aggressive when you have a chance to close out a hole. Don't take a needless chance if the match is close.

No need for a handicap here 'cause the person you're competing with plays off exactly the same number. If you're a 12, you're a 12—doesn't matter what ball you play. A final note—no giving yourself putts. Make 'em all and your game will be better for it.

Miniature Golf

No windmills or clown's mouth here, just a suggestion to help the short game. Instead of planting the flagstick and walking straight to the next tee (where you'll be forced to wait and wait while the group ahead of you tees off and then burns 10 more minutes looking for lost balls before finally hitting their seconds), go back and spend some quality time working around the green.

Make each of the 18 "holes" a par 2, and practice getting up and down from various spots around the green. Not even the best pro could finish an even-par 36 for the round, but making a run at it will hone your green-side recovery skills, arguably the most important aspect of the game. Play from a couple of bunkers, hit from the short side of the green, in front of it, behind it. Purposely give yourself bad lies and buried lies. Breaking 40 for 18 would be excellent, 41 to 45 good, 46 to 50 average; 51 or more, and you need more work. Downtime on a golf course doesn't have to be idle time. Play Miniature Golf to go with your regular game.

Two for One

How does a mulligan on every shot sound? Too good? Two for One is your game. Basically, it's the solo version of Best Ball. Hit two balls off the tee, and then play the best shot. The routine is the same for approach shots, sand shots, putts, or any other shot until the ball is holed. Hit two and play the best one. A player should be able to cut his or her handicap by half or more given a second chance on every swing. But if you card a score 10, 12, or 15 shots lower than your previous personal best, make sure to keep it to yourself, or, at least, explain to people the reason for your sudden drop from 90 to 75.

The beauty here is that players get a chance to instantly fix any problem. A mistake in swing mechanics or lapse in judgment can be assessed and corrected immediately, no waiting until the next time you're confronted with the shot. A do-over can also help reinforce a positive pass at the ball. Remembering what went right and then repeating it right away will help ingrain a good muscle memory.

"The thing about playing alone is that a man can practice all his options. Should he chip or pitch, hit a five or a six, does this putt break left or right, can I cut the corner of a dogleg? And this will serve him well in future matches because you should never try and hit a shot you haven't practiced. Everybody sees Phil [Mickelson] hit that flop shot, and he makes it look so easy that they try it when they play the next time.

"And what happens? They've never hit the shot before in their life, and they either hit 50 yards over the green or take a big divot and don't even move the ball two inches. I can hit that shot because I used to try and get the ball as high as I could by hitting it over palm trees and make it land soft. Same thing goes for a hook or a fade.

"You gonna tell me a guy who has never hooked a ball around a hazard in his life is going to magically turn the ball in mid-air the first time he tries because he read a book? No. You must practice these shots whenever you get a chance on the course, and when you play alone you get a lot of chances. Don't be too bold and hit a shot in a money match until you've worked on it a couple of times by yourself."

To make Two for One more demanding and a useful tool for improving your game, don't always play both balls the same way. Hit your first ball just as you would normally around the course, but experiment with the second. Hit a driver, then follow it with a 3 wood off the tee. In the fairway, hit a normal 8-iron approach, then try to knock down a 7 iron or hit a hard 9 iron on your second ball. If you're torn between a high hook and a low fade, try them both so that you get a feel for each shot.

Just be careful that double dipping doesn't become a bad habit when playing with other golfers. Playing two balls is, after all, not legal in any way, shape, or form under USGA rules. Any player will tire of a partner who continually drops a second ball out of his or her pocket and hits it again for the heck of it.

Worse Ball

The 180-degree, complete, exact, polar opposite of Two for One, Worse Ball gives a golfer two chances on every shot, but you have to play the worse of the two each time until the ball is holed. The guess here is, unless you're a 5-handicapper or less, you won't come within 15 shots of your normal score. So why play? Practice, practice, practice. But it's practice with a purpose.

Golfers are on the course hitting real golf shots and scrambling to make the best score they can on every hole. A golfer will develop far more quickly learning to play difficult shots as opposed to easy ones. It's also a matter of getting comfortable with trouble. Most players adopt a defeatist attitude when they find themselves in the rough, a bunker, blocked out by a tree, or faced with an unusually long iron shot. Learning to play from outside your comfort zone or in trouble will help develop recovery skills and in turn boost confidence.

Because hitting two good shots in a row is hardly impossible, Worse Ball doesn't always mean having to hit from trouble or a terrible lie. But it will increase the level of difficulty on every shot, and that little bit of extra work will make a big difference when you go back to playing only your good ones.

Worse Ball is also a cinch to improve your putting. Anybody can make it once; doing it twice is a real test. "In all the pro-am events I've played in over the last 40 years, thousands of them, I've never seen an amateur hit a putt again after making it," says Chi Chi, "but they all putt the ones they miss two or three extra times. Learn to make the same one twice, especially the ones from 15 feet and in, and you'll make a lot more of them."

Oil Leaks

In almost every round, a time comes when the game gets away from a golfer. Occasionally all 18 holes go well start to finish, but more often than not you'll need to stop an oil leak. Stop the bleeding. Get off the bogey train, as it were. First thing to do when in trouble is to take a few seconds, breathe deep, and concentrate on slowing down. Frantic equals fast which equals fatal, so stay calm.

Next, remember that you didn't suddenly forget how to play golf and that a change in fortune is one good swing away. "In the game of golf," says Chi Chi, "you are not going to succeed every time. That's how life is, too. I just tell myself I will do better next time. Next time is my favorite phrase of all time. 'I'll do better next time.' Always reinforce positively with next time. Do not say 'if,' say 'next time.' And believe it." Don't worry about making a big number or getting lost strokes back on the next hole. Concentrate solely on the shot at hand. Think positive and block out everything but the target. Most oil leaks are nothing more than a wandering mind.

Opposite

Sometimes we all know the right thing to do, and we go ahead and do the opposite anyway. This game encourages it. We're not telling golfers to play anything but smart golf; we just want to encourage them to look at alternatives. The best way to do that is by determining the correct club for each shot . . . and then *not* using it.

The hope is to get golfers to use their imagination and create shots they might not see originally. Chipping with fairway woods, hitting a bunker shot with a putter, flop shots, or pitching past the pin and letting a slope on the green bring it back to the pin are all creative shots originated when somebody went against the norm.

"In his prime, Seve Ballesteros was a magician from 100 yards and in not because he made shots nobody else could make but because he made shots nobody else could think of," Chi Chi says admiringly. "I know instantly what play I am going to make when I get to my ball; the reason I take extra time is to think of any other way that would make the shot easier or give me a better chance at birdie than the obvious one."

Once again, playing alone is a great time to experiment with your game. No fear of failure, and if a particular shot does turn out poorly, you'll know better next time. Every great inventor learned a lot more from his or her failures than from his or her successes. Golf should be no different. To truly know your game, you need to know what every club in the bag can and cannot do.

Chi Chi's Best Shot Ever

In his six-decade career, Chi Chi Rodriguez has authored many strokes of genius, and yet he doesn't hesitate when asked to name his favorite. It came on the 72nd hole of the 1991 U.S. Senior Open at Oakland Hills Country Club in Birmingham, Michigan, with Chi Chi trailing Jack Nicklaus by one stroke.

"I had 175 yards, and there was no way to stop the ball on the green. The best shot in the world with a 5 iron would have bounced over the green. So what I did was take a 6 iron and hook it so that it hit between the two bunkers in front of the green and jumped up to the pin. I hooked that ball 50 yards. I mean it made almost a U-turn in midair and ended up a foot from the hole.

"Then my caddie came up to help me read the putt, and I said to him, 'Get away, you're just trying to get on the TV. I'll handle this one buddy.' It was the greatest shot I ever hit. To tell you the truth, I was a little mad after that shot because I really thought I had made it." Chi Chi and Jack would finish tied Sunday, with Nicklaus winning an 18-hole play-off, 65-69 the following day. Still, Chi Chi's incredible 6 iron is forever part of U.S. Open lore at the monster.

One Club

Eighteen holes, one club, have at it. That's the game. Shove a handful of tees in one pocket, a couple of balls in the other, get a stick, and fire away.

"That *Tin Cup* guy's got nothing on me, boy. In that movie where he shot even par for nine holes with a 7 iron, I can do it with everything from a 3 iron to a 7 iron," exclaims Chi Chi. "When you grow up as poor as I did, and we were so poor I drank milk with a fork to make it last longer, you get a good club, you use it all the time. I would have been a good guy to caddie for in the days when I was a young caddy—not much to lift."

One Club can be an absolute hoot (alone or in groups), and you'll be surprised how much mileage you can get out of a single club. Most par 3s are reachable. Unless you're playing at PGA Tour distances, you can get home in three on par 4s, and par 5s should never take more than four swings to reach the green.

Stick to irons when playing One Club—the game doesn't really work with woods, and you'll discover you're toting a lot of extra weight. You'll also find you play a more controlled game because of equipment limits. If you can't hit 250 yards with a 7 iron, no use throwing out vertebrae trying. One Club also has teaching value that will be discussed further in chapter 9. If you can make one club do a little bit of everything, it's a great security blanket.

"I can use my 4 iron to lift your wallet out of your back pocket."

As for Chi Chi's one club of choice, he says, "I would play with a 4 iron. I can hit it anywhere from 110 yards to 210 yards. I can hit high or run it low. Bend it right or turn it left. And if there's money on the game, and you are betting me I can't beat you with just one club, then I can use my 4 iron to lift your wallet out of your back pocket, too."

Head Games: Quick Course Management

"When I was a young man, I was so daring on the course that, if you would have put the pin on the Titanic, I would have gone to get scuba gear," says Chi Chi. "Now I think about things a little more. Golf is half intelligence and half physical—50/50 mind and muscle." Here's a quick guide to thinking your way around a course:

On par 3s

Aim for the middle of the green and try to work the ball toward the pin.

Keep the ball below the hole.

On par 4s

The first priority should be hitting the fairway.

Don't be a hero out of trouble. Advance the ball the best you can safely toward the green. If you can reach the green in three, you always have a chance for par, and you should do no worse than bogey.

On par 5s

Be aggressive off the tee. An extra shot is built in to recover if your drive goes awry.

Don't go for the green in two unless you're positive you can make it.

When laying up, lay back so that you have a full swing for an approach shot.

On all holes

Tee up on the side of trouble, then don't dwell on it. Lining up with a hazard opens up more room to avoid it.

Always, always, always go for the percentage shot under pressure.

chapter 5

Tournaments

Just look at all these fabulous prizes—high-tech drivers, gleaming sets of irons, newfangled putters, dozens of balls, airline tickets, dinner for two at Chez T-Bocks, a free foursome at Cypress Point (okay, that's wishful thinking), pro shop gift certificates. No end is in sight to the loot available on the "amateur" tournament circuit. Charity golf events are a summer staple, as are club championships, member/guest events, and after-work leagues. Even if a golfer never makes it to the Tour—and rest assured 999,999 out of a million won't—he or she is sure to play in something more competitive than his or her weekly Sunday morning outing—or at least more populated.

Tournaments are every player's chance to experience the drama of looking at the leader board, feel the rush of asking around to see where your team stands, breathe the charged-up atmosphere of playing golf against a full field. Competing against a single person or partners is one thing; taking on two foursomes on every hole, 144 players, is quite another. Even matching up against three or four other foursomes can be a gas.

Many people are satisfied at tournaments with merely picking up their tee package during registration. Sure the hat, shirt, handful of tees, sleeve of balls, and beverage koozie are nice gifts, but if you're going to invest five or six hours of your afternoon in something (not to mention a substantial entry fee), why not win?

"Golfers should always try to win. It's that simple. You should always play to win, or else go sit in the clubhouse and read the paper. Play golf for enjoyment?" asks Chi Chi. "What is more enjoyable than winning? The thing about playing in tournaments is people try too hard. It should be the easiest thing in the world. If you rely on me and I rely on you and we rely on the other two guys, then there is no pressure because, given four chances on every shot, even a group of chimpanzees can shoot under par." Well, even for the most evolutionized of the primates, it may not be that simple, but keys to success in tournament play include order, attitude, ability, and strategy.

Most tournament players are familiar with a Scramble format, but the next few pages list many additional games to make the golf season a little less monotonous. Also included are games for organizers running events that last two or more days. So sign up and buck up for a charity event or a school fund-raiser, take a three-day golf vacation to a nice resort, play in some of the clubs or men's or women's association events—just make sure to find three friends and get involved.

Golf on Television

Why buy an expensive golf video when you can get a four-hour lesson for free on television? Watching tournament golf on television can actually help improve a golfer's game. Who better to imitate than the world's best players? Watch and learn from their swings, their setups, their tempos, their demeanors. Take notice of their routines and how they study a putt or examine every shot option before making a play. Not everyone can swing like a pro, but anyone can try. Find a player who has a similar swing to yours and study it. "Yogi Berra, one of my favorite players, said, 'You can observe a lot just by watching.' And I agree," says Chi Chi. "Imitating a good player is good for the game."

Also pay close attention to the commentators. Because golf coverage bounces from player to player, announcers are forced to explain each shot and what's required by the pro in a quick and concise manner. These mini-lessons can be beneficial because they get straight to the point and don't overwhelm the viewer with volumes of technical information. "Chi Chi has a decent lie in the bunker, but the lip might be a problem. He's just going to open up the face of his club, move the ball ahead in his stance a little, and slide the club under the ball." Simple is best in teaching.

Championships

No new games here, just a review of the two most popular ways to play—match and medal. Most golf clubs hold a championship under each format during the year. Medal play usually lasts more than one round, with the first round used to put players into flights for the final round or rounds. The championship flight is generally the top 32 scores, A flight the next 32, and so on through the D flight.

Medal play is the game you see on television every weekend and all four Majors without the oversized novelty check and bad-looking blazer awarded at the end of the tournament. Tee it up, play smart, and go low—or at least don't go too high.

Match play championships pit players head-to-head over the course of a couple of days and have an NCAA basketball tournament feel to them. Quite often match-play tournaments begin with 18 or 36 holes of medal play, to establish flights, and then shift to individual matches. Because match play is really a series of two-person tournaments, it helps to pare down large fields into more manageable numbers before beginning head-to-head competition. Even in a 32-person field, a player will have to win four matches to claim a championship.

Concentrate on your ball, but be sure to keep track of your opponent's position during a hole, as well, and play accordingly. Winning a hole or having it handed to you counts exactly the same. Put bad holes behind you quickly (remember, no matter how bad, they only count as one). Never give up on a hole 'cause a miraculous hole out is always just a swing away. May you be at least one up after 18 on all your matches.

Scramble

The gold standard of golf outings, the Scramble format is a Best Ball for all. Four musketeers armed with dynamic gold shafts—one for all and all for one. The rules are simple: Four players tee off, and the best ball is chosen and marked. All players then hit their next shots from that point, and the process is repeated until the ball is holed. Players can move their ball within a club length of the original lie, no nearer to the hole, and the lie cannot be improved. That means balls in the rough can't be moved into the fairway, out of hazards, or onto the green from the fringe. Scrambles are always, always, low-scoring affairs. Breaking 60 is almost a requirement for winning. Play aggressively. Swing hard. Aim for pins. Stroke putts boldly.

Scramble teams should develop an order of attack and stick with it. It's best for weaker players to hit first and consistent players (that doesn't mean big hitters) last. This formula gives the early hitters a chance to swing without the pressure of carrying the team and also gives them a chance to feel valuable. If a short or errant player always has to follow the better player, his or her role is diminished to "Good ball. Guess I don't even need to hit here."

Likewise, a big hitter is a great asset to any group, but anchor duties should always be left for the straightest, most consistent player. The key is to always have at least one ball in the fairway. If the anchor person can be counted on, then the long knocks of the world are free to swing from the heels and hope. If you're fortunate enough be in a group with a player who can hit it both straight and long, then take that golfer to dinner. If you are that player, don't eat too much.

The order of play on the tee doesn't have to be the order used from the fairway. In fact, often it's a good idea to let the person who hit the chosen tee ball have first go at the second shot to keep him or her in the rhythm of the hole. Courses are also filled with great drivers who can't hit an iron worth a lick, so don't be afraid to switch the batting order so that, again, the most consistent iron player hits last. That insurance blanket will help oil up the swings of the other players, as well. Get a safe shot in the middle of the green, and then zero in on the stick. On par 5s, set up a comfortable layup shot for safety, and then let 'er rip. "Swing hard," says Chi Chi, "in case you hit it."

Around the green, be sure to choose the easiest shot for all players and not just the shortest. Stay away from bunkers unless absolutely necessary because most players aren't comfortable in the sand (though we hope to change that by the end of chapter 10). Likewise, the shortest putt isn't always the easiest putt. A 15-footer below the hole will always be easier than a 10-foot slider.

On the green, make sure whoever is chosen to putt first gives the rest of the group a good strong read. The first putter is the teacher, and everybody on the team should go to school. Make sure the first putt is strong enough to get to the cup but not so bold that it rolls through the break. If the first ball drops, more power to the team, but ideally it should give a good read and end up close enough to the cup that it can easily be holed with a second putt if needed.

For that reason don't let a terrible putter hit first. Bad putters need help, and giving them a chance to look at the speed and direction of the putt with their own eyes is the best advice. Repeating—*bad putters second, not first!* Once a team gets one in gimme range, remaining putters should be aggressive. Make a solid run at the hole 'cause it's one of the few times you don't have to worry about making a three- or four-footer coming back.

Most often in golf, the word "scramble" means recovery or scratching out a score from bad places. In a Scramble tournament, it should mean birdie, birdie, birdie.

Speeding Up Scrambles

Pace of play is always an issue in a Scramble—players searching for and retrieving balls, picking which tee shot to play, putt after putt, after putt, after putt. The quickest way to speed up a Scramble is to birdie every hole, but barring that, here's a time-saving suggestion. Play with "par as your partner."

As soon as a team or a player reaches par (net), he or she is finished on the hole. Pick it up. Advance to the next tee, please. Because Scrambles are low-scoring tournaments, anything that's not a birdie or eagle isn't really going to help. Make your par or take your par, but then move on. With par as your partner, a Scramble should take no more than four and a half hours to complete. That saves at least an hour, perhaps one and a half hours that can be better used, say, at the 19th hole.

Also, in the event of a tie, go to a scorecard play-off. Start on the 18th hole or the number one handicap hole, and compare scores backwards until one team wins a hole and, in turn, the tournament outright. Golfers should always grind extra hard on the final hole and the toughest hole on the course just in case it comes down to a play-off in the scorer's tent.

Bloodsome Scramble

Yes, it can get worse! In a Bloodsome Scramble, the same rules apply as in a regular Scramble except for one teeny tiny, small, little, barely even noticeable modification. Instead of playing the best ball after every shot, a team must play its worst ball. Enjoy, because you will see parts of a golf course you never knew existed. Breaking 80 is the big barrier in this game, and 90 will show itself on a lot of scorecards. Think of it as "one miss, all miss."

A Bloodsome calls for teams to play every bit as conservatively as they would aggressively under regular Scramble rules. Weaker golfers should play their normal games, while good players will have to scale back. For this reason, a Bloodsome should be a once-in-a-while event. It's good at the club for a laugh or to break up the normal routine, but for golfers plunking down a sizable sum to play for fun or the rare chance to play a lavish course, it can be a little too punishing. Not to mention that it can take hours and hours to play because every last putt must be holed. Bloodsome is not friendly to final scores or the clock.

Designated Driver

A simple but pressure-filled twist to a regular Scramble, Designated Driver requires each team to play at least four tee balls from every player in the group. The order is set with the first person listed on the scorecard hitting on number one, the second on two, the third on three, and the fourth on four with the wheel continuing throughout the round. The last player listed, for example, would hit on numbers 4, 8, 12, and 16. The regular Scramble format then applies until the ball is holed.

The beauty of Designated Driver is the drama. The tee ball has no three-person safety net to cover mistakes. The designated driver alone is carrying the hopes of the team on the box, and everybody else is just carpooling along on the initial swing. And if you don't think that'll make for some collar tightening or shorten a few swings or produce never-before-seen shanks, your thoughts will change after 18 holes.

A word of advice from Chi Chi: "If you are confident that the hole sets up for your game, then swing away hard. But if you have even a little doubt or your nerves start to act up, be conservative with your shot. Your teammates can more easily bail you out from a shorter shot in the fairway than a long one from in the trees. Remember, the woods are filled with long drivers."

Shamble

Here's a game to get the most out of your golfing dollar. The Shamble is Designated Driver played backwards. All golfers tee off on every hole, and after the best drive is chosen, all golfers play their own ball the remainder of the hole. Think Scramble off the tee—real golf the rest of the way.

Two nice benefits of a Shamble: First, with occasional exceptions, golfers get to play approach shots from a decent position on the fairway. Second, it feels more like a regular game of golf; and if a player has plunked down a generous fee for a spot in the tournament, it's nice to be able to play your own ball and see the whole course.

The real fun in a Shamble comes in the various ways to keep score. Because each team has four scores on every hole, the options are plenty. Teams can take the low score only or count all scores, net or gross. The team total can consist of the high and the low score; or, as in diving, throw out the high and the low, and count the middle two scores. Tally up the first and third best balls. Be creative.

Tournament Side Games

Here are a few extras that add excitement to the main game in a tournament:

- Longest drive—For the big hitters
- Shortest drive—For the not-so-big hitters
- Straightest drive—Rewards accuracy over length
- Mulligans—$15 apiece or two for $25
- Closest to pin on par 3s—Truly tape-measure shots
- Hole-in-one prizes—Win a new car or VCR
- Beat the pro—Ante up and win if you're inside the pro's tee ball
- Hit the green—Enter for a few bucks and get back double on the dance floor
- U.N. hole—For a price, putt for birdie at any of the five flags

Cha, Cha, Cha

The name should be a giveaway—a Cha, Cha, Cha is a favorite of Chi Chi Chi Rodriguez. Each member of the foursome plays his or her ball as in a medal-play event with full handicaps. The cha, cha, cha comes in the bookkeeping of the game. On the par 3s, only the lowest score is counted; on the par 4s, the two lowest scores are recorded; and on the par 5s, the three lowest scores are tallied. If the tournament is played on a normal par-72 layout featuring two threes and two fives on each side, par for a Cha, Cha, Cha is 152 (4 holes × par 3 × 1 player = 12, 10 × 4 × 2 = 80, 4 × 5 × 3 = 60, for a total of 152).

Cha, Cha, Cha is a great tournament to get all the players on a team involved, and it's fun to watch as the strategy evolves. Teams need to be aggressive on par 3s and more conservative on the long holes, the opposite of a normal round of golf.

"If there had been a famous baseball player in my country named Cha Cha, then I might have become Cha Cha Rodriguez. My given name is Juan Rodriguez. But as a boy, my favorite player in all of Puerto Rico was a third baseman for the Cangrejeros de Santurce named Chi Chi Flores. The Santurce Crabbers [English translation] are like the New York Yankees of Puerto Rico. I liked Chi Chi Flores because he always tried very hard. He always gave 125 percent. I liked him so much that I would always pretend to be Chi Chi Flores when we played games, and pretty soon everybody started calling me Chi Chi. He was my idol, and I still love baseball today.

"In my day, I was a pretty good player. I was a pitcher who could throw the ball in the mid-90 miles per hour. I played with many of the great Puerto Rican players who made it to the American major leagues, such as Roberto Clemente and Orlando Cepeda. One of the guys I used to throw to eventually caught Sandy Koufax, and he said to me, 'Chi Chi, you threw at least as fast as Koufax.'

"Baseball is a great game. But when I was in the army, I went to the baseball park, and there was a guy named George Spencer [George Spencer pitched eight major league seasons with the Giants and Tigers between 1950 and 1960], and he was hitting baseballs. George asked me if I wanted to play golf or play baseball. And I watched him hitting baseballs, and I thought if that guy hit me he could kill me. And I had never thought of a guy hitting a line drive and hurting me because I never was hit very hard when I was pitching in Puerto Rico, you know, people could hardly hit me at all. But I saw those line drives, and I just kept heading for the golf course. That was the last I thought of it."

Progressive

Like Cha, Cha, Cha, Progressive, or Sixes as it's referred to in some club circles, is a game where accounting is almost as key as golfing. In Progressive, all team members play their own ball tee to the green, with the round divided into six-hole segments. On holes 1 through 6, the team score is the lowest of the four balls. On holes 7 through 12, the two lowest scores count. And on the final six holes, 13 through 18, the three best scores are added up. The key to Progressive is to attack the course and go after birdies early and then play it safe to avoid big, score-wrecking numbers late in the round.

Hole	1	2	3	4	5	6	7	8	9	10	11	12	13	14	15	16	17	18	In	Tot	Hcp	Net
Gold	400	426	450	383	183	393	550	190	590	420	173	449	599	426	155	376	400	600				
Hdcp	13	7	1	17	15	9	5	11	3	12	14	4	10	8	18	16	6	2				
Par	4	4	4	4	3	4	5	3	5	4	3	4	5	4	3	4	4	5				
Player 1	(4)	(4)	(3)	(4)	4	(4)	5	(3)	(4)	(4)	(3)	4	(4)	(4)	(3)	(5)	(5)	(5)	37	72	0	72
Player 2	5	4	4/3.	4	4	6	5	(3)	(5/4.)	(4)	3	(4/3.)	(5)	(5)	(3)	(4)	(4)	(6/5.)	38	78	4	74
Player 3	5	5/4.	5/4.	4	(3)	6	(5/4.)	4	6/5.	4	4	(4/3.)	(5)	(5/4)	(4)	5	(5/4.)	(5/4)	41	84	8	76
Player 4	6/5.	6/5.	5/4.	5	4/3.	7/6.	(5/4.)	4/3.	6/5.	5/4.	(3/2)	6/5.	6/5.	6/5.	4	(5/4.)	(5/4.)	7/6..	47	95	16	79
Team	4	4	3	4	3	4	8	6	8	8	5	6	14	13	10	13	12	14	22	41	76	(139)
Progressive par	4	4	4	4	3	4	10	6	10	8	6	8	15	12	9	12	12	15	23	48	75	146
																			1-6	7-12	13-18	Total

El Legado Golf Resort
Home of Chi Chi Rodriguez

Team counts: Best ball holes 1-6
2 best balls holes 7-12
3 best balls holes 13-18

Date ____________ Scorer ________________ Attest ________________

Blind Nine

Don't let the name fool you; players get to keep their eye on the ball. Blindfolds are not required, at least not when hitting. In Blind Nine, teams play a Scramble format, but only 9 of the 18 holes count toward the team score. Which 9? Well, it's not up to you. Outing organizers select a combination of three par 3s, three par 4s, and three par 5s to make up the blind 9 before the tournament tees off.

This format is best for tournaments with a limited number of entries because a full field event will produce too many similar scores. Although using seven-eighths or three-quarters of a team's average handicap will help avoid that sort of logjam, the drawback then becomes that golfers' handicaps determine the winner more than the golfers themselves.

As for strategy in Blind Nine, go for broke on the short and long holes because a majority of them will count in the final score, and fire at pins on par 4s, too, 'cause you never know which birdie may make the difference. If your squad does wind up making one of those killer bogeys, say a little prayer that the hole isn't in the draw, and maybe you'll end up dodging a bogey bullet.

Money Ball

Got to have the Money Ball! In this game, each foursome is given a money ball, usually something in a lovely pink, a stunning orange, or glowing yellow, which rotates from player to player throughout the 18 holes. On each hole, one golfer plays the money ball while the other three team members compete in a traditional Scramble. Scores on the money ball and the Scramble ball are kept separately and added together to calculate the team score at the end of the round. Low score takes home all the awards and neat free stuff.

The key in this game is getting the money ball all the way around and back home. If a team loses its money ball, it's out of luck and out of the tournament, although in some events lost money balls are given a score five shots higher per uncompleted hole than the highest returned money ball.

"For me, I hit my money ball on Sundays. Tiger Woods, he likes to wear red during the final round of a tournament for luck. I was the first player on the Tour to dress in the same color all the time on a certain day. I always used to wear green on Sunday because that's when they hand out the checks and green is the color of money. If you ever see a color picture of me in a book or some place in a magazine and I am wearing green, then you can take it to the bank—the picture was taken on a Sunday."

If you choose, Money Ball can be played entirely as its own tournament with an award for the low score. The game can also be played as part of a Best Ball with the money ball counting for half the score and the team's low ball on the hole counting for the other half.

Play the money ball wisely. Get it through all 18 holes, and you're a cinch to beat half the field. Look at the scorecard carefully when establishing your team's money ball order. Keep poor players away from water holes, and put your best players on the highest handicap holes. If it means taking an iron off the tee or even putting a ball 10 times on a par 3 to keep alive, do it. The money ball must live at all costs.

Tombstone Tournament

See you were right. This game is going to be the death of you. In a Tombstone Tournament each player is given a number to shoot for based on his handicap and par for the course. The number and player's name are written on a piece of paper, and the player carries it with him during the round. Best way to figure the number is par plus three-quarters handicap, meaning a 16-handicapper playing on beautiful Lake Ballbegone Country Club's par 71 north course has a target score of 83 (12 + 71 = 83).

Golfers tee off on the first hole (a shotgun start won't work) and play until they reach their number. And, well, we all know what happens when your number is up. R.I.P. The player takes a tee and pegs his paper (tombstone) in the exact spot on the course that his ball lies after his final shot. The golfer

completing the most holes and any extra distance on his final hole wins. If a player completes all 18 holes and has strokes left, he goes back to the first tee and continues playing until he reaches his number. An alternate method for scoring players who complete an entire round is to award first place to the player who finishes the most strokes below his number.

In lieu of a tombstone, many tournaments use a flag to designate the end of a golfer's day. In either case, the final three or four holes on the back nine of a full field event will look like a golf graveyard. Tombstone is no different from any other medal-play event—the name just seems more fatal; consistent play is crucial; and triple bogeys, dare we say, are killers!

Chicago

The tournament format of broad shoulders. Chicago gets the whole team involved the whole time. In Chicago, each player is given a point quota based on his or her handicap, making it imperative that all golfers have a verified handicap in this format. Point quotas are set as follows: 39 for a scratch player, 38 for a one, 37 for a two, 36 for a three, and so on down to a three for a 36, two for a 37, and one for a 38 or worse. Hey, everybody has to shoot for at least one point during a round. The sum of each golfer's quota makes up the team's quota. A team composed of 5-, 10-, 15-, and 20-handicappers would have a quota of 106 points (5 = 34, 10 = 29, 15 = 24, 20 = 19). Points are then awarded for each score made on a hole as follows:

Bogey = 1 point
Par = 2 points
Birdie = 4 points
Eagle = 8 points
Albatross = 16 points

The goal is for each of the players to reach his or her quota and, if possible, exceed it. Golfers who fail to reach their quota have the difference between their point total and their quota subtracted from the team score. The winning team is the foursome that scores the most points beyond its quota.

Chicago, in addition to being a fine city, is a fine format that allows every player a chance to get the most out of his or her round and experience the pressure to produce for the team on every hole. And that pressure mounts as the round progresses and valuable points are still out there for the taking. On a 7,000-yard golf course, Chicago can be golf's miracle four miles.

Calloway System

If you've ever uttered the words, "Except for two really bad holes, I played great today," this is your game. The Calloway System allows players to toss out those annoying triple bogeys and other scorecard eyesores. Instead of using handicaps, net scores are figured by throwing out a certain number of holes based on a golfer's total score.

Let's say Paul Washer throws an even 100 at the field. He can subtract his three worst holes of the day. If those holes were a 6, 7, and 10, his net score is 100 minus 23 for a smooth little 77. The lower the gross score, the less a golfer gets a break. If Barbara Ballstriker cards a nifty 79, she discards only her worst score on any hole. The table of deductions is as follows:

Gross score	**Subtract**
73 or less	0 holes
73 to 75	1/2 hole
76 to 80	1 hole
81 to 85	1 1/2 holes
86 to 90	2 holes
91 to 95	2 1/2 holes
96 to 100	3 holes
Continue one-half hole increments for every five strokes.	

Hole	1	2	3	4	5	6	7	8	9	10	11	12	13	14	15	16	17	18	In	Tot	Hcp	Net
Gold	400	426	450	383	183	393	550	190	590	420	173	449	599	426	155	376	400	600				
Hdcp	13	7	1	17	15	9	5	11	3	12	14	4	10	8	18	16	6	2				
Par	4	4	4	4	3	4	5	3	5	4	3	4	5	4	3	4	4	5				
Calloway #1	6	5	(8)	6	4	4	7	3	6	(7)	5	5	(7)	6	5	5	5	6	51	100	3 holes	78
Calloway #2	4	4	5	3	3	4	(8)	3	4	5	3	5	5	4	4	4	4	5	39	77	1 hole	69
Pts-A	+4	+2	+2	+2	+2	+1	+2	+2	+4	+1	+1	+2	+2	+2	+2	+1	+1	+4	+16	(+37	pts)	(+1)
Chicago - A	3	4	5/4.	4	3	5	5	3	4/3.	5	4	4	5	4	3	5	5	5/4.	40	76	3/36	pts
Chicago - B	5/4.	4/3.	5/4.	5	3	4/3.	5/4.	4/3.	6/5.	5/4.	5	5/4.	6/5.	5/4.	4	5	6/5.	5/4.	46	87	13/26	pts
Pts-B	+1	+4	+2	+1	+1	+4	+2	+2	+2	+2	—	+1	+2	+2	+1	+1	+1	+4	+14	(+33	pts)	(+7)

El Legado Golf Resort
Home of Chi Chi Rodriguez

Date ____________ Scorer ______________ Attest ______________

Chicago scoring:
Bogey = +1
Par = +2
Birdie = +4
Eagle = +8

The Calloway System is best used in tournaments where a large number of competitors either have no handicap or are estimating their handicaps because they're not sure. The idea is to level the playing field, while not penalizing a player for one bad hole or a brain lock in judgment. Every golfer has a scoring flareup on occasion, and the Calloway System helps cushion that blow. The format is also a swell way to sift out any sandbaggers or bandits in the field who purposely inflate their handicaps to increase their chances of winning.

A local rule often made to the Calloway System is specifying that any hole may be discarded except the 18th. The pressure to finish a round well or burn up on the closing hole should never be legislated out of any game.

String

Who knew a simple piece of string (or yarn or twine) could become the 15th and most effective club in a golf bag? In this game, each team or each player in the foursome is given a length of string. The string may be used at anytime and in any direction to improve a lie. The catch? Each time you use the string, it has to be trimmed by the same distance the ball was moved. Shift a ball six inches out of the sand, cut off six inches of string. Move a ball one foot from the rough and into the fairway, lop off another 12 inches. Take an inch of relief out of a divot, take an inch of your string.

If you wish, use your string to sink a putt, but remember: Rarely does a golfer have enough string to sink a putt of any significant length. The best time to unfurl your string is for bad lies, shots blocked out by trees or shrubs, bunkers, or unplayable lies. As versatile as your string is, it cannot be used as fishing line. A ball lost in a water hazard remains lost, and it's a penalty stroke to put another ball in play.

Most players are given only a yard of string to start, so use it judiciously. Teams playing a Scramble format may receive a foot or two per player to begin the round. Individual or team game, once the string is gone, play resumes under normal tournament rules, be it a medal-play event, a Scramble, or a Shamble.

Strings can be used as a substitute or as a supplement to handicaps, but you'll need a lot of string to even things out. Even giving an extra yard per stroke won't bring a scratch golfer and a 20-handicapper closer together. High handicappers don't generally hit it just a couple of yards off line—they hit it way, way off line. Besides, giving golfers too much string only encourages them to act on their thoughts to hang themselves after a particularly horrific shot. On the other hand, play really well at String and you can spin a ripping good yarn in the clubhouse.

Shoot-Out

Please no 19-somes on the tee without permission from the starter. A game of Shoot-Out begins with 19 golfers, yes 19, or 19 twosomes playing alternate shots on the first hole. Highest score net (or gross, your pick) on the hole is out. The remaining 18 golfers or teams play the second hole, and, again, the high score goes home. Play continues in the same manner, with the field cut by one after every hole until the tournament is left with two players or teams dueling it out for the win on the 18th hole.

Because so many players are involved in the competition in the early going, ties will need to be broken. This is done by holding a green-side "chip-off." Each contestant involved in the tiebreaker hits from the same designated spot, and the golfer ending up farthest from the pin is eliminated from the game.

"To win in a shoot-out you must have two things: the touch of a thief and the smarts of a fox."

"Until you get down to five players or less," says Chi Chi, "there will be a chip-off on almost every hole, and if you don't have a good short game, you will be on the sidelines very quickly. You don't have to try and hole every chip. Just try and get the ball to die somewhere close to the hole. Not until there's only one or two players in the chip-off do you have to worry about being too fine.

"And always be smart. Remember that you're not trying to beat all the other guys on every hole. You are only trying to beat one guy on every hole, so you can advance. In a shoot-out there are only two places—tied for first place and last place. Play smart and avoid last place. Don't worry about being low man until the final hole. Shoot-outs are easy for me. I just lurk in the weeds until the end and then I pounce like a tiger, and the guys I beat they all go, 'Chi Chi Rodriguez? Where the heck did he come from?'"

Because so many players are involved in a shoot-out, the game can be quite time consuming, so many times the events are trimmed to 10-person fields playing nine holes. Shoot-outs are a staple of PGA and Senior PGA Tour events early in the week. Pro and local celebrities team up in alternate-shot format. If you can get to a Tour event and watch, you'll be amazed at how wonderful athletes who can shoot baskets, throw footballs, and score goals in front of tens of thousands of people crater under the pressure of a small tee-side gallery.

Get Out

Here's another game where the end of the round can come at anytime on any hole. In Get Out, foursomes compete against par in a Scramble format. Teams start on the first hole and continue to play as long as they make par or better on each hole. If the foursome records a bogey (which is hard to do and is *almost* a sin in a Scramble—no, it *is* a sin in a Scramble), their day is finished. The team completing the most holes wins the tournament.

Because bogey is so rare in a Scramble, the field of teams won't be pared down dramatically in Get Out. The winner will be decided as in most all other Scrambles, with a team shooting the low 18-hole score (figure a 54 or that vicinity) winning the event. A hint in playing Get Out—be careful on par 3s. The short holes allow very little room for recovery.

14 Clubs

The USGA allows 14 clubs during any sanctioned round of golf. This game just divides that allotment up *among all four players in the group.* Fourteen clubs separated into four bags. No sharing. Two players carry four clubs, the other two players get three, and all teams play a regular Scramble.

No rule exists against duplicating clubs, but carrying four drivers and four putters at the expense of long or middle irons isn't exactly Einstein strategy. Make sure to take one club from every country for starters (i.e., a wood, a long iron, a middle iron, a short iron, a wedge, and a putter), then fill out the rest of the set with clubs each player is most comfortable with. It's crucial to have at least one swing on every shot where the club selection matches the shot required if a team wants to score well.

As for versatility, a 3 wood is more useful than a driver. The 3 iron can be used off the tee from the fairway and on the green as a putter substitute. Seven irons are effective on almost any shot and can be used to fish balls out of water hazards. A good lob wedge can play out of a bunker all the way back to short par 3s.

Greens Keepers' Revenge

Not every Scramble has to end with a winning team shooting in the low 50s. Greens keepers who work from dawn to dusk hate to see their beautifully cared for and manicured course give up scores that resemble fall football temperatures, and so this game gives them a chance to fight back.

Start by placing the tees as far back in the box as possible. The tee markers should be just wide enough for a player to take his or her stance, and the ground between them should be as uneven and divot filled as possible. Fairways should be narrowed to less than U.S. Open width, say 18 to 20 yards across, and the rough should be grown up so high that you can hide a Plymouth Duster in the grass.

Bunkers should be left unranked and if possible have some sort of animal tracks in them. The greens should be mowed to within 1/16 of an inch of their lives and triple rolled by an employee weighing no less than 350 pounds so that they register 14 on the stimp meter. Pins should be placed in the most impossible positions. Six inches on the green, fine. On a severe and blatantly unfair slope, perfect. On a crown that couldn't hold a marble, thank-you.

Greens Keepers' Revenge should be the hardest, most unfair golf course you've ever played. And after you've played it in a Scramble format, go back and scrape your own ball around that monster. Now you know what a U.S. Open feels like. Then, while enjoying a beer in the mixed grill, try to figure out how the pros break 70 on that kind of layout.

Golf Courses Designed by Chi Chi Rodriguez

- TPC Tampa Bay—Tampa, Florida (signature)
- Moss Creek—Dayton, Ohio (signature)
- Dorado Del Mar—Dorado, Puerto Rico (signature)
- Shimofusa Country Club—Japan (signature)
- Palm Cove Golf Club—Palm City, Florida (signature)
- El Legado Golf Club—Guayama, Puerto Rico (signature)
- Badlands—Las Vegas, Nevada (with Johnny Miller)
- Ballymeade—Cape Cod, Massachusetts (with Jim Fazio)

"When I design a golf course, I want to put it in a beautiful place," says Chi Chi. "I want it easy to maintain and I want it to be enjoyable so that everybody from senior ladies to top amateurs to top pros can have a good time. A golf course should be what the people want, not what the designer wants.

"As for me, if I wanted to play one last round in my life I would go to Winged Foot in New York. It has been a great golf course from its first day and it will still be great 200 years from now."

Head Games: Competition and Composure

To play well in a golf tournament, or any sport for that matter, players must crave competition and then keep their composure. Chi Chi Rodriguez became one of the best golfers in the world because he wasn't afraid to take on the best golfers in the world. He looked forward to the challenge of measuring his game against theirs or competing against anybody who wanted to test his. Successful players look forward to competition. For some people, the desire comes naturally. For others, the quality is developed—they must learn by playing and, perhaps, losing, until they become match tough. Never has there been a great golfer who didn't want to compete and who didn't fight tooth and nail to win every time out.

Composure is a key component and really can't be separated from competition. Composure means leaving each shot, good or bad, behind. It's not getting down over a bad break, a bad lie, or a bad day. It's a belief that you will win every time out and that you deserve to win. It's managing your emotions first and your game second. Keep your composure, and competition and pressure become a pleasure.

chapter **6**

Side Bets

Long before Chi Chi Rodriguez earned a living with his golf clubs, back even before he used them to make some spare change, he spent hours plowing in the sugarcane fields near his home in Puerto Rico for $1 a day. "I carried a stick with a good sharp nail pounded into the end of it," says Chi Chi. "Then if the oxen started to get off line, you know, turn off the course, I would take my stick and poke them with the nail and they'd straighten out. I was fortunate; I didn't have to persuade the team with my stick very often. An ox is a smart animal. He knows where he's going when he's hitched up."

And this has to do with golf . . . how? "Well, not all people want to play a full money game when they go to the course, so sometimes golfers need a little poke to get them in line when it comes to making a bet." For any number of reasons a golfer may be less than eager to take on a game. Golfers who play infrequently may not wish to play anything but a straight game because they don't get out very often. Other golfers just aren't comfortable enough with their game or confident enough to risk money. Still others find themselves too light in the wallet to wager seriously after paying greens fees; shelling out for a sleeve of balls or three; buying a new Corinthian, all-weather, leather golf glove, hat, shirt, spikes, and a high-powered infrared range finder from the pro shop.

Although Chi Chi is not advocating the use of a nail attached to a 1 iron to prod partners into making a golf bet, he is suggesting a small side bet or two. Try some of the games listed here to help test yourself—sort of stick your toe in the shallow end of the gambling pool. Get your nerve up playing Greenies, Sandies, and Flagsticks, and go from there. No handicaps are needed, and booking the bets is a cinch. Bets are commonly worth a quarter or a buck but can always be raised to the level of one's tax bracket.

Greenies

A player hitting the green in regulation on a par 3 wins the bet. If two or more players find the dance floor, closest to the pin wins. Golfers must then validate all greenies by holing out in one or two putts. A three jack means no jack. If nobody hits the green, nobody wins, and the bet can either be carried over or left behind.

Chi Chi's Awards

Here's a list of prestigious awards Chi Chi Rodriguez has won "on the side," outside of golf:

- 1982 Father of the Year
- Roberto Clemente Cup
- Salvation Army Gold Crest Award
- National Puerto Rican Life Achievement
- "Caring for Kids" Award
- Bobby Jones Award
- Jackie Robinson Humanitarian Award
- Civilian Meritorious Service Medal
- 1994 World Sports Humanitarian Hall of Fame Inductee
- Grand Marshal of the 106th Tournament of Roses Parade

Oozles and Foozles

Find yourself on the short holes at St. Andrews, and the locals play Oozles and Foozles instead of Greenies. Same rules, same game, different name. Closest to the pin on par 3s wins a bet (oozle), provided he or she goes on to birdie or par the hole. If the golfer should three-putt or worse, he or she foozles and now *must* pay each of the other members in the group one bet.

Wall-to-Wall Carpeting

If a golfer makes a clean sweep of all par 3s on the course, he or she is said to have laid wall-to-wall carpeting, and all his or her Greenies or Oozles winnings are doubled.

3-2

A 3-2, or 32, bet is really the equivalent of laying three-to-two odds that a player will three-putt. If the challenged golfer does, indeed, three-putt or worse, he or she pays two bets. If, however, he or she manages to two-putt or sink the first one, he or she receives three bets in return.

This can be a one-on-one bet, or any and all partners may join in if the player putting is willing to accept the risk. Though not obligated by any USGA, federal, or state statute to accept a 3-2, a putter who passes on the bet should be heckled mercilessly and called chicken, yellow, coward, or some other name with enough bite to make the player accept the bet the next time it rolls around.

"A three putt is just about the worst thing in golf. I hate them. I could make the longest putt you could think of, and if it's a third putt or for bogey, I can't bring myself to do the sword dance. I was playing a tournament one time, and a woman asked me why I didn't do the dance on a hole after a pretty long putt. Well, I had just made a double-bogey six, and I said to her, 'Lady, you can't make a monkey dance without giving him a banana.' Three putts and big numbers, they make even the bravest man in the world cry."

Sandies and Super Sandies

Here's a chance to make that bad shot that landed in the bunker pay off. Sandies are getting up and down from a bunker for par. If golfers choose to, they may agree among themselves beforehand to pay out sandies regardless of the gross score on the hole. Hit it out of the trap and one-putt into the cup wins a bet. Holing out from a bunker in one shot pays double in Sandies. Super sandies are any pars, birdies, or better made from fairway bunkers.

Moles

Moles are the ugly opposite of Sandies. A player leaving his or her bunker shot in the sand pays out one bet. Leave a second shot in the sand, it's two bets and so on until the poor lad or lassie finally extricates himself or herself from the bunker. Feeling rich or just ornery?—double the bet for every shot left in the sand.

"Amateur players hear the guy on TV say that a bunker shot is the easiest shot in the game, and they don't believe him 'cause they can't do it," says Chi Chi. "They think it's a bigger lie than the check's in the mail. But it's true. It should only take one shot to get out of the sand. Check out chapter 10."

Ferrets and Golden Ferrets

This is actually a good rodent problem to have on a golf course as opposed to gophers, squirrels, and chipmunks. A golfer gets a ferret and wins one bet for holing out from off the green without using his or her putter. This includes any and all chips, pitches, bumped fairway woods, ricocheted shots off port-o-lets, and miraculous shots slam dunked from back in the fairway. Golden ferrets are shots holed from a bunker and, as mentioned in Sandies and Super Sandies, pay double.

Dunce Cap

No money is involved, but public humiliation is. Dunce Cap starts by finding the ugliest and gaudiest hat known to mankind and then making the player with the worst score on the hole wear the hat while playing the next hole. A player continues to wear the hideous headgear until someone else in the group loses the hole outright. Hats that work best are usually seen on Mom Easter morning, on The Village People, or on any head attending the Kentucky Derby on the first Saturday in May.

Murphys

Miss the green? Give ol' Murphy a call and make some money. A player declaring Murphy has just bet every other player in the group that he or she can get up and down from his or her position off the green. Rough, bunker, under the ball washer, doesn't matter—one chip or pitch up and one putt in wins the bet. Fail to make your Murphy, and you pay a bet out to all your partners.

Opponents may reject a Murphy bet and would do very well to assess each situation before accepting. Some green-side shots are considerably easier than others, and rarely does anybody Murphy from a bad lie to a short, downhill pin.

Be careful if you get in a game against a player with a killer short game. These magicians can make quite a tidy sum on what seems like a small wager. If you see one of your partners starting to miss greens on purpose, you may just want to tip your cap and move on to the next hole.

Ten Timeless Golf Insults

1. You're still out.
2. Hit it with your purse next time.
3. Hole's gonna play long from there.
4. Does your husband play golf, too?
5. Chili dip's good, but I prefer queso.
6. Wanna try for heaven? You just moved earth.
7. Two more like that and you'll be on the green in par.
8. Wow, you just missed a hole in one by three strokes.
9. In Vegas, they pay good money for making a hard eight.
10. You're not playing with new balls, are you?

Flaps

Get a little rush of blood to the head? Hit a shot a little too pure? Discover too late you've taken too much club? A simple shout of "flaps" before the ball lands, and the bet is made. For those who prefer real estate references to aviation, the word "house," as in "hit a house," may be substituted for "flaps."

Shouting "flaps" is declaring to all that you can get up and down from wherever your ball comes to rest. Lest this be a one-sided affair, any partner may counter "flaps" with a shout of "double" after the shot lands and before it stops rolling.

If the player makes his or her flap, he or she receives a bet from all partners. If the flap is unsuccessful, the player loses to all partners. The winnings and losses are doubled for all partners who declared "double."

Flagsticks

Perhaps you've seen these on a golf course. They're sticks with flags attached to them, and they stand in the cup. Flagstick bets can be won in two different ways. First, players earn a stick for any tee or approach shot hit within flagstick distance of the cup. Second, players receive a stick for every putt sunk from outside the length of the flagstick.

Depending on the height of the flagstick (and they do vary some—in Great Britain and Ireland, they're usually much shorter than in America, and many courses, home and away, use extremely high flagsticks on holes with severe uphill approaches), the game will either favor putters or iron players. Shorter flagsticks make it harder to win a bet off the tee or from the fairway but easier to win one putting. Taller pins increase the chance of sticking an approach shot but decrease the chances of draining a putt. Next time out, use the flagstick as both a target and a unit of measure.

Barkies, Fishies, Froggies, and Bambis

Welcome again to Chi Chi's wild kingdom. He's basically Marlin Perkins in soft spikes and Jack Hanna with a better short game.

Barkies—Pars or better made after hitting a tree. Players finding themselves deep in the woods may declare "Arbor Day" and bet the rest of the group double that they can make par from their lie.

Fishies—Pars or better made after hitting a ball in the water. And if you've never thought about how tough a chore that may be, consider that, if you rinse a ball on a par 3, you have to hole out on the next shot for par. Gurgle it on a par 4, you almost certainly need to one-putt. And if you manage to make five after splashing down on a par 5, you should kick yourself for giving away a birdie.

Froggies—Pay out regardless of score. All that's required is that a player's ball skips successfully across a body of water. Creek, stream, river, lake, pond, pool. Pool or a pond, pond be good for you.

Bambis—Pars or better made after hitting an animal. Deer, squirrels, rabbits, and the course dog that's always asleep under the huge willow tree near the seventh green are all Bambi candidates, but the most common creatures struck in Bambi are *people*. Sure, hitting another golfer counts, it's just not encouraged. So, even if you need the money, please have the courtesy to shout "fore" to those humans in harm's way.

Wiz, Duck, Sheik, and Lumberjack

The goal in this group of games is simply not to be the last offender. Bad things occasionally happen during a round, and it's fine if they happen to you, as long as someone else in the group suffers the same fate before you get back to the clubhouse. Think of this as playing tag with trouble and you don't want to be "it" after 18 holes.

Wiz—last person to hit a ball out of bounds pays a bet

Duck—last player to hit a ball in the water owes the rest of the group

Sheik—last player to find a bunker loses

Lumberjack—last player to hit a tree off the tee is out cash

Metoo

Like that shot, did ya? Me too! In fact, it was so terrific I'm also going to play my next shot from there. That's a Metoo. A player is allowed to swap his shot for his favorite among all the others in the group at anytime on any drive, approach, or putt. Simply move your ball next to your partner's, and play the hole in without penalty.

The number of Metoos should, again, be agreed on before the round begins and, in some instances, can be used in lieu of handicap strokes. Playing Metoos as a handicap substitute will actually quicken the pace of play. Instead of combing the acres looking for lost balls or shots gone terribly awry, just play a Metoo from the best ball and continue on without delay.

Bus Driver

Bus Driver is a game where it pays to be a passenger. The bet occurs twice during the round, the bus running once on each side, and is based on honors off the tee. It's quite simple, really. The golfer teeing off last in the group on the 9th hole is the bus driver and must pay everyone else in the group a bet. Same goes on the 18th tee box—last in line to hit opens the billfold. Each of the wagers is generally a little more pricey than normal side bets, roughly four or five times the amount, because it really encompasses the entire front or back nine.

Because the bus driver is essentially the last player to lose a hole outright before reaching the final tee on each side, strategy in the game, obviously, starts about two or three holes back. The player with honors on 15, 16, or 17 wants to keep his or her position or at least halve the high score among his or her partners to avoid falling all the way back, while the last player in the rotation must make aggressive swings and attack the hole in an effort to better all, or at least one, score in the group. The USGA encourages golfers to walk while playing golf; carts are fine, but you definitely don't want to drive a bus.

The Greats

Nothing is more fun than winning a bet, but it's even better to do it in the same manner as one of the game's all-time greats. So give these games a try.

- Nicklaus—making par or better after hitting the longest tee shot in the group
- Arnie—making par or better without hitting the fairway
- Hogan—making par or better after hitting both the fairway and the green in regulation
- Seve—making a par or better from an adjoining fairway or off the green
- Watson—making a par or better by chipping in from an impossible lie on a par 3
- Crenshaw—making par with just one putt
- Pavin—making par or better with the shortest drive in the group
- Sarazen—making a double eagle anywhere, anytime
- Chi Chi—making a par or better and counting up your score in Spanish

Where's Tiger Woods you ask? "In a class by himself," says Chi Chi Rodriguez.

"Until Tiger came along, I thought Jack Nicklaus was the greatest player ever. Sam Snead was the best ball striker I ever saw. He was the Michelangelo of golf. Ben Hogan was second, with Byron Nelson pretty close to both of them. Me? I'm probably in the top 10. But Tiger Woods, he is the complete package. He has the intelligence of Nicklaus, the guts of Arnold Palmer, the beauty of Sam's swing, the shot-making ability of Hogan, and the patience and temperament of Gandhi. He is the best—even so young, he is the best."

Soccer Caddy, Noonan, and Mulligans

This is basically a cheating threesome.

Soccer Caddy—a player is allowed to give his or her ball a good swift kick in an effort to extricate it from trouble

Noonan—a player may scream "Noonan" at any point during an opponent's swing or just before a putt

Mulligans—a player may disregard a bad shot and replay it without counting the extra stroke

Because all of these acts are either unsporting or out and out illegal, players in a group must set an allowed number, usually no more than three, on each offense before the round starts. Players in desperate straits may purchase extra caddy kicks, noonan screams, and mulligans from opponents if they believe the investment may help them win more money in the long run.

Golf's Golden Rule

The USGA rulebook contains 34 rules. And remarkably, it takes more than 150 pages to explain them. "I love our rules," says Chi Chi. "You never lose anything because of a person's subjective judgment as in baseball or football or basketball. I quit being a big NBA fan because the referees call too many subjective things. In our sport, a rule is a rule, period. The problem is not enough people understand them, they are too complicated to read. So here is my golden rule of golf—*After you tee the ball up, do not touch it again until you take it out of the hole.* Follow that rule, and you will always be within the written rules of golf."

24-Second Clock

Here's a little-known rule not found in the USGA rulebook but rather lifted from the NBA rulebook: Three times during any round, a player may replay a shot without penalty, provided she can retrieve her ball and place it back in its original position and hit it again within 24 seconds. Putts are not included in the game. Seems fun and simple enough, but by the time a player sprints to track down her errant shot and gets it back in the exact spot where she hit it to begin with, fatigue and a time crunch can often produce an even worse shot.

The evil twin of the 24-second clock is that players have 24 seconds to request that partners replay any terrific shot. Down in a match, and your opponent stiffs an approach or unloads a 300-yard drive, simply ask to see it again.

Head Games: Find the Fun in It

When was the last time you deliberately went out to play a bad round of golf? When was the last occasion that you purposely hooked a drive in the woods, hit a ball in the water, or missed a three-foot putt? Exactly. You never have. And that should be the basis from which you start every round of golf. A good round starts with a good attitude.

Find the fun in it. You are not at work. You are not doing chores around the house. You are in a beautiful (sometimes hard-to-breathe beautiful), quiet place playing a game you enjoy. So enjoy it. Don't louse it up by getting yourself worked up or beating yourself down. Golf is the hardest game in the world, and until you put the same kind of hours into it as a professional does, you won't play like one, so don't expect to.

Everybody arrives at a golf course eager to tee off. Keep that positive frame of mind throughout. Concentrate on your game, but make sure the fun meter of your day doesn't depend solely on it. If you struggle hitting the ball, focus on other enjoyable aspects of the round—the company, nature, exercise, fresh air, getting away. Nothing makes a round of golf more fun than playing well, but nothing ruins it more than a bad attitude.

PART II

Games for Stroke Improvement

"Never take a lesson from a pro unless he's had his eyebrows in his lips."

Long before the invention of the 500-dollar-a-day golf school and the perfectly pressed teaching pro, Chi Chi Rodriguez was giving lessons for the bargain price of $3 a half hour. After curing one student of a five-year case of the shanks, Chi Chi received a bonus of $500. Chi Chi's tip—"Keep the elbows the same width apart through the entire swing: at address, during the backswing, at the top, and at impact." Sometimes, it's just that simple.

On another occasion, he pocketed a $1,000 bonus merely for teaching a career 170 hitter to break 150. What grand wisdom did Chi Chi impart to this pupil? "He was left handed playing with right-handed clubs," says Rodriguez, "so I went into the shop and got him a left-handed set." Isn't it comforting to know that sometimes it really is the clubs?—although Chi Chi figures the tools of the trade are generally down third or fourth on the list of reasons good people play bad golf.

Chi Chi Rodriguez is convinced that, no matter what problem is ailing your golf game right now, he can "turn a mule into a race horse." Sorry, but it's not you he has all the confidence in, it's himself. Giddy up. The man has, figuratively, "had his eyebrows in his lips," tasted the pressure of tournament golf at the highest levels, faced everything from crucial drives in Majors to critical putts in the Ryder Cup. Rodriguez's swing has held up, and he's succeeded under the most extreme heat the game can offer, making him extremely qualified to help fix or improve your swing.

"Golf is like business: You have certain basic things that you must do to hit good shots," says Chi Chi, "and there are too many gimmicks going around now, guys making fortunes teaching people junk. You could put horse manure on an ice cream cone with whip cream and a cherry on top, and people will buy it if a top-30 Tour pro is selling it."

In a sport where people are passionate, often times possessed, about improving their game, beware of the quick fix or miracle cure. In fact, the more intricate the wizardry, the less likely it is to help. "Keep it simple," says Chi Chi. "Those are the words that should echo in your head. That is maybe the best swing thought a golfer can have—keep it simple. People are overtaught and overloaded with information. By the time the amateur reads a book and a magazine, watches a video, talks to his neighbor next door, listens to the person hitting next to him on the practice tee, he can't possibly process it all. Paralysis by analysis they call it." Simplify!

"There are six basic things that you must teach, and you should not get out of those basics," explains Chi Chi. "The six basics are a good grip, good posture, good ball position, good alignment, good take-away, and a good follow-through. If you have those six basics, then you will succeed. Four of those things you do before you even start to swing, so you should be able to get those things right without really trying."

Simple—and further explained in the following chapters. What you won't find in the pages is the perfect swing. Chi Chi Rodriguez swings the club one way, Tiger Woods his way, Duane Dimplepattern another way. The idea is for you to find your swing and perfect it. Golf swings are as individual as signatures and fingerprints. Lee Trevino's swing isn't as pretty as Gary Player's, but both worked splendidly. Jim Furyk makes as distinctive a swipe at the ball as any pro who's ever played the Tour, and no coach would dare try to teach it to another student, but it serves Furyk just fine. "The best swing," says Chi Chi with conviction, "is something that gets the job done every time.

"I have played this game for almost 60 years, and still I don't know everything. I know a lot but not all there is to know. Only God knows everything. So, do not be afraid to experiment. Learn these basics, but also make them fit you. Too many players read too many books and try to follow each word to the letter. This is a mistake. Books, even mine, should only be used as a general guide. The six steps are fundamentally sound, but everyone needs to make minor adjustments to fit their body and feel comfortable."

Chi Chi Rodriguez developed and got comfortable with his swing as a boy in the hot sun of Puerto Rico. Following his discharge from the army at age 21, he returned home to Puerto Rico and took a job at Dorado Beach Resort where, for $80 a week, he shagged range balls, shined shoes, and stored clubs seven days a week. Then in 1959 the resort hired legendary Florida pro Pete Cooper as head professional. Chi Chi's game was on its way to the Tour. "Pete Cooper is the greatest golfer ever to come out of Florida," says Chi Chi, "native Floridian, not of all the players who moved there over the years, and he was a great teacher and a friend to me. He helped hone my skills and got me ready for the Tour. I am a combination of many teachers, but Pete gave me the best lessons of anybody I ever worked with."

Ed Dudley

"I got my first job in professional golf from Ed Dudley," recalls Chi Chi. "He was the head pro at Dorado Beach before Pete Cooper. Ed is the man who is really responsible for putting me on the PGA Tour. He was also the first head pro at Augusta National Golf Club and served as PGA president in the 1940s. Speaking of presidents, at Augusta, Ed helped cure President Eisenhower's slice. Ed Dudley was a great player, too, and just a great and generous man, period. He was, and I tell people this, like a second father to me. Not only did he hire me, but he also helped raise my salary by making me an assistant, he gave me the down payment for my first car, he gave me the money for a down

continued ☞

payment on my first house. Until I met Ed Dudley I had never eaten a steak. I was afraid of it. I was used to eating rice and beans but, man, when Ed cooked those steaks, it was the best thing I had ever had in my life. One time when I was at Ed's house I was looking at all the beautiful gold and silver trophies, some of them even had diamonds. Ed was a fantastic player. And as I was admiring all his trophies he said to me, 'Chi Chi, if you want those you can have them.' And he was serious. I said, 'No thanks. If you just teach me to play golf I'll be good enough to win my own trophies.' We both made good on the deal."

Chi Chi's successful relationship with Cooper taught him a valuable lesson about lessons. "Make sure you find the right teacher for you," cautions Chi Chi. "Just because the head pro charges more for a lesson than the assistant doesn't mean you won't do better with an assistant. Maybe he's closer to you in age. Maybe you understand the terms he uses to describe parts of the swing better. It does not matter how good the message is if the amateur can't understand it. People shouldn't be afraid to switch pros if they don't think they're getting a good result. But it's important, if you want to develop into something more than just a recreational player, to find a regular pro who knows and can help you with your swing." Just make sure that at some point "he's had his eyebrows in his lips."

It was while working under the tutelage of Cooper at Dorado Beach Resort that Chi Chi began giving those 30 minutes for $3 a session on his own. (Forget the bargain prices. Do you suppose at the time any of those lucky students had any idea how famous their instructor would become one day?) Giving 20 or 25, sometimes even 30 lessons a day, Chi Chi realized that the best instructions are given in a straightforward and plain manner. The key was to make the student understand the message, not show him or her how much he knew. He also noticed that occasionally, after a dramatic improvement in their game, his pupils would leave him and try another, more expensive teacher, only to return to him with their game in shambles.

"A golf pro is like a doctor," according to Chi Chi. "People always think that if they spend more money they get a better doctor, but that's not always the case. Sometimes they just charge them more, and because of the cost patients think they got a better cure and they have to go back in a week 'cause they are still sick. A good doctor is a good doctor—the size of the bill shouldn't matter. Same thing with a golf pro."

And also like medicine, golf advice is best dispensed in small, controlled doses. "A doctor gives you one or two pills at a time," says Chi Chi, "not a whole handful. Too much at once, whether it's pills or golf advice, will make you even sicker than when you started. You give them one thing to learn one day, and when they learn it you move on to the next thing the next day or the next week. Any change needs to feel natural before moving on." Chi Chi's goal is to get you and your game healthy. And he'll do that with a simple swing philosophy that's grounded, literally, in the ground.

"The first half of the first lesson for any amateur should not involve a ball," Chi Chi insists. "The person should be doing nothing but taking swings and taking divots. Hitting the dirt. People need to learn that it is okay, that it's necessary, to hit the ground. You can't hurt the ground, and the grass will always grow back. And once you make the commitment to learn golf, you must practice and you must play. There is no substitute for playing."

Reading magazine articles and books is fine (clearly, or you wouldn't be holding this particular one right now), but they're no help if you can't understand them or take the help to the course. A golfer's mind and muscles learn best when they are learning together. Practicing and playing. If a "secret" to the game of golf truly exists, it's practicing and playing. In the next six chapters, Chi Chi feels he's combined the two into games that are both helpful and enjoyable.

chapter 7

Fundamentals

"Gimmicks, gimmicks, gimmicks," says Chi Chi. "Golf is not gimmicks, golf is basics." Ironic that a man who is known far and wide for his flamboyance is as vanilla as they come when the topic is teaching the golf swing. Succinctness and simplicity are the cornerstone tenets of his philosophy. If Chi Chi had charged by the word for his lessons, this man, who will talk to the tee markers if he has no gallery following him around, wouldn't have made even three dollars a session.

Grip, posture, ball position, alignment, take-away, follow-through. Where Hogan went with five fundamentals, Chi Chi teaches six basics, choosing to include ball position as a separate skill. But he shares a belief with his childhood hero that breaking 80 is a realistic goal for any golfer who is serious about the game.

Though seemingly quite simple, each element explained here is not a shortcut. Each is vital to building a solid, repeating, winning golf swing. And once learned, developing each skill to its fullest is a direct result of a person's dedication. "And hard work doesn't cost nothing except sweat," says Chi Chi.

Grip

Good golf starts with putting the club in your hands correctly. This comment may seem akin to pointing out that each day begins with the sun rising in the east, but it's easy to overlook the obvious, and building the best golf swing begins by holding the tool for the job appropriately. The grip is not the most glamorous part of golf, but when done right it's a thing of beauty.

"I used to tell all my students, and now I tell the amateurs I play with before Senior Tour events, if you buy a book on golf instruction buy the thinnest book you can find. The thinner the book, chances are the easier and more elementary the instruction. It can do one of two things: help you more or hurt you less. Both are good compared to the alternative.

"The first book I wrote was in 1967, and it had 78 pages, and many of those pages had pictures on them. It cost only $2.95. I guess I can't help it, all my life I give away my golf knowledge for about three dollars.

"Ben Hogan's book [*Five Lessons: The Modern Fundamentals of Golf*] is terrific and no thicker than my finger. Ben Hogan knew more about the golf swing, worked harder on his swing than any other pro ever. I mean he really had to work hard to become a great player, and if he could explain everything he knew in a very few pages, then that's proof enough for me.

"Sam Snead—Sam could talk about the swing for hours, too, and he was great at helping other pros and all his people at his club in West Virginia [Snead was associated as a pro at the Greenbrier Resort for 66 years], but his swing was so perfect and so natural it couldn't be copied. We should all have Sam's swing, but it's easier to get Hogan's."

Get the grip right, and improvement is sure to ensue. Get it wrong, and there's not much chance for a successful shot. Yes, occasionally, a golfer with a bad grip can play well, but chances are the swing isn't pretty and it took many, many years of practice to perfect. Though turning a bad grip into a good grip is not an easy task, it's far easier than learning to play around the bad grip. Embrace the idea that a good grip will hold your entire swing together, start to finish.

There are three basic grips—the overlapping, or Vardon; the interlocking; and the 10-finger, or baseball, grip. The first two grips are almost universally used, and the third very rarely and most often by very young players or older players looking for a little extra power.

Chi Chi Rodriguez, Sam Snead, Ben Hogan, and Arnold Palmer are overlappers. Jack Nicklaus, Tiger Woods, and John Daly interlock. Try them both, and stick with the one that feels more natural. In all cases, the position of the left top hand is fairly consistent.

Begin by laying the shaft of the club across your left hand where the fingers join the palm. Wrapping your fingers around the shaft will then naturally press the club across the top of your palm from the crook of your index finger to the pad below the pinkie. The thumb should wrap around and be placed down the right side of the shaft. Think about always keeping the shaft as near to the base of the fingers as possible.

If the left hand is on the club correctly, the V made between the thumb and the forefinger will point at your right shoulder, and the first three knuckles should be visible. Putting the left hand in the proper position near the end of the shaft with the V aligned and the knuckles showing will give a player a good strong grip and help to get maximum power from the left arm.

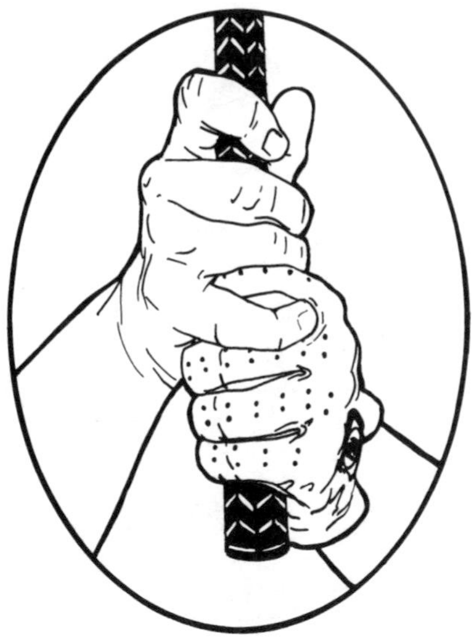

Overlapping grip: The pinkie on the bottom hand overlaps the index finger on the top hand. Grip pressure should be firm but not tense.

In an overlapping grip, the right hand is placed on the club facing the target with the shaft placed between the base of the fingers and the first knuckle. The right pinkie overlaps, resting in the channel made by the left index and middle finger. (see figure at right). The right-hand move was best explained by legendary Texas teacher Harvey Penick, author of *The Little Red Book,* who said simply, "shake hands with the club." Just as with the left hand, the V formed by the thumb and forefinger should point at the player's right shoulder. This is considered a strong grip. If you find yourself hooking the ball too much or too often, simply rotate the Vs a small amount so that they point more toward your chin.

"Even though I have very small hands, and I only wear a large ladies' glove," says Chi Chi, "I use an overlapping grip because the extra finger on the shaft from the left hand gives me extra control. Plus my hands are closer together, so I feel as if my grip and the club combine as one. I need to feel the club as much as I can. Most people with little hands and short fingers like mine use an interlocking grip. Jack [Nicklaus] has small hands and he interlocks, but I like the control and comfort of an overlap. It also feels most natural to most beginners. I've done pretty good with it so far. You will too."

If the overlapping grip doesn't feel right, try interlocking, which helps tie the hands together for power and control. To form an interlocking grip, place your left hand on the club, as previously described, then point your index finger down and away from the shaft. As you place your right hand on the club, the left index finger fits in the webbing between your right pinkie and ring finger. Now grip the club snugly with your index finger and pinkie forming the interlock around the shaft (see figure, above left). The thumb remains in the same position as in an overlapping grip. With the left and right hands entwined, the grip helps the hands work together in harmony throughout the course of the swing.

Interlocking grip: The pinkie finger on the bottom hand entwines with the index finger on the top hand. A good grip holds the hand and club together as one.

Play ball! The right hand in a 10-finger grip grasps the club exactly as it would a baseball bat (see figure, below left). In fact, the left and right hand pretty much mirror each other. Make sure to keep the hands tight together because nothing is there to unify the grip. This most popular way of gripping a club in golf's early years disappeared right around the start of the 20th century.

In general, when gripping the club, the shaft should be held firm but not so tight that the muscles in the forearms become tense. Holding the club too tight will tighten the rest of the arm muscles and not allow them to swing freely. Tension is the enemy, the big enemy, in a golf swing. If you're gripping the club with the proper pressure, someone should be able to come along and pull the club out of your hands with a good solid tug.

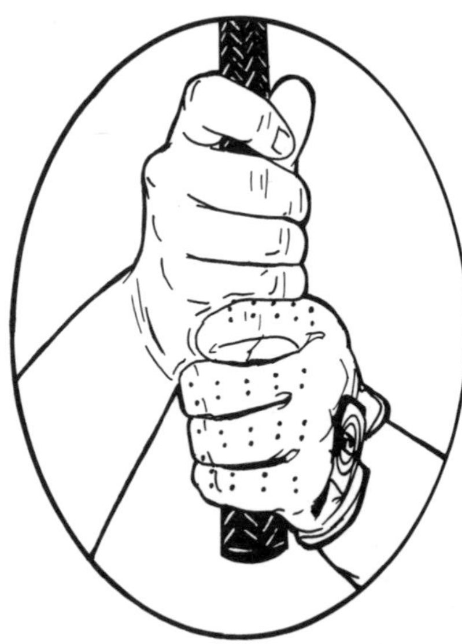

Baseball grip: All 10 fingers grip the club. Keep the hands butted together for control. In all grips point the Vs at the right shoulder.

The left hand generally holds the shaft a bit firmer, as it, along with the left arm, is the power behind the swing. The right hand should be snug but, really, only along for the ride. A good test of grip pressure is to make sure you can feel the weight of the club head. If your grip is too tight, the club will feel very light and uniform in weight. "My friend Sam Snead used to say, 'If people held their fork the way they hold their golf club, they would starve to death.' A golf club should be held as a bird or a family pet is held—strong enough to keep it in your hands but not so strong that you would hurt it," says Chi Chi.

Hold Everything

"The biggest complaint I hear from people trying to learn a new grip or improve an old one is 'it doesn't feel right,'" says Chi Chi. "So my recommendation is to practice your grip on everything and anything until it does feel right. Put a Vardon grip on your garden hose. Interlock when raking leaves or holding the dog leash. Once or twice an hour, just form a good, sound grip sitting at your desk. Keep a club with you while you're watching TV, and repeatedly practice putting your hands on the club correctly.

"I started with an interlocking grip, and when I changed I kept saying to myself, 'I can't play golf like this.' But I kept practicing and overcame my fears. It took me more than a decade—13 years to be exact—before I came up with exactly the right grip. Getting comfortable with a grip is a combination of routine and repetition and can be worked on anywhere at anytime. Holding everything will help improve your grip on the one thing that matters—the club. And hopefully it will not take you 13 years."

Posture

Nowhere does the body language in golf speak louder than standing over the ball. Poor posture ruins more golf games than bad whiskey and bad wives combined.The shape and quality of every swing are rooted in a player's stance, and if the angles are all wrong at address, they're going to be disastrously incorrect at impact. Set up with proper posture, and the swing should flow smoothly. However, if your body is in a bad position to begin with, the resulting swing becomes a chain reaction of corrections that is nearly impossible to repeat effectively.

The first step in building a good sound stance is by walking up to the ball and introducing yourself to it just as you would to a stranger. Confident, straightforward, center yourself in front of it, standing tall but not too close. What you certainly wouldn't do is twist around, hunch over, or otherwise contort your body into some sort of pretzel.

Square yourself to the ball and place your feet shoulder-width apart, with your weight distributed evenly on each foot.This is the key to getting good balance and keeping the hips free so that they can make a full turn. Stand as upright as possible without being stiff; we're not measuring for height here, but you want to take full advantage of the leverage the Lord gave you.

Flex the knees slightly, an inch or so, as if you were going to sit down on a stool, and point them in just a little.This allows for a nice free foot and leg action. Remember, slightly, *slightly* flexed knees—we don't want squatters.

The right foot should remain square to the ball, with the left foot turned out toward the target a few inches. Think of a clock, and point your left foot at the 11. The position of the right foot will help to safeguard against a backswing getting too long, and the left-foot move helps ensure a full weight shift. "The exception is for the small golfer like me," Chi Chi stresses. "For smaller golfers, the left foot should be slightly pigeon toed in on the longer clubs. The foot serves as a brace for the downswing. If the brace breaks, the swing breaks. For normal-size golfers, the left foot slightly turned out is best."

Bend toward the ball from your hips, keeping your lower back nice and straight. Your arms should now hang down freely to grip the club. No need to reach for it. The length of each club will guide you as to how far you should

Perfect posture helps produce perfect swings. Stand tall and square to the ball, with feet shoulder-width apart and knees flexed. You should feel balanced and relaxed.

be standing from the ball. Put the club in your hands and the club directly behind the ball.

The left arm should be straight, with the elbow pointed at the left hip. The right arm has an ever-so-slight bend in it and is in line with the right hip. Both arms are extended but not stiff. Think about being relaxed and comfortable. As mentioned in Chi Chi's cure of the five-year shanker in the part II opener, keep the arms close together and the same distance apart throughout the entire swing.

The head bends slightly to give a good view of the ball, and it's imperative that it remain as still as possible and behind the ball throughout the swing. "Nobody can keep their head absolutely still on each shot," says Chi Chi. "It's physically impossible. But you have to concentrate on keeping it as still as possible during the swing because it is the key, the center, to keeping everything in balance."

The entire framework should feel perfectly balanced, relaxed, and comfortable. If your partner came up and gave you a shove, you should be able to stay in your stance. If the shove sends you staggering or nearly knocks you over, you need to reset up and adjust your weight for better balance.

Get Comfortable

"You gotta feel comfortable," advises Chi Chi. "If you feel uncomfortable, then, man, you've got the wrong stance. From my experience, I recommend only what is comfortable. On this point, I am very firm. I tend to keep my right knee tilted inward a little more than most golfers. This is not critical to hitting the ball long. It's just something that is comfortable to me.

"The stance I teach should feel comfortable for everybody unless they have some type of physical problem. If it's not, go through each step to make sure there's no tension or strain on your body. It is a basic athletic position much like the starting point in any sport—a free throw in basketball or a baseball batting stance. A good golf posture should be so good and so comfortable you could stay in it for two hours if you had to. Developing good posture is easy, and you should feel at ease over the ball. It's not a coincidence that the best players in the world look the most natural over the ball. Jack Nicklaus, Tiger Woods, Ernie Els."

In addition to the square stance previously described, you also have heard, no doubt, many times about open and closed stances. The benefits of both will be discussed in further detail in chapters 8 and 9. For the purposes of this chapter, however, only the mechanics of each are important.

In our ideal square stance, the toes on each foot are on a line parallel with the intended target. To make an open stance, simply move the left foot a few inches back from the line and the right foot a few inches over it. The golfer is "opening" himself or herself up to the target. The hips and shoulders also adjust to this new line. This stance will help produce a left-to-right, or "sliced," ball flight.

The closed stance is the exact opposite. The right foot is moved back from the original line and the left foot nudged over it a bit, thereby encouraging a right-to-left, or "hooked," ball flight. Looking for a quick correction for a slice?—close your stance.

Ball Position

Contrary to many golfers' beliefs, ball position is not about moving one's ball out of a divot or the rough onto a better piece of turf or better lie. That's cheating. Ball position in its legal and teaching sense refers to where it's positioned in the stance, and it is a significant, though often overlooked, component of a good setup and nearly as important as the grip. Good aim begins even before takeoff. Start the ball in the wrong place in your stance, and the shot will undoubtedly finish in the wrong place on the hole.

With the longest clubs in the bag, driver and 3 wood, the ball should be played just a shade (a half inch to an inch) inside of the left heel. This allows the hands to stay behind the ball at impact and allows the club to make contact at the correct angle of attack—the very bottom of the swing, maybe even a little on the upswing.

As a player works his or her way through the golf bag, the ball should move back in his or her stance in small increments as the clubs get shorter and more lofted. This coincides with the stance narrowing and becoming more open as the golfer clubs down.

Because the swing remains basically the same on all shots, these adjustments are merely a simple matter of physics. The shorter the club, the shorter the swing radius and the closer a player must stand to the ball, thus the narrowing of the stance. Because the shorter swing takes less time to execute, clearing the left hip through the hitting zone becomes a problem. Opening the stance helps alleviate the problem by getting the left hip out of the way before the swing ever starts.

A good guide is woods off the left heel, long irons two or three inches inside; and continue moving the ball until it's exactly in the middle of a player's stance for a 5 iron and two or three more inches back for full swings with a 9 iron or pitching wedge. Be sure to double check your ball position before every shot—don't let it sneak too far forward when you're not looking.

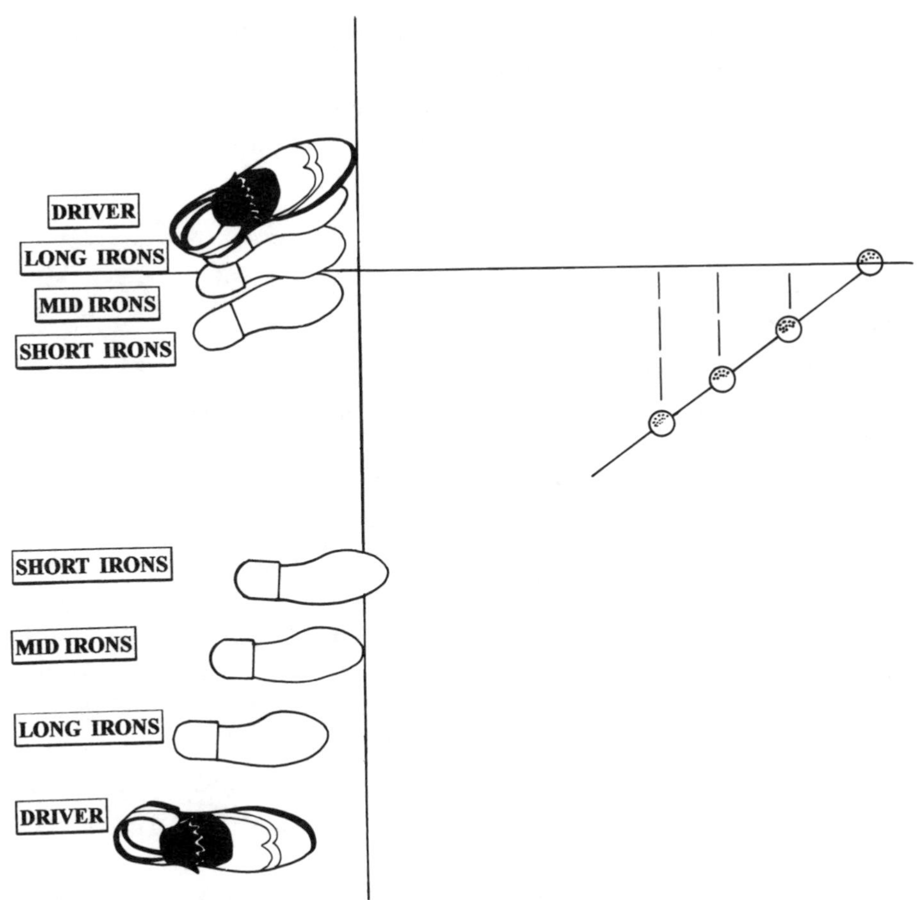

As the clubs get smaller, a player's stance gets narrower and more open. The ball position gradually moves from the front foot to the back.

Hit Your Pitch

"As a man who was a very good baseball player before becoming a professional golfer, I can tell you hitting a baseball well is much harder than hitting a golf ball. Why? Because a baseball is a moving target and a golf ball is a sitting duck. In baseball, a player waits and waits for just the right pitch to hit, waits for a strike before he swings. A golfer, he gets to swing at a strike every time. But what amateurs do wrong too often is get the ball in a bad spot and end up swinging at ball four.

"It is imperative that the ball is in the right spot. It's just sitting there waiting for you to hit, so it's very easy to line it up in the strike zone. Make sure to get your pitch to hit every time by putting the ball in the proper position in your stance and then making a good swing. Remember—only hit strikes!"

Ball position is also crucial when playing in wind. For shots into the breeze, take an extra club or two, widen your stance to help with balance, and put the ball back in your stance to help hit a low-boring shot. Downwind, take a little less club, still keeping the stance a little wider, then move the ball forward toward the left heel to help hit it a little more on the upswing, and let it ride the jet stream.

Alignment

Because everybody needs direction in life and even the finest struck ball in the world will land in the water if it's aimed there, alignment is the final preshot component of the setup. Start by standing behind the ball and picking a target. Off the tee, it may be a bunker on the right side of the fairway, the third pine tree from the left, or a church steeple in the distance. Even on the easiest, most wide-open driving holes, find something to aim at; and the more specific the point of reference, the better. Make it the rake in the trap. It'll help you focus and give the mind's eye a distinct picture.

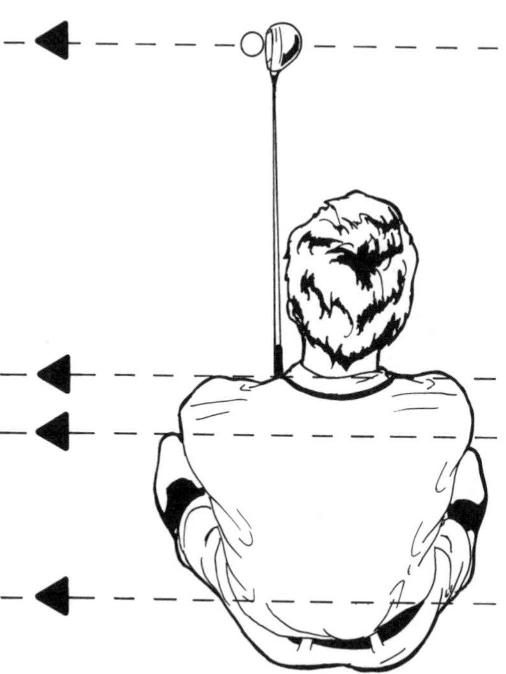

In perfect alignment, the shoulders, hips, and feet are all parallel with the target line. A good square clubface will then travel along the same parallel line.

On par 3s and approach shots, the target may or may not be the flag. Because of the slope of the green or wind conditions, it might be the edge of the putting surface or an azalea bush on the back right-hand side of the green. Again, find the spot and zero in on it.

Place your club behind the ball with the face pointed square to the chosen target. Now take your stance, and align your body along a line parallel to the target. Start with your feet, then make sure your hips and shoulders are along the same parallel line, as well. If, in an effort to get comfortable, you need to move a little bit, try to set up just a shade left of the target. Working yourself to the right is no good.

To check the aim of your setup, simply take your club and lay it across your thighs. If you are aligned correctly, the shaft of the club will be pointed directly at the desired target. Putting a club on the ground to check your position is common but not as effective because it can't tell you if your torso is off line, and the key to good alignment is making sure the feet, hips, and shoulders are all headed in the right (read same) direction.

Most players have lousy aim, so even when they hit an excellent shot, it doesn't go where they planned. Amateurs tend to work themselves a little too far to the left and then end up hitting it right trying to compensate. To help practice getting square to a target, take your stance along a crack in the sidewalk, the boards of a hardwood floor, the edge of a rug, or a line running through the living room carpet—any line will do—then check to see what target you're pointed at. Do it over and over again, and eventually the repetition will teach your feet and eyes to work as one on the course.

Chi Chi's Preshot Routine

"Part of ensuring a good setup is going through the same routine before every shot. Building a solid repeating swing is impossible without repeating the movements leading up to it. The familiarity of this preshot routine also helps mentally to put a player in a comfortable and confident position.

"Even when I know exactly what I want to hit, I still make my caddie take my bag off the golf cart and bring it to me in the fairway, so I can take the club out of the bag myself. That's the start of my routine, taking the club out of the bag. Then while eyeing my target, I put my grip on the club. As I take my stance, I review to make sure my grip is correct. Sometimes I will strengthen or weaken it depending on the shot I wish to play. I then square myself to the target, and only after getting square do I adjust my stance to allow for a fade or a draw. My final move is a smooth side-to-side waggle. Rarely do I take a full practice swing unless it's an unusual shot that I haven't hit in a while. Then I set the club behind the ball and go.

"Though it seems lengthy, my preshot routine takes only 8 or 10 seconds. Like the swing, a preshot routine should be simple and repeatable. Don't make an afternoon of getting to the ball, setting up to it, and standing over it. Standing over the ball too long only increases the chances of tensing up and overthinking. Get your shot, commit to it, and swing. Do this for every shot on the course or at the practice range."

Take-Away

And now the movement begins. The chain reaction of events that, when done well, appears to be one seamless motion—a smooth golf swing. Don't complicate things. Always remember that the goal of the take-away and the entire backswing simply is to put the club in a good position from which to hit the ball. Nothing more, nothing less. Do not get too concerned about the length of your backswing. A longer backswing does not necessarily translate to longer shots.

John Daly goes way back. Jack Nicklaus, in his prime, got the club perfectly parallel with the ground. Chi Chi Rodriguez has a comparatively short backswing and yet, despite his small build, has always been one of the longest hitters in the game. "Because of my size, my swing will never be as long as

Hands, arms, shoulders, hips: Start the club back low and slow, then simply pick it up in a smooth arc taking it as far back as your body comfortably allows.

Tom Weiskopf's, who is a very tall player," says Chi Chi, "but it's the right length for me. More important is that my swing has always been the same length. It was a short swing when I was a boy, and it is the same amount of short now in my 60s."

A good take-away always follows in the same order: hands, arms, shoulders, hips. The first three (hands, arm, shoulders) start nearly in unison. Separated only by fractions of seconds, they appear to move simultaneously. A simple rhythm of anatomy—hands connected to the arms, arms connected to the shoulders.

Take the club away along the target line (it should feel as if your arms are doing all the work) about two and a half feet, and then, keeping the left arm straight, simply pick up the club and swing it back in a smooth arc as far as

The left arm should stay as straight as possible during the take-away. With the hands at waist height the toe of the club should be pointing straight up.

The hands at shoulder height have already cocked naturally and the shoulders are turned nearly back from the target. The weight has shifted properly to the back leg.

your body comfortably allows. A person's flexibility in the shoulders and hips will determine the natural length of his or her backswing. "I feel my arms," says Chi Chi, "but I'm thinking more about a smooth, slow turn of the shoulders and hips."

At "the top" of your backswing, your shoulders should be turned away with your back facing the target, and the club, ideally, is also pointed at the target on a line parallel with your stance. Your left shoulder should be touching or gently tucked under your chin. A proper turn will naturally shift your weight onto the right foot. Your body is now "coiled," and the club is "set." Simple. Think no more of it.

If you are comfortable and balanced and the club is in good position at the top, skip down to the next section about the follow-through. If your analytical side needs more information, here is a full explanation of what happens in the brief time from address to the "set" position.

Drawing the club back with the hands, arms, and shoulders helps to bring the left knee and left hip in behind the ball. Getting the left knee behind the ball is crucial to the backswing. Hitting from "behind" the ball is part of generating power and thus distance. But the move needs to be natural not forced. The club should be traveling on a slightly inside line to help get it behind your head and set up a good position for the downswing.

As your hands raise and approach your waist, the natural turn of the shoulders begins to turn the hips. Don't turn the hips too soon, or you'll lose power

In the slot: At the top of the swing the hips and shoulders have made a full turn and are filled with potential power. The club points at the target.

and throw off the entire swing sequence. Let the shoulders give them a tug to get started.

At the same time as your hands are reaching your waist, a natural wrist cock should occur. If the toe of your club is pointed straight north to the heavens, God bless, the position is correct, and the wrists are sufficiently cocked. "Wrist cock, poppy cock!" Chi Chi exclaims. "Amateurs don't need to make a dramatic, separate movement to cock the wrists. If they do, they've now overcocked and put the club in a bad position." Done properly a spectator won't be able to notice any certain spot where the wrists are cocked.

From the waist to "the top," a straight left arm brings the club up while the hips and shoulders continue to rotate right in a move that completes the weight shift from the left to the right leg. Because the hip turn is rooted in a good, firm stance and we don't want to move our feet, the hips stop rotating at about 45 degrees. The shoulders, now turning independently of the hips, continue to rotate until they are nearly 90 degrees, or perpendicular, with the original line of the stance. The club will now be in its normal position at the top of the backswing.

The left heel may or may not be raised off the ground. It's fine in either position. If it is raised, it should have come up naturally (do *not* make a conscious effort to pick it up) and be no more than an inch or two off the ground. A raised heel will usually add a little length to the backswing. In an effort to develop the arc of a much larger man, Chi Chi Rodriguez's left heel raises higher than most, and he gets his left knee farther behind the ball—both moves allow him to generate maximum power.

Be careful not to get too tensed up or stiff during the backswing. The idea of "coiling" is not to get wound so tight that the muscles can't do their job. A golfer's body should be taut and firm and ready to release its energy. Think of stretching a rubber band. Pulled back too far, it loses its elasticity and may break or snap off in an unwanted direction. Pulled back gently, it is taut and loaded with power that is easily aimed and released.

I've Got Rhythm

"The one thing all great golf swings have in common is great rhythm. They may each look a little different, some faster some slower, but they all have a beautiful tempo from start to finish. Players should work on their rhythm. Simply swinging a golf club back and forth in an easy, gentle manner with no extreme changes in speed will help. Concentrate on keeping an even flow from take-away to follow-through. The golf swing doesn't contain any sharp, outwardly dramatic movements. It's a lyric to be hummed, not shouted or screamed.

"Some people have more natural rhythm than others. I was lucky to be born with the genes that make up the golf swing. Sam Snead had the greatest natural tempo ever. They said watching Sam was like 'watching syrup poured from a bottle.' Sam did have the sweetest, most graceful swing in history. Nick Price has a fast tempo, but it's good for him. Bob Murphy is considerably slower, but his swing reflects his personality. Most of them do. People who drive fast and put on their shoes fast usually swing fast. People who move slow and have easygoing personalities tend to swing slow.

"But great tempo and rhythm doesn't mean underdoing it. The golf swing is still an athletic act, and you must swing with enough force to drive through the ball. Tiger Woods and Phil Mickelson are two guys who look as if they are trying to hit the ball hard, but their tempos are both perfect throughout the entire swing. Swinging too easy is just as bad as swinging too hard. You may not lose as many balls, but you won't score any better."

Follow-Through

Now, finally, it's time to hit the ball, which, after all, is why we came to the course in the first place. This is the most crucial part of the swing because, obviously, it is the payoff; but it also should be the easiest because if the body and club are in the correct position, it's a simple matter of bringing the club head down to meet the ball and hitting off a strong left side.

Getting the club down from the top occurs in the exact opposite order of taking it away. On the downswing, the hips lead followed by the shoulders, arms, and hands. The body uncoils, with the power transferring from the shoulders down through the club to impact with the ball.

To initiate the downswing, make a gradual turn of the left hip and shift your weight onto the left foot, and in the same movement begin to bring your right elbow back down to your body. Just like that, you're on your way back down to the ball. It's the turning of the hips that is the essential move in starting the correct chain reaction of the downswing. It should feel as if you're planting the left foot. The left shoulder, arm, and hand follow a fraction behind and travel back to the ball as one unit. Strangely, the sensation shows up in your left hand. "It should feel as if you're making a tremendous pull downward with the left hand," explains Chi Chi. Remember, this is only a feeling. To actually lead with the hands is to lead to disaster.

A slight hip turn starts the downswing. "Planting the left side is the most important part of the swing," says Chi Chi. From the top down think mainly about hitting the ball.

To practice this move, start from the top of your

swing; and, forgetting about your arms and hands, make your hip turn, and watch as the arms and hands naturally drop toward your waist and in the direction of the ball. Move the hips first, and everything else will come along in good time. Move the hands and arms too soon, and the timing of the swing breaks down, resulting in either a big slice or a ball yanked too far left.

Now that you're on the way down, *only think about hitting the ball.* Gravity and centrifugal force are your friends and will do most of the work and naturally shift the rest of your weight. The left arm is extended full and accelerating downward along the target line to and through the ball. *Stay down through the ball.*

The back of the left hand and the palm of the right hand both face the target to keep the club face square and hit with maximum force. Your grip pressure should be exactly the same as when the swing started. Do not squeeze the shaft any harder on the downswing, or at impact—it will only add shot-

"At impact," says Chi Chi, " a golfer *must* be hitting against a solid left wall." Left foot planted, left arm straight, clubface square, head behind the ball.

wrecking tension to the swing. Keep in mind that the hands work together at impact, and don't let one overpower the other. Think of yourself as a baseball player trying to hit the ball over second base into center field.

At impact, the entire left side of the body will be aligned and generating tremendous power. "I call this the perfectly solid left wall," says Chi Chi. "It is impossible to find a good player who does not hit off a strong left side." Left foot planted strong and braced the entire way up the leg to the hip. The left shoulder, arm, and club shaft are also nearly perfectly aligned as they blow through the ball. "The wall must be strong," says Chi Chi. "Do not let it crumble."

After the ball is away, both arms should remain fully extended out and in front of your body, with the right shoulder coming underneath the chin on the follow-through. The force of the swing will bring the torso around toward the target. Pick the head up, and bring the arms through to a nice, well-balanced high finish over the left shoulder. If you choose, you may hold the posture an extra couple of beats in one of those perfect made-for-TV Tour finishes.

Of course, more is going on here than stated, and for you type-A personality technicians, here's a step by step.

During the downswing, the hips are not only turning but also moving laterally, along with the right knee, toward the target. The right elbow remains close but not cramped against the left side, allowing the right shoulder to come down and under in the proper manner. This puts the club slightly inside the line and allows the player to hit from the inside of the ball, with the club swinging out to the target. A key to hitting a shot straight or with a slight draw is "dropping" the club inside and hitting out. Chronic slicers come over the top, from the outside in.

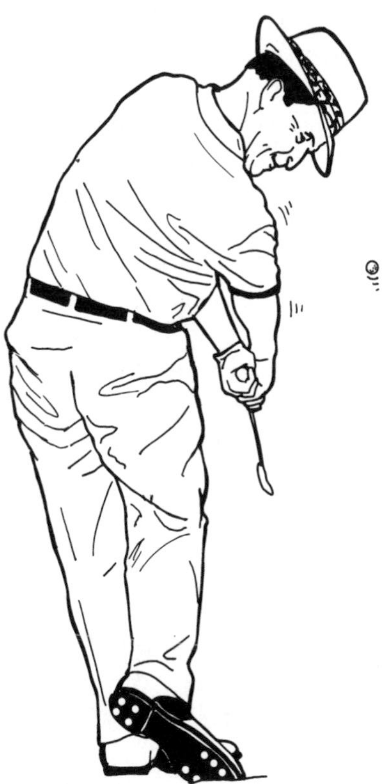

Following through. After impact the arms continue fully extended out in front of the body causing a natural rolling of the forearms and wrists up to a classic high finish.

As the hands move below the waist, the hips continue to rotate and clear out of the way, along with the entire left side, just before impact to make room for the arms and hands to pass through and strike the ball along the target line. "Just as the wrists cock naturally," explains Chi Chi, "they uncock in the same simple manner. If you get the hands and the club head meeting the ball in the same position they were at in address, then the wrists have done their job fine."

Contact is made with the club hitting down into and then through the ball, all the power of the hips, shoulders, arms, hands, and club lining up at impact. Make sure to hit the little ball before the big ball. Golf ball first, earth second. A divot is taken after the ball is struck, not before! And, again, keep your grip pressure constant from the start of the swing through the finish. Do *not* choke the club on the way down.

Keep Your Eye on the Ball

"The biggest myth in golf is that a player must 'Keep his or her eye on the ball.' It's a bunch of bull, not to mention it can't be done. Everybody, even the best pros, loses sight of the ball for a fraction of time during his or her swings. David Duval and Annika Sorenstam aren't even looking at the ball at impact. Curtis Strange peeked up a little early, too, and he played great enough to win two U.S. Opens. The best pros have such a dependable, repeating swing that they can hit a decent shot if they were blindfolded. The USGA machine nick-named 'Iron Byron' hits a perfect shot every time, and it has no eyes at all. Most often when people hit a topped shot or fail to get it in the air, it's not because they fail to keep their eye on the ball. Most often it's because they don't stay down through the shot.

"An amateur must maintain good posture through the swing. If the knees are unflexed and the player stands up, he will top it because the club is raised higher than the ball. Same thing if the player's shoulders come out of the swing too soon. If a player tries too hard to get the ball up in the air and tries to scoop it, he will top it because he is hitting too much on the upswing. Keep your eye on the ball the best you can, but concentrate more on staying down through the entire swing to be your best."

The ideal position of impact has the weight completely shifted onto the left leg, the hips cleared, and the left arm straight. The hands are slightly in front of the ball, and the head is behind it. The heel of the right foot is raised a couple inches off the ground, and the right knee (leg) is driving to the target. In a great golf swing, the chin is directly over the right knee when contact is made. All the power stored up from the backswing and generated during the downswing is now in a perfect vertical line and transferred down the shaft and into the ball. "Sometimes I look as if I am falling back away from the ball when I hit," says Chi Chi, "but that is only because I generate so much force up against my solid left wall that it has a recoiling effect on my body, so the reaction looks as if I'm going backward."

After contact, it is essential to continue through, with the arms fully extended out in front of the body to a high finish. This cannot be emphasized enough. Don't put the brakes on the swing after impact. Let it flow all the way through the ball and out toward the target to ensure the club head remains square and the ball is hit with maximum velocity. A baseball player doesn't stop his swing right after bat meets ball. He continues on until the bat follows all the way around his body. Think of your own game and how many times the club finishes in a poor or unnatural position on mis-hits. There's a correlation. A good follow-through is the exclamation point to the quality moves that came before it. Likewise, focusing on a sound follow-through will help keep the club in good positions leading to it.

The key to a consistent golf game is based entirely on a consistent swing. These six simple steps, when followed and practiced with care, will help produce quality golf shots time and time again. Perhaps, more important, they will greatly reduce the number of poor or really bad shots a player hits, thus lessening the frequency of double and triple bogeys on the scorecard. Every golfer will hit a number of really fine shots during the course of a round. The winner is almost always the golfer who hits the fewest number of bad shots. Learn and develop a sound, consistent swing, and you will not only hit well but also miss well.

A Golfer's 12-Step Program

1. Take a good strong grip.
2. Make sure your stance is square, athletic, and relaxed.
3. Put the ball in the proper position for the club you've chosen.
4. Check your alignment with the target.
5. Make a nice smooth take-away and turn to get behind the ball.
6. Keep the head still.
7. Pick the club up to the top.
8. Start the left hip back and feel the left hand pull down on the club.
9. Think only about hitting down and through the ball.
10. Keep the head still. Still.
11. Picture the powerful left-wall position at impact.
12. Stay down and keep the arms extended through follow-through.

"Just by listing a dozen things, I am violating my own golf philosophy," worries Chi Chi. "I don't want the amateur or any golfer to think about all those things and swing the club at the same time. Thinking of one or two things is hard enough. Think of 12, and you'll maybe miss the ball. Pick one and concentrate on it. Then, the next time, try another until they all become second nature."

Head Games: Visualize

"Before I hit any shot, I first see it and play it in my mind. I can't do it any other way. I pick the club and I pick a target, and then I visualize how the shot will look getting from my club to the target. The truth is the 6 iron I hooked in the '91 U.S. Senior Open to tie Jack [Nicklaus] disappointed me a little because I pictured it going in and it stopped two inches short for only a birdie.

"Everybody should make these mental pictures before they swing. Think about exactly what you want to do with the shot, how it should look and how you will execute it. You will be surprised how strong the mind can be in shaping a good shot. When the muscles remember the right movements then the brain controls the game.

"Visualization is a technique all of the golf psychology people are teaching now. But I have been doing it so long now that my brain is like a computer. When I'm in the zone where I see everything clear as a bell, nobody can beat me. What I hit is what I see, and what I see is what I hit. Learn a good swing, then see the shots in your mind and trust them in your hands."

chapter 8

Off the Tee

Q: Chi Chi, what's the most important club in your bag?

A: Canadian Club!

Q: Stop. You're a riot. What's the most important *golf* club?

A: Oh, that's easy. The driver.

The driver not only fuels Chi Chi's game but it's also the lightning rod for his golf-clinic humor. Hitting it 265 yards straight as a saint from a folding chair, he'll tell you, "For most amateurs, the best wood in their golf game is a pencil. They especially like the ones that come with erasers on the end."

Belting another monster ball off the tee while kneeling, Chi Chi jokes, "I figured I had a better chance in golf if I was praying and swinging at the same time. I even invented a stance for a Jim and Tammy Faye Bakker swing. You get down on only one knee, in case the IRS shows up and you have to run."

One more? Sure, he has a million. Slicing one ball and hooking another in rapid succession so that they cross and nearly collide in midair, Chi Chi moans, "That looks like a pro-am I played in last week. It was a Scramble, and our team was so bad off the tee that one guy hit it out of bounds on the second hole and we had to use his drive." When it comes to the driver, or any other wood, Chi Chi kids because he cares. "Those long clubs put food in my mouth and roofs over my family's heads, and I have a big family."

The short game may be where golfers score, but hitting the tee ball is where they derive self-confidence. Getting off the tee is the key to making birdies and easy pars. Fail to get off the tee successfully, and a world-class short game is reduced to trying to save par and avoid bogeys. And the pressure of relying solely on the short game for an entire round can be draining and eventually damaging to the scorecard. Nobody gets up and down every time.

"The driver is the most important club in the game because it sets up everything. It's my biggest weapon," preaches Chi Chi. "Hitting it long and straight is a big confidence boost for starters. After I hit a good drive, I feel I can hit any shot. And hitting the driver well means shorter iron shots into the greens. Driving it past your partner is beneficial because it means you get to see what club he hits and how the elements might affect the ball. It also allows you to see how the ball reacts when it hits the green. You get a free look at the speed, firmness, and contours of the green."

"In truth, the short game only saves scores; the long game is the key to lowering scores."

Not to mention that driving well is the single biggest factor in getting players to return to the golf course. Making a long putt is nice, but nothing on earth compares to the pleasurable feeling that one gets from a purely struck driver soaring off into the distance.

Chi Chi's Driving Tips

- Take a good grip, but avoid squeezing too hard. Tighter doesn't add distance.
- Use good posture with the hands and head behind the ball.
- The shoulders line up with the inside of the heels, making for a little wider stance.
- The ball should be in line or just an inch inside the front heel, with the rear foot set back a bit to form a slightly closed stance.
- Tee the ball up high. Air provides much less resistance than the ground.
- Swing hard. I hit the driver at about 95 percent of full power (keep a little in reserve) and hit the ball on the upswing. This will add distance and prevent "pop-ups."
- Take a nice long walk to your second shot.

Don't fret if that walk to your second shot isn't as long as you'd like. "Short knockers" have a place in the golf world, too, and they needn't worry about their "short"-comings. "Hitting long is terrific," says Chi Chi. "I am a long hitter myself. But the farther you hit it, the farther it can go into the woods, the farther it can go out of bounds, the farther it can go into the water too. Big hits can only be a benefit when they stay in play."

Despite the obvious advantages, outside of the pro game, distance has become somewhat overrated and oversold. Three hundred–yard drives are nice but, despite all the promises from ball and club manufacturers, not the norm for most golfers. And trying to hit it 300 yards when you can't will only ruin your swing. It gets too fast or too long or too twisted or too tight, all those bad things that can happen when a player tries too hard and overswings.

If a golfer can hit his or her drive 225 yards, he or she can play any course in the world from the white tees. A player who can drive it consistently well 250 yards will have no problem stepping back to the blues. Working the math can make it less intimidating: a 375-yard par-4 is driver 9 iron, 400 yards should play driver 7 iron, 425 yards calls for a driver 5 iron. All are manageable holes and distances. So what are you waiting for? Peg it and play.

Grip It and Rip It

Hit the driver. Hit it hard. And hit it on every hole. Remember, the object here is to develop your skill with the driver, and hitting it 14 times during a round will do it. In golf, familiarity with a club does not breed contempt, it breeds better golf. The best way to get used to a club is to use it.

A huge side benefit of this game is that you will quickly learn that, as much fun as "grip it and rip it" sounds in commercials and in the locker room, it's not the soundest or smartest philosophy. It can be a crash course in course management. Want to find out what you're up against on every hole and what the course architect had in mind? Pull the driver every time and explore. Soon you'll find out which bunkers you can reach and which ones you can clear, which water hazards you can carry and those that you cannot, which doglegs can be cut and which need to be worked around. The designers may have provided a generous landing area on every hole, but it may be just a 3 wood away and sharply narrow just beyond.

As you play the round, keep track of the holes where the driver was the right play and where it was the wrong play. Keep the scorecard handy for review during future rounds. Don't do it every time out; but occasionally stick a few extra balls in the bag, then play Grip It and Rip It. You'll be a better and wiser player for it.

Be the Three

Leave the driver in the bag. You have a date with a 3 wood, again, and again, and again. Instead of the driver, hit the 3 wood off of every tee box. The repetition will improve your skill with the club and, as with Grip It and Rip It, give you a bonus lesson in course management.

Many times you'll find it's worth sacrificing a little bit of distance to save penalty strokes or keep the ball in play for the second shot. The 3 wood may also leave you in a better approach position. Better to hit a nice, full wedge from 110 yards than a three-quarter finesse shot from 87 yards.

If you're playing alone or in a twosome and you're slowed by course traffic, take advantage of the downtime to hit two balls off every tee—first with the driver, then with the 3 wood—and mark down on the scorecard the results of both. A pattern for smart play should develop. Ideally, we all want to be a confident driver of the golf ball, but the 3 wood can be a savior of a round when the big stick starts going wayward.

Triggering the Move

"No golf swing, especially with the woods, can begin from a dead stop; you must trigger the move to start. Some players use a forward press (tilting the hands slightly forward before starting back). I use a brief side-to-side waggle. Whatever. Some movement is necessary to get everything in motion. Think of a billiard game. Before a shot, a player moves the cue gently back and forth through his hand before initiating the strike of the white ball. Same thing in golf. Jack Nicklaus moves his head to the right. Some pros wiggle the hips. Find your trigger and stick with it."

Pay Fair

This game is as simple as keeping track of how many fairways a golfer hits during the course of a round. Tee it up and hit it straight. Distance is not an object.

The bet is fixed, with the player hitting the most fairways getting $5 from each of the other golfers in the group and a bonus buck added for each additional fairway hit. If player A hits 11 fairways (a very good day, we should add) and player B hits 10; player C, 7; and player D, 6, then player A would receive $15 ($5 per person) plus $1 from player B, $4 more from player C, and another five spot from player D. If the land of Lincoln ($5) is too rich, the game can be depreciated to dollars and quarters.

Fairways

Fairways is a one-shot, short-grass equivalent to a Skins game. Par-4 fairways are worth a set amount, say $1. Because fewer of them exist, par-5 fairways are worth double. All golfers in the group tee off, and the golfer whose ball lands in the fairway wins that fairway. If two or more golfers make it onto the mown grass, the fairway carries over just as it does in Skins.

The money continues to add up until somebody wins a fairway outright. If fairways are carried over on the last hole, all players hit another tee shot, with the ball closest to the middle of the fairway declared the winner. If the group behind is pushing you and you don't have time for a second ball, then the most accurate of the balls in the fairway on the first shot wins the bet.

Golfers may elect to break ties by measuring the longest drive, but that will always tend to favor one or two players in the group. Unless all golfers hit the ball about the same length, let accuracy be the deciding factor so that everybody has an equal chance. Fairways must be played with woods, a 1 iron, or an equally appropriate club off the tee. No lobbing a 5 iron down the middle to pick up a few bucks.

Fairways to Heaven

Blessed are the straight hitters, for they shall inherit the course. Fairways to Heaven is a fantastic game to sharpen your driving game and test your nerves. It takes both accuracy and timing, with the added pressure to hit it straight when it counts. In Fairways to Heaven, each player in the group antes up a bet on each of the par 4s and 5s. The amount is usually a quarter or a dollar, but feel free to wager $10 if you're part of the six-figure income crowd.

continued ☞

An order of play is set and followed for the entire round, with the bet rotating from golfer to golfer. If the money player hits his ball in the fairway, then he wins the money in the pot and a new kitty is started. If he misses the fairway, the pot carries over and is increased as everybody antes up again. If the next money player finds the fairway, he collects the pot. Miss it, and the prize money continues to grow. Hitting the fairway pays but *only* if it's your turn in the rotation.

A game of foursomes will always include two extra fairways, and those are played with the first and second players teaming up on one hole and the third and fourth players partnering on the other. If either player of the partnership hits the fairway, he wins the pot and they both split the take.

Big Drives

"The longest drive I ever hit in my life was on the second hole at the Desert Inn Golf Club in Las Vegas. We used to play the Tournament of Champions there in the '50s and '60s, and the winner got $10,000 in silver dollars. They used to bring all the coins out in a wheelbarrow. I was playing with Jack Nicklaus, and I hit the ball, downwind, 430 yards. That is the honest truth. I outdrove Jack by 100 yards on that hole.

"The best driving week I ever had was when I won my first PGA tournament. I won the Denver Open in 1963 with a score of 276, and I will always remember that I won, in part, because of good, steady play with my woods. I reached a 590-yard par-5 there with a driver and a 7 iron.

"The first time I was in Denver, the guard would not let me on the course. I went to the gate and said I'm Chi Chi Rodriguez the golf pro, but he wouldn't let me in. I said, come on, I am Chi Chi Rodriguez the golf pro. Again, nothing. I said it to him one more time, and he didn't move. Finally, I told him I'm Chi Chi Rodriguez, Arnold Palmer's caddie, and he said, 'Come right in.' "

The Way I Play: Power With Drivers

"There are many reasons I am able to hit the driver with tremendous power for such a small man. Hitting off a firm left side is the start and most critical part. As I've said, I make what I call the perfectly solid left wall. The left side of my body is straight and strong starting from the left shoulder straight down to my left foot.

To get a feel for this stand against a wall or door frame in your house and put your left foot, leg, hip, and shoulder against a wall and push against the wall. It is that force that will help make monster drives when channeled into the ball.

As I mentioned earlier I also raise my left heel a little higher than normal and make a slightly bigger turn with my hips and shoulder to compensate for my height. These are small changes that add extra yards by lengthening the arc of my backswing.

Then, as I always tell students, amateurs, or galleries, I swing hard in case I hit it.

The secret to remember, though, is that when you grip it and rip it you must stay relaxed. The farther you want to hit it the more relaxed you've got to be. I am like a baseball player. The power hitters who hit the ball the farthest have strong swings but very light grips, like Barry Bonds. Bonds chokes up on his bat but he doesn't hold it like he's choking it. I always stay loose. No tension.

I generate enormous speed with my legs, knees, and hands. The sensations I get on the downswing are of my left hand pulling down hard on the club and my right shoulder making a strong move toward the ball. Together the movements give an even, complementary, smooth-looking swing. If you work at it anybody can learn to move fast through the hitting area. But never sacrifice smoothness for speed. The uncoiling of the body needs to flow naturally, not be herky-jerky. Learning the timing of it takes a lot of practice and patience.

Though my swing is anything but perfect, it is a perfect example that unconventional is okay. Golf tips are guidelines and you need to experiment to fit them to your body, swing, and style. If it's natural and works, it's right—for you.

Physically, though I am only 5 feet 7 inches, the biggest key to my tremendous length is the strength in my forearms and wrists. As a boy I became very strong from using a machete in the sugar cane fields. Plowing behind an ox also gave me strong hands; even though they are small they are strong. And when I caddied I used to carry the bags, two at a time, on my forearms because I didn't want to wear out my shirt. We were poor and I didn't have many clothes and I couldn't afford to ruin a shirt working. Today's pros weight train all the time in the fitness trailer. If they want a real workout they should grab a machete and head for the fields."

Aim Game

Do you know where you're driving to? The Aim Game helps you keep track. That you can make money at the game, as well, is just a bonus. Points are awarded as follows:

Ball in middle of the fairway = 4 points
Ball in left or right half of the fairway = 3 points
Ball in first cut off the fairway = 1 point
Ball in the rough = –1 point
Ball in fairway bunker or woods = –2 points
Ball in water = –3 points
Ball out of bounds = –5 points

Keep track of your driving points on every hole and during every round, then watch and compare your point total with your overall score. You'll soon see the pattern is inversely proportional—the more driving points, the lower your score; fewer points off the tee, more strokes at the end of the day. To wager on the game, merely put a price on each point, and pay the difference to the best driver of the day.

Also, make a note of what type of hole tends to give you trouble. Always too far right on a dogleg left, work on drawing the ball. If you struggle on a left-to-right-shaped layout, practice hitting a gentle fade. Let the Aim Game help point you in the right direction. And, men, if you keep finding yourself getting lost with your driver, don't be afraid to pull over and ask a pro for directions.

Total Driving

In a formula similar to the PGA Tour's total driving statistic, this game takes into account the accuracy of the Aim Game and combines it with a distance element. Record points just as you would for the Aim Game, then add these points for length:

Less than 150 yards = 0 points

151 to 200 yards = 1 point

201 to 225 yards = 2 points

226 to 250 yards = 3 points

251 to 275 yards = 4 points

276 or more yards = 5 points

The points for distance count regardless of where the ball ends up. Whether it's in the fairway or the trees, 265 yards off the box is worth four points. An excellent score in Total Driving is usually equivalent to par for the course—70 or 72. Reach 80 in Total Driving, and you will most certainly have broken 80 on the scorecard for 18 holes. Betting on Total Driving is the same as in any point game—the difference between the higher and lower scores is multiplied by the value of each point.

Drawing Class

In Drawing Class, the goal is to sculpt a smooth, controlled right-to-left ball flight. Control is the key component. If you hit a ball right to left but can't manage the movement, then you've hit a hook. Hooks are harmful, and huge hooks will make a golfer swear off the game twice a month—or at least swear a lot!

"Hitting a draw off the tee is so simple it ought to be illegal to charge a lesson to teach it."

"When I want to hit a draw," says Chi Chi, "I turn my hands a little more to the right to strengthen my grip. I close my stance [dropping the right foot back from the target line and moving the left one slightly forward] and aim a little more to the right of the target to account for the right-to-left ball flight. I stand a little farther away from the ball to help take the club back a little inside the target line, and on the downswing I think of the ball as a clock face and try to hit it from seven o'clock to one o'clock. The follow-through stays extended down through the ball and extended a little more outside. Some players like to purposely shut the club face, but if you make the correct swing the face will shut properly on its own, and it doesn't need any more help from you."

Not every hole on a course sets up for a draw, but in Drawing Class you hit one every time anyway. Learning any new shot, especially a draw, takes some scribbling to get it right.

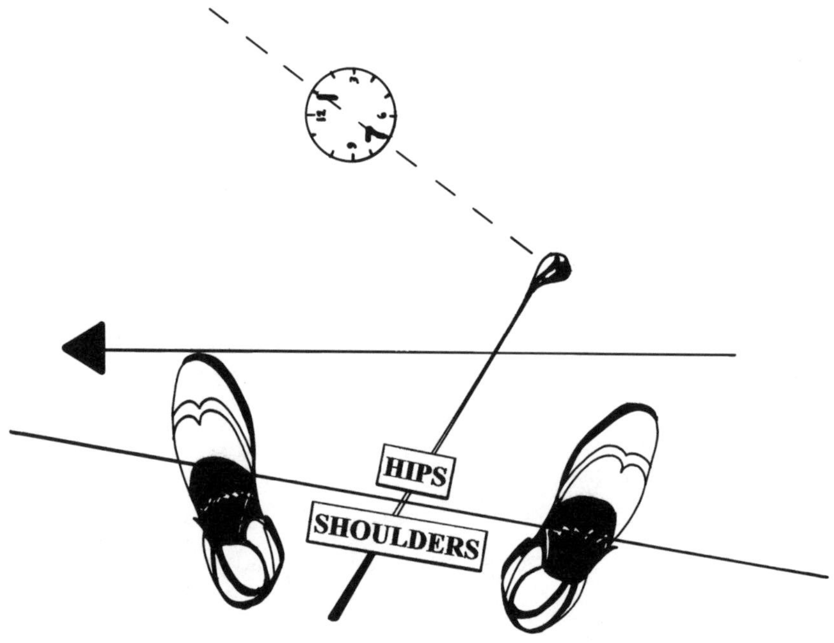

Fade Away

Because not everybody is an artistic type and can draw, the other option is to learn how to fade the ball. In Fade Away, a player hits the ball left to right off every tee regardless of how the hole sets up. What about the straight shot, you say? Like Ben Hogan, Chi Chi believes that "any ball hit perfectly straight is an accident. I would not recommend for the amateur to the move the ball all the time, but it is a good skill to learn. Hitting it straight is fine and works well for most golfers; however, if you are coming to play with me on the Tour, then you better know how to work the golf ball."

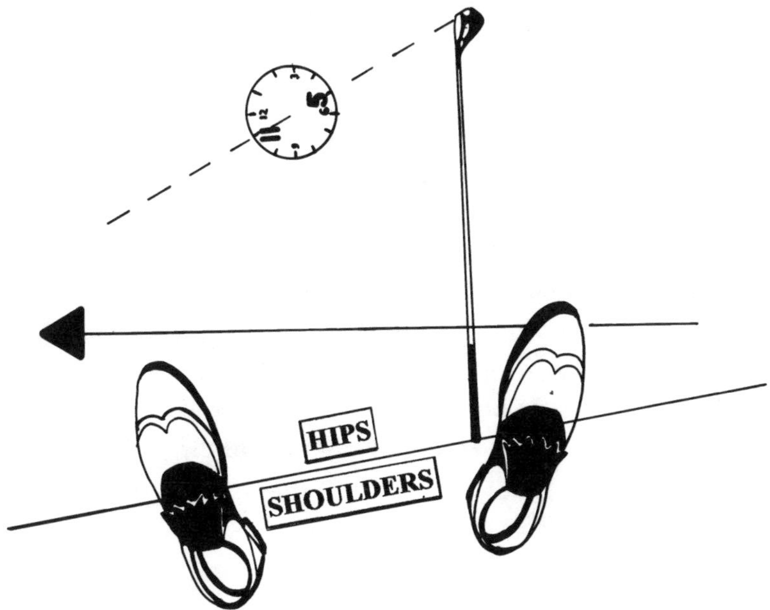

A fade is nothing more than a draw hit backwards. The moves are exactly opposite. "When you want to hit a ball left to right [a fade], simply open your stance by sliding the left foot back and moving the right one forward," instructs Chi Chi. "Since you are opening yourself to the target, aim a little bit to the left because the ball will come back around to the right. The grip rolls over a bit to the left from normal. Move a bit closer to the ball, so the club goes back a little to the outside on the take-away, and on the downswing you hit the ball from 5 o'clock to 11 on the clock.

"Anytime you want to move a ball, either the fade or the draw, the follow-through is even more important. If you do not stay down and make a clean,

continued ☞

fully extended follow-through to the finish, the ball will not curve in the air, and you will leave it way too far out to the right or left of the target."

A note of caution—Fade Away should be played with great care. Curing a slice is the hardest thing in golf, and hitting one on purpose can lead to bad habits. Slice sparingly to save aggravation in the future. "I had a student one time in Puerto Rico," Chi Chi recalls. "This man sliced so bad and so big and so often that I finally had to tell him, 'Buddy, until we fix your swing, any vow you make to God in heaven out here on the course is only good for 24 hours. Then you can recant if you wish.' "

To a Tee

Golf tees aren't that heavy and don't cost much, but they can weigh heavily on the quality of your tee shots. "When I was caddying as a young boy in Puerto Rico," says Chi Chi, "I watched the pros all the time, picking up even the smallest of tips, trying it; then if it suited me I kept it and if it didn't work I let it go. And one of the smallest tips I learned and experimented with that paid big dividends was how high to tee up the ball and where to tee it up."

Take a round and see what ball height fits you to a tee. Peg it high and let it fly. Tee it low and let it go. Adjust the tee depending on circumstances. Chi Chi likes to tee it very high. Very, very high. He has specially made tees for his driver that are nearly six inches high. Families of squirrels are left homeless to make these tees. They're tent stakes actually. His caddy has to file the sides off them so that the ball sits cleanly and he can get his club on it. Chi Chi tees it high for two reasons: air offers less resistance than the turf and his driver is an amazing 54 inches long.

"I tee it extra high and tilt the ball back a little downwind. Into the wind, I drop the tee down only slightly because I still want to hit the ball at the lowest point of my downswing and tilt it forward. I always tee up on the side of trouble in the fairway to give myself more room to hit away from it. And I always make sure I hit from a nice level part of the tee box."

Moving Boxes

Though the USGA frowns on it, it is not a criminal offense to switch tees during a round. Moving Boxes encourages it for the betterment of your game. Begin your round on the first hole hitting from the forwardmost set of tees. If you make a birdie or par, then move back to the next set of tees on the second hole. Another birdie or par, and move a tee box farther back again. Bogey or worse, move up one set of markers.

This ebb and flow of the game continues throughout the entire round—moving back until you reach the tips if you're playing well, getting stranded on the red tees if you're playing poorly. Yes, even for men, the ladies' tees are in play in Moving Boxes. All courses have at least three different teeing grounds, and these days most new and high-end courses come with as many as six.

continued ☞

Because the goal is to get better, the target score doesn't have to be par—it can be adjusted, should be adjusted, to personal preference and skill level. Make bogey or double bogey ground zero if that's what it takes to "get moving."

Moving Boxes is designed to improve driving by putting more pressure on the tee shot as you move back farther on each hole. A drive on a 325-yard hole isn't nearly as crucial as it is on a 425-yard hole. Play well, and the pressure increases to let out a little shaft; hit it long or be faced with making an excellent iron shot to stay in the game.

Head Games: Confidence and Trust

"Confidence and trust. You cannot have one without the other in golf. When I'm on the tee, I'm confident I will hit a good shot because I trust my swing. And I trust my swing because I have confidence I can hit my driver.

"Confidence and trust come from practicing good fundamentals. I am committed to every shot, and I know I will do the right things. That's why I don't get nervous; I know I've practiced to do it right. It is not possible to hit a good drive if you are uncertain about what you are doing. The brain has to tell the body, and if your mind is indecisive the muscles will be, too. Once I decide the play I will make off the tee, I stick to it and hit it with a single-minded purpose. No doubts—that is part of thinking positive.

"One of my amateur partners was having a lot of trouble with water hazards during our round, and he asked me, 'Chi Chi, what do you think about when you see a water hazard?' He was obviously sad and serious, but I couldn't help myself and replied, 'I think, man, I hope there are no alligators in there.'

"The weekend golfer is afraid of hazards, and he doesn't need to be. Do not get scared. Aim away from them or, if you have the distance, hit over them. During your swing, the head is supposed to be down concentrating on the ball, not looking at hazards on the course. Do not let water or sand or rough control the thoughts in your mind. When I line up the shot on the tee, I see nothing but fairway."

chapter 9

Approach Shots

In golf, as in life, a great deal of success is determined by the approach we take. "My approach has always been to go at the pin," says Chi Chi. "There's never been a flagstick I couldn't find." That bold, confident style has always been the foundation of Chi Chi Rodriguez's iron play—aggressive approach shots.

Think of irons as the middlemen, the clubs that do the dirty work between the drive for show and the putt for dough, the worker bees that cover the broad expanse of real estate that goes unmentioned in the phrase "tee to green." In most instances, you can't get from one to the other without an iron. Drivers and putters get all the press, but irons are every bit as important. Few things in the game are as rewarding as watching a well-struck iron zero in on the pin and few things as demoralizing as a perfect drive wasted because of a bad approach shot.

"Three putts and double bogeys from the fairway will make even the most devout minister question the 10 Commandments."

Approach shots are difference makers during a round. The difference between having a birdie putt from 12 feet or 50. The difference between routine pars and scrambling saves. The difference between a satisfying score and a second-rate one.

To that end, choosing the correct iron for the task is crucial. "The most important thing in golf," proclaims Chi Chi, "is to pull the right club. In my prime, I never used to hit the wrong club more than twice in 72 holes. I never forgave the caddie if I did, especially if he gave me a yardage that was even a little bit off. He would have been gone. I *never* saw Jack Nicklaus hit the wrong club in my life. Never, in all the years I played with him. Jack. Jack was not as accurate as I was hitting a golf ball toward the pin with his irons, or Snead. Snead was always on target. If Sam Snead had pulled the right club all the time, he would have shot in the 50s many times. If you get the right club, you should never be more than 5 yards off line in any direction, short, long, left, right."

A power player off the tee with an iron in his hands, Chi Chi Rodriguez is an artist, the course his canvas. "To be a great ball striker, you must paint the shot in your mind," says Chi Chi. "I see the picture complete, then make the proper brush stroke. If there is trouble short, I finish long. If the trouble is long, I finish short. If the pin is on the right side of the green, I fade the ball in left to right. If it's on the left, I draw the ball. If the pin position is on the back of the green, I hit it low and run it back. If the flag is up front, I hit it high and stop it. Straight shots work fine, but my brain and hands will not allow me to play one that way." With his iron-play tips on the following pages and games to help you improve your approach shots, Chi Chi Rodriguez hopes to turn you into the Picasso of pitching wedges, the Monet of middle irons.

Long Irons (2, 3, and 4)

"No series of clubs in the bag scares amateurs more than long irons," says Chi Chi. "True, they are more difficult to hit but not impossible. There is not much difference in the swing with a long iron and the swing with a driver. Only small adjustments are made in the stance [feet a little closer together], ball position [ball farther inside left heel closer to the middle], and backswing [club doesn't go quite as far back because it's shorter]. The two key elements are to swing hard and try easy.

"You must swing almost as hard as you would with a wood because you are still using a big club and you still need to hit against the solid left wall. Baby the 2, 3, or 4 iron, and your shots will spray all over the course.

"An easy attitude is also a key. What happens to an amateur with a long iron is that they are very far from the green and they worry that they have to make a perfect shot, so they feel pressure and try too hard. Couple this with the anxiety of holding a club they are not entirely comfortable with and fear sets in, and fear results in tension. That is why you need to try easy. Hit the ball well, and it will travel as far as it needs to; you don't need to help it with extra effort. Then, do not try to be too fine with the final result—any long-iron shot on the green is a good shot; let that be enough. Try easier and trust your swing."

Middle Irons (5, 6, and 7)

"Middle irons require a change in mind-set. Where long irons, like woods, are power tools for achieving distance, middle irons are instruments of control and accuracy. You cannot and should not make them do the same things.

"With middle irons, the stance continues to open toward the target, and the ball position continues to move back as the clubs get shorter. These slight modifications make it easier for a golfer to hit down and through the ball. Remember, ball first, then the dirt to take a divot.

"The swing with a middle iron must, again, be aggressive. Baby the clubs, and they are still long enough to fly off in the wrong directions. The caution here is not to try too hard to get the ball up in the air. Long-iron players try to hit too far. Middle-iron players try to hit too high. Hit a long iron well, and it will fly far enough. Hit a middle iron well, and it will fly high enough. You don't need to help them. Clubs come with the right loft for the job. Just allow them to do it."

Short Irons (8, 9, and Pitching Wedges)

"Short-iron shots are scoring shots. Hitting them well sets up winning chances; playing them poorly squanders opportunities and does costly damage to confidence. I am completely focused on accuracy, not power, with the short irons. Because I'm not going to hit the ball as hard, maybe 80 percent tops in most cases, I don't worry as much about the strong left wall. There is not much of a turn and not much movement in the lower body. With other clubs, the legs and arms do most of the work; with these, the arms and hands are in control.

"So what I do is narrow and open my stance and put the ball in the middle to back of my stance. These moves compensate for the shorter shafts and the shorter backswings that are part of hitting short irons. It is critical to remember when hitting short irons that the knees stay flexed so that you can get down and stay down to the ball.

"Making a smooth, simple swing will take full advantage of the short iron's natural loft and produce high, soft shots. Then you must practice to develop good distance control. Every yard you can hone your skill is a putt three feet closer to the hole.

"When I first moved back to Puerto Rico, my teacher there, Pete Cooper, had me hitting short irons almost exclusively. Hundreds and hundreds of wedges every day from 100 yards and in to help me develop accuracy, timing, and touch. In every round, you have many more shots from 100 yards and in than you will from 300 yards and out. Show patience, and practice with the short clubs, and your scores will get smaller, too."

Tiger Tees

Don't have a 7,000-yard golf course in your area? Can't blast it from the back boxes? Even from the tips, your home club is no more than a driver—short-iron challenge? Well, you can't make any more land, but you can create more space by playing from the Tiger Tees. Back up by clubbing down. Tiger Tees helps improve long-iron play through subtraction—less club off the tee means more club on the approach shot.

The change in math occurs because a player tees off using a 3 iron instead of a driver. A 380-yard par-4 that plays driver–8 iron for the average player (250 + 130 = 380) becomes a 3-iron–3-iron play from the Tiger Tees (190 + 190 = 380). The numbers add up the same, but losing 60 yards off the tee box

means 60 more yards to wrestle with from the fairway, which means more reps with the long irons. More reps mean more improvement.

Clubbing down by just 60 yards per tee can add more than 800 yards to the overall length of a course. And don't stop at 60 yards; work the math on every hole to try to put a long iron in your hand. On par 5s, hit three 4 irons instead of driver–3 wood. On short par 4s, use a 7 or 8 iron off the tee so that you're still faced with a challenging long-iron approach. Moving back to the Tiger Tees will take the fear out of those evil long irons, and a bonus of lightening your golf bag is added: You don't have to carry any woods during the round.

Go Low

The opposite of Tiger Tees, the goal in Go Low is to have the shortest approach shots possible into the green. It's a game that gives short irons a workout. To play Go Low, simply move to the forwardmost tee boxes on the course and blast away. Don't worry about the embarrassment of playing from the ladies' tees; worry about hitting good 9-iron shots. This isn't a macho game, it's a wedge game.

If some of the holes get too short for a driver or even a long iron off the tee, say, a 290-yard par-4, great. Work with a combination of middle irons and short irons. The idea pretty much is to play a game of lawn darts without the possibility of a puncture wound. Go Low should sharpen your short irons to the yard. "If you hit two good shots," says Chi Chi, "you should never be more than 15 feet from the pin. Think birdie, birdie, birdie."

Birdies are the bonus, the game inside the game, to Go Low. Because the game is predicated on short, manageable shots, it promotes scoring opportunities. These opportunities will, often times, translate into a chance for career-best rounds. Yikes! Nothing will constrict a golfer's throat like the chance to shoot his or her lowest score ever. "Forget money. You want to see a guy choke for nothing?" says Chi Chi. "Watch him play the last three holes when he has a chance to shoot a really low score." Go Low will help simulate that pressure whether it's to shoot even par or break 80, 90, or 100. Stand up to that pressure and a player's confidence grows. Fail in that situation, and the player knows he or she needs to work harder on controlling his or her nerves.

Go Low can also be a cure for low confidence. If you're struggling, move up and play a round from in close. This will give you some easy shots, some looks at birdies, and the feeling of playing well again. Wagering? Playing closest to the pin for a dollar on each hole will not only add extra interest and excitement to the game but also put a little pressure on fairly easy shots.

GIR

Greens In Regulation—a simple, straightforward, standard PGA Tour statistic. The game of GIR is just as simple. All players ante up $5, and the player that hits the most GIR wins the pot. Hit 70 percent of greens in regulation, and you're playing GIReat! Better than almost every pro, in fact.

Accuracy pays. And you'll be surprised what else it reveals. The winner in GIR will almost always be the straightest player off the tee and the one with the lowest overall score at the end of the round, too.

GIR Power

Not all GIR are created equal. GIR Power pays not for the most greens hit in regulation but rather the best greens hit in regulation. This game is target practice for points. Farther the approach shot, greater the reward. GIR power points are awarded as follows:

Approach from 200+ yards = 7 points
199 to 175 yards = 5 points
174 to 150 yards = 4 points
149 to 125 yards = 3 points
124 to 100 yards = 2 points
99 to 50 yards = 1 point
Inside 50 yards = 0 points
Miss inside 100 yards = –1 point
Miss inside 50 yards = –2 points

The player with the highest GIR power total wins and the payout is the difference in points at a predetermined price. Don't be afraid to make points worth a little more than you think you can afford, a dime to a quarter, a quarter to 50 cents, 50 cents to a buck. Points aren't as easy to accumulate as you might think. The average Tour player hits about two-thirds of all greens in regulation, and a majority of those come from between 100 and 175 yards. If you find yourself with 40 GIR power points, you'll not only break the bank but also be ready to try the Tour's Qualifying School.

Know Your Distance

Keeping in mind Chi Chi's fervent belief that "the most important thing in golf is to pull the right club," it follows that knowing exactly how far you can hit each club is essential. It's impossible to know if you have the right club if you don't know exactly how far you can hit each of them.

"Tiger Woods," says Chi Chi, "went from being merely the greatest player in the world to the greatest player in the world every week once he learned distance control with his irons. One time in a tournament, Ben Hogan asked his caddie how far it was to the pin, and the caddie says to Hogan something like 142 or 143 yards; so Hogan, he turns to the guy, and says, 'Which is it?—142 yards or 143 yards?' Hogan knew. I know. Great players know. You *must* know exactly how far each club will go."

Figuring out distances can be worked on at the practice tee, but because range balls are made mostly to take a beating and aren't the same quality as the balls you use during a round for shot making, they need to be refined on the course. Make use of markers on the course—sprinkler heads, 150-yard stakes or trees, yardage blocks in the fairway—to help gauge distance.

Keep careful track of how far you hit each iron during a round and under what conditions. As you begin compiling the information, always try to hit a normal full shot, not an easy, cozy swing or a swing where you give it a little extra. Once you establish a good, reliable yardage for every club, then you can begin adding and subtracting distance to it.

Know Your Distance isn't so much a single-round game as it is a round-by-round gathering of data that will help you learn the range of your golf game. Knowledge is power, and knowing you have the power to hit a full 6 iron 155 yards or an 8 iron 127 yards will improve your scores.

Club Distance Guide (in yards)

Lob wedge: 30–**50**–60
Sand wedge: 60–**80**–100
Pitching wedge: 90–**100**–115
9 Iron: 100–**120**–125
8 Iron: 120–**130**–140
7 Iron: 130–**150**–160
6 Iron: 150–**160**–170
5 Iron: 160–**170**–180
4 Iron: 170–**180**–190
3 Iron: 180–**190**–200
2 Iron: 190–**200**–210
5 Wood: 190–**200**–210
3 Wood: 210–**225**–240
Driver: 230–**250**–270

Distances are for the average male player; some golfers hit each club considerably farther (number on right) or considerably shorter (number on left). Use this as a guide and then adjust it to fit your game.

The Perfect Lie

Imagine a world where every drive ends up in the fairway. Nice, huh? The Perfect Lie refers not only to the ideal position for a ball in the fairway but also to a dishonest placement of the ball in the short grass if the tee shot fails to get the job done. In this game, tee balls not hit in the fairway are picked up and moved to the fairway, with the distance the shot is off line subtracted from the length of the shot as a penalty.

continued ☞

Hook a drive 20 yards left into the trees—go find the ball and walk it directly back right to the edge of the fairway, then walk it back 20 yards and play your second shot. A tee shot settling in the rough 5 yards off the short grass is carried in a straight line back to the fairway and then walked back 5 yards and dropped. The result is a chance to hit iron shots of a good, clean "perfect" lie and have a nice, clear shot every time. This means more practice hitting full-approach shots and less punching out of the rough or having to swing from in the woods.

The benefit is that good shots give you a chance to hit shorter irons, while bad ones generally offer the opportunity to polish long-iron play. It's proportional, really; the farther a ball travels off line, the more club that will be required to reach the green. The reward is an all-around better golf game. Although, if you find yourself walking too many balls back to the fairway, review the last chapter on tee shots, and come back to approach shots once your woods are straightened out.

Be careful to play The Perfect Lie when you're not being pushed by the group behind you. Seeing players pick up their ball and walk back toward the tee can be time consuming and confusing. Play but don't delay.

Of course, in The Perfect Lie, a golfer must fess up and tell the truth about his or her golf score, since the game tends to give a distorted picture of the final total. Do keep track of how many penalty strokes or drops you would have taken during the round when playing the game, and you'll see what a difference just putting the ball in play can make. Long is good. Straight is just as good. Long and straight are a money-making combination.

The Way I Play: Irons and Accuracy

"There is only one instance when I am not aggressive with my iron shots—when I have a two-stroke lead on the 18th hole and there's water on one side of the green. Hah, hah. Then I happily land my ball in the middle of the green nice and safe.

The swings I make with my long irons are very much the same as my woods. The tempo and force of the swings are similar because I am trying to hit the ball far. It is with medium and short irons that I back off a little and will sacrifice some distance for accuracy with these clubs.

When I am playing my best golf I am never farther than 10 feet from the hole with a 5 iron on down. In fact, I know it is time to head to the practice tee if I play 18 holes and don't have at least six shots inside of *five* feet.

I always, except with that two-shot lead, try to work the ball into the pin. Drawing the ball by making a little more inside-out swing than normal. Swinging outside-in to fade the ball. Actually I don't work the ball as much as I did back in my prime because the golf course designers don't allow you to do it. All the greens are elevated with lots of humps and very few pin positions and there is little cause to hit anything except a high straight shot.

Players like Sam Snead, Lee Trevino, Dave Hill, Tony Lima, Jack Nicklaus, and Julius Boros were terrific shot makers. I have no doubt there are great shot makers on the PGA Tour today but for the most part their talents are kept hidden because the courses don't require them to make special shots. Tiger Woods still tries to move the ball almost every time he hits it, and that is one more thing I like about him.

As good as my aim is, I do not work on my accuracy as much as I work on ball flight. This is very, very important to me. Not only do I need to control my ball's movement right and left but also up and down.

I like to use my 2 iron for practicing my trajectory. It is the most difficult club for me to hit. So when it is going good I know the rest of my clubs will be good, too.

For higher shots I take a wider stance and put the ball slightly forward in my stance. To hit it low and cheat the wind I narrow my stance a little, put the ball back in my stance and reduce the amount of wrist action in my swing. This gives me the abbreviated follow-through that you see on punch shots."

Be Full of Yourself

Not a game, just a reminder. "Give each shot your *full* attention," says Chi Chi. "Be *fully* committed to each shot. Try to leave yourself a *full* shot into the green whenever possible. Give *full* effort all round, every round. Take nice, *full* deep breaths to enjoy the outdoors and stay calm. Be *full* of self-confidence when you play. Keep these thoughts in your mind, and your golf will always be *full*-filling."

My Favorite Club

Hopefully yours isn't Canadian Club, at least not until after the round. Not only does everybody have a favorite club, everybody *needs* a favorite club! Think of it as your magnetic north. Use it as the ultimate staff of quality in times of good play. An anchor to excellence if all goes bad. The one club that, in a pinch, can lead you home or, at least, back to the main road.

The favorite club is usually one of the middle irons (5, 6, or 7), and if you learn to hit it well it's quite possible to structure an entire game around it. Having one club you know you can hit on the green every time is a great security blanket, a comfort that will creep into the rest of your game. Learn to use it and lean on it.

During a round of My Favorite Club, do a little math at the start of each hole, and figure exactly how far you need to hit your tee shot so that you leave yourself the right distance back from the green to use your favorite club for the approach. Let's use an average 7 iron of 150 yards. If the hole plays 400, use a driver off the tee. For a hole measuring only 335 yards, hit a 3 or 4 iron off the box to set up a 7-iron approach. A good number cruncher can set himself or herself up for a shot with his or her favorite club a dozen or more times during an 18-hole round.

Keep in mind that the idea of My Favorite Club is not to set a new personal best score; it's simply to improve your game in the long run. Pick a club, or let it pick you, then work with it, play with it, practice with it, sleep with it. There's not a great deal of difference between a swing with a driver and a swipe with a 6 or 7 iron. Develop a fail-safe swing with your favorite club, and then work to develop the rest of the clubs in either direction. One good club in the bag cannot overcome 13 bad ones, but it can improve them and carry you to a serviceable round if required.

Chi Chi's All-Star Golf Bag

The championship has come down to one club and one shot. Here are Chi Chi's picks to make the winning play:

Driver: Miller Barber—"Long, straight, and never missed."

3 Wood: Ben Hogan—"Clutch with any club, Ben hit the brassie especially well."

4 Wood: Billy Maxwell—"Not many remember Billy, but he could hit a fairway wood."

1 Iron: Sam Snead—"God cannot hit a 1 iron? He needs a lesson from Sam."

2 Iron: Jack Nicklaus—"The greatest long-iron player ever."

3 Iron: Arnold Palmer—"Always aggressive. Arnie could play any shot with his 3."

4 Iron: Byron Nelson—"So consistent they named a hitting machine after him."

5 Iron: Don January—"A beautiful, tall player who could get down to the ball."

6 Iron: Hale Irwin—"Irwin with a middle iron is a guaranteed makeable birdie putt."

7 Iron: Lee Trevino—"Take away Lee's 7, and I'd have won 10 more Senior events."

8 Iron: Fuzzy Zoeller—"Swings an 8 as easy and sweet as his demeanor on course."

9 Iron: Ray Floyd—"Money with this club. For his, yours, or anybody else's money."

Pitching wedge: Chi Chi Rodriguez—"I can make it do everything except talk out loud."

Sand wedge: Chi Chi Rodriguez—"I was blessed with great hands for the short game."

Putter: Billy Casper—"Billy could make a 40-foot putt just by winking at it."

Work

Golf should be a game, not work—unless Work is the name of the golf game you're playing. In Work, in addition to applying regular handicaps, players can discount an extra stroke by declaring, then attempting, a more skilled shot. "Declaring" your intention on a shot means explaining to the rest of the group exactly how you plan to pull it off. Think of it as showing your work on a math problem. Strange, perhaps, but it's the only honest way to do it, and the explaining out loud will actually serve as a good review.

If Chi Chi Rodriguez declares he's going to play a high fade, he then explains to his partners, "I'm going to open my stance a little, swing the club from the outside in, and move it up in my stance just a bit to add height to the shot and help land it soft."

Declare you're going to fade the ball into the green, subtract one. Declare a high draw, and take one stroke off your total. Declare you're going to go two clubs down to account for an uphill lie, earn a bonus pop. Essentially, by declaring your intention to work the ball, you get the shot for free.

The rub is that your partners get to judge if the execution of the shot is worthy of the bonus. A low hook may not reach the green, but if it was executed properly then the stroke saver should still apply. If you declare a divot shot and follow it with a cold top that travels 15 yards, well then, the shot counts one just like all the rest.

The game Work is so named because it takes some work to get good at it. Here's a list of qualifying shots and tips for playing them:

- Fade: Open stance. Aim right of target. Outside-in club path. Hit from 5 through 11 on the clock face.
- Draw: Closed stance. Aim to left of the target. Inside-out club path. Hit from seven to two on the clock face.
- Low ball: Ball played back in the stance. Hands stay ahead of the ball. Make solid, square contact.
- High ball: Ball moved forward in stance. Slide club under. Hit hard to let ball climb up club face.
- Uphill lie: Take more club than normal because the hill will add loft to the club and cause a higher trajectory. Fit stance to slope. Put more weight on back foot. Ball position toward front foot. Swing up with the slope, but don't pull up off and catch the ball thin.
- Downhill lie: Take less club than normal because the hill will de-loft club and cause a lower trajectory. Fit stance to slope. Put more weight on

the front foot. Ball position toward back foot. Swing down with the slope of the hill, but don't drive into the ground and catch the ball fat.

- Ball above feet: Choke down on the club. Stance is a little more upright. Aim right of target to allow for a natural-draw ball flight.
- Ball below feet: Hold club as far up shaft as possible. Stance is bent more from the waist. Aim left of the target to allow for natural-fade ball flight.
- Divot or loose lie: Take a good firm stance. Choke down on the club slightly. Restrict backswing and lower body movement. Sweep the ball away to hit it flush; don't attack down into it.

Executive

Executive, or par-3, courses are a fabulous way to play golf and improve your short-iron play at the same time. Most short courses offer a good variety of holes so that you can work on long, middle, and short irons over the course of 18 holes. Plus, at affordable rates and two hours tops, they can save you both time and money. Most cities and towns have an executive course in the area, and a golfer should try to find a couple of hours once a month at minimum to get out and tighten up his or her iron play on a track full of par 3s.

"The more times you can put a club in your hand, the more natural its feel becomes," says Chi Chi. "This is especially important on the shorter clubs and with shorter shots. Feel and touch are crucial. I have played golf so many years that, anymore, shots from 100 yards and in go from my brain straight to my hands."

A helpful hint for short courses—leave the woods in the trunk and that includes tees. While it's a good idea to peg the ball on par 3s during a normal round, ditch them for executive courses. This helps to better simulate fairway conditions.

As suggested in the previously listed game GIR, put a price on the ball closest to the pin on every hole. Another alternative is to play a variation of Skins. Hit the green, win a skin. If two or more players hit the green, the skin carries over to the next hole. Outright winner of a green skin wins the greenbacks.

Rescue Ops

Because sometimes even the best players find themselves in places they'd rather not be, practice hitting the "impossible shots" on occasion. Work on rescue operations whenever you get a chance. These are positions that can't be mimicked on a driving range, so you have to be inventive and work on them on the course.

Waiting on partners to hit? Drop a ball behind a tree or bury it down in the rough, then practice the play. Purposely give yourself a buried lie or a left-handed shot, and hit it while you're waiting for the line at the snack shack to dwindle. Idle time on the tee? Hit some shots off hardpan or pine straw while you wait. The best way to prepare for the worst is to deal with it before it happens.

"The first rule to remember when getting in trouble," says Chi Chi, "is to remain calm. If you panic, then you will not play a good shot. If you are calm, then you start from a good foundation to start the recovery. The second rule is just try to play a shot good enough to get out of the trouble. Do not be a hero unless you're absolutely sure you can pull off the shot. And chances are you cannot or you would not be in the trouble you are in in the first place. I never in my life had to play an impossible shot unless the one I hit before it was worse than lousy. And I've never tried to play an impossible shot that I haven't tried in practice."

Knowing you have a plan for getting out of trouble and getting comfortable with it is critical to making a good play in a bad situation. Learn some escape routes, and you won't be so quick to resign yourself to a bad score on a hole and a debilitating confidence blow to your entire round.

Rescue Ops can be as simple as taking your medicine. A player can recover from a bogey far easier and a lot quicker than from a triple or a snowman. "When adversity becomes the opponent," says Chi Chi, "then patience and attitude become more important clubs than the ones in the bag. Golfers hit themselves into trouble, but you have to think to get out of it."

Throw It

"When my amateur partners get angry during tournaments, I try to get them to calm down and make them happy by telling them, 'Mister, for the money you're spending to play, you ought to enjoy yourself.' If that doesn't work, sometimes I tell them to throw the club. Hard. Then they laugh and we keep playing. But in truth, throwing a club is a great way to learn the golf swing.

"To throw a club and really make it go, you first have to get the club back in good position, not too high or too low. It's then usually followed by a textbook weight shift from the back foot to the front foot. As the person gets ready to let the club fly, they have a nice, not too firm, grip on the club, and they plant their front leg to establish the strong wall. To make it travel any great distance, you need to make a fully extended follow-through and release. All that's really missing is a bend at the waist and a ball.

"While throwing a club is very bad sportsmanship and I would never, seriously, recommend it on the course, try it sometime in a field or wide-open space. Feel the sensations. Who knows? Your anger may be the start of your happiness."

Head Games: Between Shots

How long does it take to play a round of golf? "About four hours for the round and two minutes for the golf," jokes Chi Chi. It's true. Swinging the club takes only a few seconds—it's the walking and the waiting that eat up all the time. How a golfer handles this downtime between shots can make a big difference in the final number on the scorecard.

To begin a healthy "between-shot" routine, start by letting go of the last shot right after it lands. The quicker you can wind down from the previous shot, the quicker you can move onto the next one. Take a calming breath, relax, and enjoy your walk to the next shot. Keep your head up and a bounce in your step. Posture is critical at all times, not just address. Don't be afraid to share a joke or story with your playing partners; enjoying the company is a key part to enjoying the game.

As you walk to your ball, think of the options available for the upcoming shot and start formulating a plan. Will it need to be played high to clear a bunker, or low to avoid a tree branch? When you decide on a shot, review the best way to play it and get to it. Don't overthink your swing. Keep it simple. Hit the ball and begin again. Don't dwell on the bad. Don't do back flips over the good. Steady and positive keep body and mind at their best.

"The thing to remember is that you can't concentrate and keep your teeth clenched for an entire round," says Chi Chi. "Even Hogan, Nicklaus, and Tiger, the most focused players I've ever seen, take a mental break occasionally. I try not to take the game too seriously until it's time to play a shot. I have fun and then I focus in—fun and then focus. I talk to the gallery or my partner or my caddie while walking between shots, then concentrate hard for the few moments it takes to size up and execute a shot. This approach keeps me happy and mentally fresh for 18 holes. And if my brain is not tired, my body is not tired."

chapter 10

Short Game

Ask Chi Chi Rodriguez about his tremendous length off the tee, and he'll regale you with stories about his boyhood days in Puerto Rico "digging ditches, cutting sugarcane, and plowing fields"—work that built up tremendous strength in his forearms and wrists. Quiz him about his killer short game, and he'll simply hold up his hands, wiggle his fingers, and say, "Many are born; few are chosen."

They are not particularly pretty hands; they're surprisingly small with little crooked fingers. He wears a ladies' large golf glove, sometimes a ladies' medium. "All of my family had small hands," says Chi Chi. "My mother and father had small hands. My hands look arthritic, but actually they've looked like that all my life. When I was a child, I had a disease called rickets. That is a disease from bad nutrition, from not having enough food. But I am happy. Even though they are small, my hands are full of feel. God blessed me with great touch. And since I became a professional golfer, I have never gone hungry again. You gotta feel it in the hands, man."

Though quick to credit his gift, Chi Chi prides himself on having further developed it. "It is wrong to be given something special and not do something with it," he says. "Some people, naturally, have more feel than others. But with hard work and practice any golfer can develop a good touch around the greens. There are golfers, like myself, for whom the short game is second nature; others develop it through determination."

A good short game is not, however, entirely dependent on ability. A player's imagination is equally critical. "When the exact play is not clear to me around the green," says Chi Chi, "then I invent one. I use the lay of the land and the loft of the club to improvise something that will get the ball either on the green or, better yet, in the hole." Combine technique with a clever intellect, and you have the recipe for a successful short game and lower scores.

More than any other aspect of golf, a good short game, whether the player is gifted or not, is the product of practice. A lot of practice. "Seventy percent of shots in golf are from 100 yards and in," explains Chi Chi. "Amateurs don't like to practice these shots because they're boring, and yet they are their most excited on a golf course when they chip a ball in the cup. I can never figure that one out, boring and exciting all at once.

"As I've said before, Pete Cooper at Dorado Beach had me hit thousands of these short shots—100 yards, 75, 50, green side, from the fringe. With every swing, I got more and more comfortable with the distance. What I did is I took my soft hands and made them smart hands, too. Now what my eyes see and my hands feel are the exact same thing. And over the years, they have saved me thousands and thousands of dollars. Every birdie or par you can steal increases the size of your paycheck on Sunday. The driver and putter win championships; the short-game shots keep you in a tournament. Give away a stroke, and you're giving away money. I love to give away money and help people, but I like to do it with a pen and my checkbook, not my sand wedge."

Practice greens and chipping areas are where short games are made. A quality hour or two spent there can be every bit as productive, if not more so, than four hours out on the course. If your time is limited, get to the practice area and get in touch with your short game. And when you're done, check your calluses. "You shouldn't have any," says Chi Chi. "If you start getting calluses while working on your short game, then your grip pressure is too tight. To really feel a shot, I hold the club very loosely. Remember, be gentle with the club."

Chip Shots

In most cases, whether the amateur knows it or not, he or she wants to chip the ball. Get it on the ground and get it rolling toward the hole as soon as possible. Putting air under the ball just increases the risk and uncertainty of the shot.

"Many teachers these days instruct golfers to use one club for all their chipping," says Chi Chi, "but I think you should let the situation and your judgment determine which club you use. The 5, 6, 7, and 8 irons are all good clubs depending on how far you need to hit the ball and how much room there is on the green to run it to the pin. The longer the shot, the longer the club; for short shots use a more lofted club."

Regardless, on any chip and with any club, let the club swing freely and do its job. Read the shot as you would a putt, and pick a spot on the green or in front of it to land the ball that you feel will allow it to finish at the hole. Then take your setup.

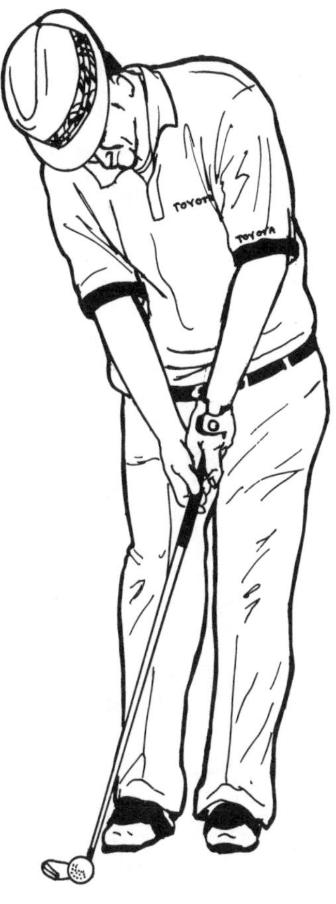

"To avoid chili dipping shots," says Chi Chi, "make sure you keep your hands ahead of the ball and don't lock up your legs."

Take an easy grip and hold the club a little farther down the shaft than normal. The feet should be close together in a slightly open stance. Your weight should be on the left foot and stay there throughout the entire swing. Though there is no real weight transfer on a chip, the legs should be kept loose and relaxed. Don't lock the knees or stiffen the legs. Keep the ball slightly back in your stance and your hands in front of the ball. *The hands remain in front of the ball and club head throughout the entire swing, too.*

The length of the backswing is as long as you think it needs to be to hit your spot on the green. The longer the backswing, the longer the shot it produces. Very little wrist action is involved when taking the club away—just a slight hinging with the right wrist. The left wrist should stay firm (and ahead of the ball) from beginning to end.

Bring the club back down to a crisp, square impact into the ball, and follow through toward your aiming spot. If the left wrist remains firm and your hands stay ahead of the ball, the face of the club will be open to the target and finish below the shoulders.

"At least once a round when playing with amateur partners, I get asked, 'Chi Chi, why do I chili-dip my chip shots?' After I explain the fundamentals of a chip, I then tell them the two biggest things that will lead to a chili dip are not keeping your hands ahead of the ball and club head or locking up the legs. Don't punch or stab at the ball. Keep your lower body relaxed and make a comfortable swing.

"Another good [quick] thing to think about is matching the follow-through to the backswing. If you take the club back to your knees, follow through at least to your knees. If your backswing goes to the waist, follow through in front of you at least to the waist."

Pitch Shots

The visible difference between a pitch and a chip is in the trajectory. Pitch shots are high shots that stop. Chip shots are low shots that run. "I pitch the ball only under certain circumstances," says Chi Chi. "First, the lie has to be very good, preferably uphill. If the ball is in a divot or downhill or on a bare lie, it's a chip shot. If I must hit the ball over a bunker, water, waste area, or some other barrier, I pitch it. Finally, if I am hitting to a soft, flat green and I can attack the pin, I will hit a high shot."

Pitch the ball only if the lie is good, in instances when the green is very soft, or you are forced to carry a sand trap, water, or some other hazard.

To play a pitch, spread the feet normal-width apart, and open the stance to the target. The ball moves forward to the middle of the stance. Where a player grips the club depends on the length of the shot. For a longer shot and three-quarter-length swing, put your hands in a normal position. On shots requiring half a swing, place your hands about halfway down the grip. For even shorter swings, the hands reach almost to the bottom of the grip. In all cases, the hands hold the club with a firm but light touch.

Likewise, the length of the take-away is in direct proportion to the length of the shot. For the longest pitch shots, which are about three-quarters of a

"The biggest difference between pros and amateurs in the short game is not ability, it's attitude. From the green side, an amateur just wants to get his or her ball close. From a bunker, they just want to get the ball out. In both cases, the pro is trying to hole out!"

normal swing, the hands rise roughly as high as the shoulders, and the wrists set themselves in a natural cocked position. For a half swing, the take-away comes back about waist high, with less hinging of the wrists.

The downswing on all pitches is a smooth, controlled movement back to the ball. Be sure to keep a good rhythm and accelerate down and through the ball. Too often pitch shots turn out poorly because a golfer slows the club at impact or tries to stab into the ball and buries the club in the turf. The follow-through should bring the club to a classic high finish.

"Even though a pitch is a short shot," says Chi Chi, "it is still a golf swing. No matter how far the club goes back, the pace of the swing does not change, and the club follows through strong and finishes high."

Bunker Shots

"Except for a putt sitting on the lip," exclaims Chi Chi, "shots from the sand really are the easiest shots in golf." Clearly not everyone shares the Hall of Famer's point of view. In fact, aside from hitting over water, nothing scares amateurs more than shots from the sand. "So then, to prove it to you, I will give you a quick lesson on bunker play that will work every time," claims Chi Chi. "Then watch your mailbox 'cause I'm going to send you a bill."

Chi Chi's 10 Bunker Basics

1. Take a good firm stance. Work your feet into the sand for a solid hold.
2. Grip the sand wedge high on the shaft to promote a full swing.
3. Open the club face and aim it directly at the target.
4. The stance should be open and feet, hips, and shoulders aimed to the *left* of the target. Keep a good knee flex and don't crowd the ball.
5. Play the ball opposite your left heel (forward in your stance).
6. Take the club back slowly and smoothly along the line of your body setup.
7. Keep the lower body still. If the feet and legs move, the sand will give and you'll lose balance.
8. Make a normal accelerating swing and hit the sand behind the ball. Three or four inches for shorter shots, an inch or two for longer shots.

"The biggest keys to playing a bunker shot," says Chi Chi, "are hitting behind the ball and accelerating the club through the sand."

9. Don't baby the shot. Cut down under the ball and through to a full, high finish.
10. Grab the putter for a tap in or retrieve the ball from the hole.

Learning these 10 principles of good bunker play will then allow you to make adjustments for any special circumstances that arise, such as the ones that follow:

- For *wet* sand, hit closer to the ball.
- For a *buried* lie, close the club face to its normal position, grip the club a little more firmly, and concentrate on a strong follow-through.

- For a *downhill* lie, play the ball back in your stance, almost to your right foot; pick the club up at a steeper angle; and make a sharp downward blow, again, an inch or two behind the ball.
- For a *fairway* bunker, take as much club as you can to clear the lip, and "pick" the ball at the point it meets the sand. If it's buried, just get it to a spot where you can play a recovery shot.

"Sand shots," says Chi Chi, "shouldn't scare you if your technique is sound. Practice them often and from various distances, and you will improve very quickly. The number one fault in this area is that people try to scoop the ball out of the trap, and that will never work. Work on my basics. The alternative is the Jack Nicklaus method. Jack, he was always criticized as being a weak bunker player. But that was only because Jack was smart enough to never hit his ball into the sand and rarely had to play a bunker shot. So, I tell you, avoid bunkers first. Failing that, try my basics."

Lagging

Is your short game ahead of the pack or lagging behind? Find out in this group game that puts a fun (read betting) twist on closest to the pin. How many shots it takes to get on the green doesn't matter; where your ball ends up on the green does. After all players have reached the putting green, regardless of the number of strokes, the player closest to the hole gets three points, second closest two points, next closest one point, and the players farthest out receive zero points. Because a good player can conceivably be punished if he or she hits an approach shot on the green from out in the fairway while his or her opponent may chip it close from off the green, a bonus point is awarded if a player reaches the green in regulation. At the end of the 18 holes, points are added up and the high player wins.

The betting on this game can be done in several ways. All players can ante up $5 or $10 at the start of the round and the winner gets the entire pot, or the kitty can be split 75/25 between first and second. Another option is to make each point worth a buck and pay out the point differential to the winner.

Re-GIR-gitation

Here's a chance to make missing greens in regulation (GIR) pay. Think of Re-GIR-gitation as an antacid tablet for those days when your iron play makes you want to throw up. Each up and down is worth a fixed amount. Start with a buck the first time you play, and see how that fits your budget, with up and downs for par paying double and up and downs for birdie paying triple. The player getting up and down (re-GIR-gitating) from off the green the most times during the round wins the bet.

The amount won depends on how sickly everybody else in the group plays. What can really upset the stomach is to hit 18 greens in regulation and watch an opponent get up and down three times for par and three more times for double bogey and you're out $9. In these instances, it's good to also have a wager benefiting good play.

Miss Me, Miss Me

. . . now ya gotta pay me! Because Chi Chi Rodriguez's goal is to improve your golf, he would never devise a game in which you would be rewarded for deliberately missing the green; but if you happened to do it on your own, well then, he'd be more than happy to help you win a buck or two.

The bet in Miss Me, Miss Me starts at a quarter, and the first person who gets up and down from off the green earns the prissy, but paying, title of Ms. Me. The next up and down doubles the bet, and that golfer takes the Ms. Me title. The prize money continues to double and the honor of Ms. Me passes from deserving golfer to deserving golfer until the end of the round, at which point the reigning Ms. Me gets paid the total in the pot from every other golfer in the group. It's much like the putting game Snake but in a good way. Earning the title Ms. Me can pay a princely sum.

It can also cause players to purposely miss greens instead of fire at flagsticks late in the round, so to avoid sandbagging, any questionable approach leading to an up and down on the final two holes must be validated. Put a 3 wood or long iron in the back bunker on 18, and you probably will be congratulated for getting up and down. Miss a 98-yard approach with a wedge at the last, then get up and down, and your opponents can request you get up and down from the exact same spot again in order to claim the prize.

Changes

"In my five decades playing professional golf, the two biggest changes have come in the last 10 years. Technology and money have changed the game entirely. I know this because I have benefited from both. The balls and the clubs are so good now it's crazy. I was a long hitter in PGA days, and I'm even longer now on the Senior Tour. Longer with age, I never.imagined it. Titanium lets everybody hit the ball 300 yards; and the golf ball is not only long but it's so aerodynamically perfect, it's made shot makers out of ordinary players.

"As for the money, when I first started out, we all wanted to play well so we could get a good-paying job as the pro at a really good club. These days, pro golfers make so much they can buy the whole club. I started out wanting only to make enough money to live well and buy my mother and siblings houses. I'm lucky to have been able to do that. And because I was born at the right time, I've been able to make more money than I ever dreamed of in this wonderful game after turning 50 years old on the Senior Tour."

Tee Boxing

Don't just stand there on the tee box waiting on the group in front of you to clear the fairway—*practice something!* Instead of complaining about the wait and sitting around stiffening up, take advantage of the delay to further develop your game. Help develop feel by hitting chip shots from one tee box to the next. Make small (dime or quarter) wagers with partners on who can come closest to the white tee markers from the blue tee markers. Depending on the lay of the teeing ground, hit from the tips to the ladies' tee markers. Play a chip shot down to one end and then a pitch shot back the other way.

Because the grass on tee boxes is mown low and tight, it provides an excellent simulation of actual short-game conditions. Experiment with different clubs and backswing lengths to determine how far a ball will fly and how far it will roll with each club. Use the scorecard and yardage markers on the tees to help figure the distance. If the blue tees on a par 4 measure 402 yards and the white tees 381 yards, you're working on your touch from 21 yards. Work the math and muscles together so that they become one and the same.

Glory Shots

If you have a wait in front and nobody pushing from behind, you don't have to rush to the next tee after putting out. Stay around the green and re-create golf's glory shots. Take advantage of downtime to make yourself a better player.

Bury a ball in the rough on the short side of the pin, and try to re-create Tom Watson's historic chip on number 17 at Pebble Beach to win the U.S. Open. Drop a ball in the front trap, and see if you can hole it out a la Bob Tway on the 72nd hole of the '86 PGA Championship at Inverness. Attempt Lee Trevino's desperation chip in for par on the 17th at Muirfield to win the '72 British Open or Larry Mize's 140-foot, sudden-death pitch and run on the 11th at Augusta to win the '87 Masters.

Working on these shots, or any other personal favorites you may have, while on a real course under real conditions will help enhance the quality of your short game. "Trevino and Watson," says Chi Chi, "when they made those shots to help themselves win major championships, it wasn't luck. They had played them and made them many, many times before in practice. It's a funny thing you learn in golf—the more you practice, the luckier you seem to get."

To put money on Glory Shots, pay a buck for holing the shot and a quarter for getting the ball inside of five feet. Pay a quarter to your partners if the shot ends up in an inglorious position.

Shag Bag

How do we get better at golf? Simple.Volume, volume, volume. Grab the shag bag and head to the nearest practice green or chipping area. If you're fortunate enough to belong to a club, head out to one of the holes at sundown and start hitting. Short pins, long pins, middle pins, uphill, downhill, side hill, sand traps and deep rough, chip shots or pitch shots—pick a predicament and practice it, 100 balls at a time.

Hit your pile of 100 balls in groups of 10, and keep track of the stats. Write down the number of times holing out, number of times getting up and down, number of others (anything over two). Hit 10, do the paperwork, clean 'em off, and start again. Repeat until you've hit your hundred. Total up the numbers and keep a running diary of your progress and improvement.

If you get up and down 25 times out of the first shag bag, work to make 30 the next time out, then 40 and 50. Some shots, obviously, are more difficult than others, and your percentage of successful shots will be lower; but every shot you make, regardless of outcome, will make you that much more comfortable when you're faced with it on the course.

Keep a detailed log of statistics for each shot type, and your strengths and weaknesses will become apparent. Tailor your Shag Bag routine to fix the problem. Soon you'll be keeping stats and records to make the Elias Sports Bureau blush, such as the following:

- Most ups and downs per set of 100
- Most ups and downs in a row
- Longest streak without an up and down
- Fewest ups and downs per set of 100
- Up-and-down percentage for all shots
- Up-and-down percentage for bunker shots
- Up-and-down percentage with the 9 iron
- Record for most hole outs per set of 100
- Record for most hole outs per set of 10
- Quickest to 50 ups and downs

Shag Bag will not only sharpen up your short game, it'll also help hone your powers of concentration. In the course of hitting 100 balls, the mind will tend to wander off—it's your job to keep it focused on fundamentals and feel.

Scatter Shot

Scatter Shot is a wonderful practice game because it offers a wide variety of tests for the short game and it doesn't take up hours of time. Take 18 balls, one for each hole, and scatter them around the circumference of the green. This can be done with exact precision to ensure a balanced representation of all green-side shots—above the pin, below the pin, short side, uphill, downhill, bunker, and so on—or the balls can be tossed randomly. Spin yourself in a circle and let 'em fly. Now that you've made your 18-hole green-side golf course—play away.

Scatter Shot can be played in either a stroke-play or match-play format. For stroke play, each ball/hole is played as a par 2, with an even-par score of 36 for 18 holes. Shoot an even- or under-par round in Scatter Shot, and you have a tremendous short game. Break 40, and you're above average; 45 is so-so; take more than 50, and you need a lot more work.

At match play, Scatter Shot can be played against an opponent, just as you would on a standard course, or against Mr. Par if you're alone. Again, all balls/holes are par 2s. Holing out wins the hole. Getting up and down earns a half. Take three or more, and you lose the hole. In Scatter Shot, beating Mr. Par can be as difficult as taking on Chi Chi Rodriguez in real life, maybe even harder.

Chipping With a Fairway Wood

"People all think Tiger Woods invented chipping with a 3 wood. Okay, maybe with a 3 wood," Chi Chi says, laughing, "but not with a 5 wood. The guy who invented that was Dave Hill. Dave Hill invented that. But I'm pretty sure, even before Tiger, Greg Norman was chipping with his 3 wood during his prime. Anyway, now that it's been invented, it's a good shot for the amateur to learn.

"You play it much like a regular chip but with a taller posture because the club is longer. You might even want to grip the fairway wood like you do your putter. The shot is most effective when chipping from collection areas and you have to play a shot up a tightly mown hill, from a tight lie or a lie against the grain of the grass. The wide, flat sole of a wood makes it nearly impossible to stub the club behind the ball, and it has just enough loft to get the ball up and on its way to the green."

Bunker Down

Sand shots are a little like CPR. It's a skill everybody should learn and know; you just hope you never have to use it. Begin by randomly throwing 10 balls into a trap, then bunker down and play them as they lie. Good lies, bad lies, plugged lies, in a footprint, uphill, downhill, under a lip—you don't get to choose, you only get to hit.

Keep score as you play each shot. A hole out wins 5 points; inside 3 feet, 3 points; inside 10 feet, 2 points; anywhere on the green, 1 point; out of the trap but still off the green, 0 points; leave the ball in the trap subtract 2 points; double it to minus 4 if it takes two or more swings to get out of the sand. Begin by trying to earn 10 points with your bunker play, and make it your goal to reach 30 points. Go ahead and make Bunker Down a competition. Play a friend, challenge a stranger, hit 10 balls for a buck a point.

"Bunkers these days," says Chi Chi, "are almost too easy to get out of. The sand is very good and consistent. The superintendents keep the traps raked and in perfect condition. If a pro gets a good lie and has enough room to the pin, he will get up and down 95 percent of the time. The trouble comes when the ball plugs or gets too close to a face or there is no room to land the ball between the trap and the pin. Practice those, too, because that is where you will save a shot or gain one on the competition."

Horse

Giddy up. Play Horse in golf just as you would if you were shooting baskets in the driveway or trading jump shots in the gym. Pick a short-game shot and send it to the hole. If you sink it, then your opponent has to match, or he or she receives a letter. First one to spell out "horse" loses. Generous sports often allow two shots on "e."

Because many golfers' short games are in the developmental stages and holing out enough shots to spell even "pig" could take all afternoon, lessen the degree of difficulty and modify the game to a closest-to-the-pin competition. But if you have the time and inclination, feel free to play "Nicklaus," "Pinehurst," "Bobjones," "Pebblebeach," or "Chichi."

If you begin with a bunker shot, the player finishing farthest out receives a letter, and the player closest to the cup picks the next shot. The game continues, with the poorer shot picking up consonants and vowels, the better shot getting honors and shot-selection privileges.

Majors

Nobody leaves the course for home until they win all four Majors—or at least give it a bold attempt. Think of it as a short-game Grand Slam. After finishing a short-game session or a round of competitive golf, take the time to sink four more shots to complete the day.

Start, as the pros do every April, with the Masters. In honor of Augusta's snow-white pillows of sand, hole a bunker shot. It could take you one swing; it could take you 25. Twenty-five is the stroke limit in Majors—more than that and your bid for the Slam fails. Move on to the U.S. Open, and drop a ball in the deepest, nastiest rough possible in tribute to the weed-stomping contest that is America's national golf championship. A chip shot from the front of the green pays homage to the bump-and-run-links style of golf of the British Open. And the PGA Championship is a pitch shot over trouble to acknowledge the great shot making and lower overall scores that highlight the final Major of the season.

Majors is not an easy game but an exceptional one for improving touch and technique. It also adds a wonderful element of pressure. The 25-stroke limit weighs on a golfer's mind a little bit more with every swing, and trying to win the Slam is a special enough achievement to tighten collars. Play by yourself or play with a friend. Play total strokes or play for each Major title outright. Beating an opponent(s) for all four championships is truly a triumph, even in short-game circles.

The Way I Play: Short Game and Feel

"The magic of my short game is in my hands and in my work ethic. I was blessed with touch and a desire to make good use of it.

Here are some of my favorite shots to use from around the green and inside 100 yards.

- *High and soft.* This shot takes the spin off the ball and will let it gently roll up to the hole. I use a pitching wedge and grip it softly near the end of the shaft. I make an open stance and stand a little farther from the ball to account for the extra length of the club. Then I make a long, fluid backswing and smoothly accelerate the club through the ball, producing a high ball that lands like a butterfly with sore feet and rolls.
- *Check-up.* This shot is the exact opposite of the one described above. I want to load up the ball with spin so it will hit and stop. To do this I stand

continued ☞

a little closer to the ball at address. I grip the club down on the shaft and hold it a little tighter than normal. I then make a shorter and quicker stroke back and through the ball. This will make the ball jump up onto the green and then check up with very little run.

- *Bump and run*. A must shot if you ever play a links course or have a good opening to a green on a windy day. I play this shot from anywhere between 40 and 75 yards from the pin. The first thing I do is choose the correct club. If I need to fly the ball farther than I run it, I will use a wedge. If the ball needs to travel the same distance in the air and on the ground, I will use an 8 or 9 iron. Finally, if I don't need to carry the ball far but it has to run quite a ways, I use a 6 or 7 iron. Regardless of the club the swing on the bump-and-run shot does not change. I take a narrow stance, shift most of my weight onto my left foot, position the ball back toward my right foot, and set my hands ahead of the ball. To swing I bring the club back about waist high using only my arms and hands (the backswing will be a bit longer or shorter depending on the overall length of the shot), then, with a pendulum-style rhythm, I bring it back down and clip the ball toward the target. The finish varies with the club stopping around the waist for a 7 iron and as high as shoulder height for a wedge.
- *Lob shot*. In my regular Tour days we never needed a lob shot because you could get at every green and pin without it. I hit the lob shot but it is a tough shot that requires a lot of skill and even more confidence and guts to pull it off.

  I prefer to use a lob wedge for this shot. Some people like to use a sand wedge but be careful 'cause if your sand wedge has lots of bounce and a lot of flange it's almost impossible to make the shot.

  If the lie is good, meaning I have enough grass underneath the ball to work with, I simply open my stance and open the club face putting the ball as far forward toward my left foot as possible. I then make a *full* smooth, almost slow-motion, swing and literally slide the club underneath the ball. The balls should pop nearly straight up and land soft with very little roll. The key is to make the full swing and keep committed all the way through the shot. Flinch and you'll scald the ball and send it shooting across the green."

Leap Frog

Ever wonder what a golfing frog sounds like? Chipit, chipit, chipit. Sorry, couldn't resist. Leap Frog is a game to help players improve distance control by working to improve the backswing. As discussed earlier in this chapter, the distance a ball travels forward on a chip or pitch is proportional to how far the club goes back. Leap frog your chip shots and pitch shots, and your game will hop up several notches.

continued ☞

For chipping, take half a dozen balls and place them close together in a row—in front of the green, behind the green, left of the green. You decide on the position. Hit the first ball so that it stops just off the fringe. Hit the next ball so that it leap frogs and lands just over the first ball. The third ball is played just over the second and so on until all balls are played.

Repeat the game several times, concentrating more on leap frogging the landing of each ball rather than where it finishes. Certainly, pick out a pin or a general direction in which to aim, but the goal is to bring the club back a little farther each time and hit the ball a little farther each time.

"Practice enough," says Chi Chi, "and soon you will give no thought to how far you bring the club back—it will just 'feel right' in your hands. I rarely bother to check the length of my backswing because I've hit so many balls in my life that my eyes and hands work together to stop the club and start it forward on their own."

To play Leap Frog with pitch shots, put a ball down 10 yards in front of the green, then walk five paces and set down another, pace five more yards and drop a third, and continue in increments of five yards until you run out of balls. Now you want to aim right for the pin and try to hole every shot. Hit the balls in order, closest to farthest away, adding a little more backswing to every shot. Again, repeat the game several times so that the swing and the distances feel natural together. If you are fortunate to have a large chipping area, continue to move as far back as possible until you are hitting pitch shots for 70 to 75 yards.

Take Your Club to Work Day

The single greatest way to get comfortable with a club is to hold it in your hands as often as possible, feel its weight, its balance, its rhythm. Spend an entire day getting to know your club. Take it to work with you or carry it around the house for 24 hours on a day off. Become one with your wedge. Get attached to your 9 iron. Bond with your blades.

Check your grip, vary the grip pressure, waggle it, take some practice swings, clip off a dandelion, whack a paper wad or pinecone, twirl it like a baton, balance it horizontally on your finger, then vertically on your palm. Hold it until it feels so natural that you don't know if you're holding the club or it's holding you. People might laugh, but after you tell them you got up and down six times during your last round and saved a great round, they'll be hauling their wedges into the office.

Going Good

"Here is my advice to you when it's going good on the course," counsels Chi Chi. "First, enjoy it. The feeling you get when you are hitting every shot clean and right on target is unmatched, so savor the feeling. Second, try and walk a little slower. A simple thing, but too often golfers playing well start to get excited, and this causes them to unconsciously speed up their tempo. Keep the good rhythm you have going. Just slow your walk a little, and it will subtly show up in keeping your swing at its normal speed.

"Third, beware of the easy shots. Everybody concentrates and thinks the hard shots through, so they are no problem. But the easy ones are where a player relaxes. Even if you hit the shot perfect 99 times in a row, don't hit the 100th one casual. That is when the game of golf will bite you, boy. Finally, just as with the bad shots, let the good ones go and move on to the next one. Good or bad golf is not played in the past or future. Yesterday is history, tomorrow is a mystery, today is today. Play only the shot in front of you."

Side-Bet Review

Looking for more short-game "action" during a round? Make a quick review of some of the side bets in chapter 6 of this book. Sandies, super sandies, moles, ferrets, golden ferrets, and Murphys all involve aspects of the short game and, of course, money.

Head Games: Thoughts and Voices

On a golf course, first thoughts tend to be the best thoughts. The little voice in your head that says, "Hit the seven," or "The putt breaks right to left," is generally correct. Give yourself credit for knowing a little about the game.

It's when golfers start hearing too many other voices and try to get too many thoughts in their heads that trouble develops. Listen to advice from friends or partners—no need to be rude—process it and use what you believe to be helpful, discard what is not. Golf is not a democracy; it is a dictatorship and you are in charge. In times of doubt, simply trust your voice and move on with it.

The golf swing is best made with a quiet mind. Make any interruption to that silence a positive one. The voice should be encouraging you to "Make a good, smooth swing," or "Put it right on the pin." It should not be saying, "Stay out of the water," or "Whatever you do, don't go left."

As for using your voice out loud, use it in a positive way, with yourself and others. Telling yourself, "You are the worst golfer God has ever put on this planet," will only lead to you playing like the worst golfer God has ever put on this planet. It's far more helpful to say, "You can play well; it'll come."

Support partners, but don't be condescending, and only give advice if asked. The most annoying voice on a golf course is the one talking during your backswing. The second most annoying voice is the one that offers unsolicited playing tips.

chapter 11

Putting

"If I could putt," says Chi Chi, "you would have never heard of Arnold Palmer."

Funny, but not exactly the ringing, self-endorsement, sales pitch you'd like to hear from the man who is about to give you a putting lesson. Which is why Chi Chi follows up his opening statement with this clarification, "I was a streaky putter. When I was going good I made everything. When I was going badly I made nothing. I would go a month, three or four tournaments in a row, where I putted great and finished really, really high in the standings. And then I would have streaks where I couldn't seem to tap it in the hole."

Chi Chi Rodriguez is not the first, last, or only pro to wrestle with the putter, an instrument of torture so evil it's driven world-class pros to retirement, Baptists to drink, Nobel Peace Prize winners to violence, and golf lovers to (gasp!) tennis. Ben Hogan struggled with the putter so badly in his later years on the Tour that he suggested eliminating the hole all together and having only pins planted in the greens. Putting entirely eliminated. The golfer hitting it closest to the pin wins. Terrible Tommy Bolt, like Chi Chi, claimed, "If I could putt even a lick, the rest of these pros could give up and go to the cabin."

It is a most remarkable phenomenon, really. The PGA and Senior Tours are populated entirely by players who cannot putt, not a single good one in the field—at least none of them who will admit to it, probably for fear that the golf gods will instantly swoop down and steal their golden stroke.

Billy Casper, a two-time U.S. Open and Masters champion, may have come closest to boasting about being a good putter when he confessed, "Oh, I make 'em once in a while." This from a player who Chi Chi says, "was the greatest putter I have ever seen in my life. When golf balls used to leave the factory, they prayed they would get to be putted by Billy."

Even stranger than the putting pessimism among pros is that right after bemoaning how everybody in soft spikes can roll it better than they do, they'll tell you putting is almost entirely about *confidence*. Yes, confidence is the key. Go figure. "Every putt I hit," says Chi Chi, "I picture it going in the hole. I always believe in my head and my heart I'm going to sink the ball."

"I have heard people say putting is 50 percent technique and 50 percent mental. I really believe it is 50 percent technique and 90 percent positive thinking. See, but that adds up to 140 percent, which is why nobody is 100 percent sure how to putt."

Confused? Good. Then when it comes to putting, you're already a pro. Now let Chi Chi Rodriguez undo the damage done by following his instructions for putting the final touch on your golf game. After all, this is the essence of the game, the ultimate goal—getting the ball in the hole.

Putting Technique

Not everybody is a natural with the putter. "God only made a few Billy Caspers and Ben Crenshaws," says Chi Chi. "Guys who can sink a putt just by staring at it." But with sound technique, a strong mind, and solid practice habits, anybody can learn to putt proficiently.

The first step on the green road to becoming a good putter is . . . to find a good putter. "You need to find a putter you can aim," Chi Chi advises. "Amateurs spend a lot of money and a lot of time picking out a putter and don't check to see if they can aim it correctly. That is a big mistake. Weight, look, lie, and feel are all very important—you must be comfortable with your putter, but don't overlook the aim. Now they have lasers they can attach to the putter to check it before you buy it. Make sure when you buy a putter you know where it's going." Once you find the right tool for the job, get to the green and get to work. The six fundamentals do not change in putting: grip, stance, ball position, alignment, take-away, and follow-through.

Putting Grip

And just as you would for a full swing with any other club, start with a good grip. How, exactly, to hold the putter has become the subject of much debate, and the schools of thought are as numerous and varied as the grips themselves—at last count that was 1,538,212. The traditional grip, index finger down the shaft, cross-handed or left-hand low, the claw, baseball grip, and the reverse-overlapping-upside-down-three-finger Vardon are all acceptable if they are comfortable to the golfer using it.

"Amateurs should start with the normal grip they put on every club, then change or experiment from there. The key is comfort. The putter and hands must feel like one. If you feel comfortable, then your grip, for the putter, is fine. Leave it be. Don't ruin a good stroke experimenting for no reason. If you make changes, don't overdo it. Change a little at a time and only if you've putted poorly for a long stretch. Sometimes the stroke is good; the ball just doesn't go in the cup."

Stance

The second step in developing a good putting stroke is the stance. And if it's numerically possible, you have even more putting stances than putting grips to choose from—feet far apart, feet next together, pigeon toed, hunched over, standing tall, squatters, and side saddle. Regardless of method, again, Chi Chi stresses comfort: "Putting is no different than any other shot. If you aren't comfortable standing over the ball, then you got the wrong stance. Find a comfortable posture and keep it relaxed, so the arms are allowed to swing freely. Beyond that, keep a little extra weight on your left foot for balance and to help accelerate the club head through the ball."

Ball Position

Ball position is also a matter of personal preference, but a simple rule of thumb is to keep the ball directly below your eyes. A little leeway in either direction is fine, but don't exaggerate it. Too far forward or too far back can lead to pushes, pulls, and mis-hits. As with any swing, the biggest or smallest, always keep the head as still as possible.

Alignment

Be sure to align yourself square with the intended line of the putt, not directly at the hole itself unless it's a perfectly straight putt. "The hole is the goal," says Chi Chi, "but it is not always the target. To hit the ball on line, you need to be standing square to it. If you set up square to the hole and then try to turn the putter to the proper line, you cannot make a consistent stroke because your shoulders and arms get all twisted."

A little extra weight on the front foot will help keep the putting stroke in balance. Make sure to accelerate the putter through the ball.

Take-Away and Follow-Through

Once in the proper position, the putting stroke should come off like clockwork—a grandfather clock. Picture and feel the rhythmic, smooth, back-and-forth action of a pendulum. The arms and shoulders initiate the take-away and control the club from start to finish. Bring the putter head back smooth and low, the hands holding the club lightly, the wrists staying firm throughout the stroke. Ideally, the wrists should not break down during a putt, although Chi Chi and his friend Billy Casper would be considered two of the more wristy putters of their generation. "Most really good putters," says Chi Chi, "will not lift the club off the ground more than one or two inches. Low and slow. No ragged movements to disturb the rhythm. Out of control or exaggerated backswings increase the chances of a putt going off line or jumping too fast off the club."

When the backswing has reached the desired length, smoothly accelerate the putter back toward the ball, remembering the pendulum rhythm. The club continues its acceleration through impact, and the follow-through should be equal in length to the backswing. A good putt is more of a gentle sweep than a bold stroke. "Acceleration is the key," says Chi Chi. "Keep the putter gently speeding up through the ball. Slow down and you're dead. If the backswing is faster than the follow-through, you will never putt with consistency."

It is important that throughout the stroke the head remains still and the putter face stays square with the ball and intended line of the putt. Keep a comfortable, smooth, shoulder-controlled swing, and putting then boils down to the speed and direction.

"If the stroke is sound, then making putts comes down to two things—the read and the speed. Learn to read greens by looking at the slopes on the green and the subtle breaks in the terrain. Will a rolling ball move left or right? Is it going up a hill or down a hill? If you are not an expert at this, you should still be able to tell the general direction a putt will move. After you've hit a number of putts, you will develop more of a knack for knowing how much a ball will break. Other things to look for are the hardness of the green (which makes the putt quicker) and the grain, height, and texture of the grass. All these things will affect the movement and speed of a putt.

"Judging the speed is even more critical than the line. If you get the ball moving in the right direction and at the right speed, then even if you miss, the ball will end up very near the cup. If you get the ball moving in the right direction but hit too hard or too soft, then you don't know what kind of position you leave yourself. Errors in speed are much harder to overcome than errors in direction. Repetition and remembering the feel are the only way to improve in these areas."

Total Putts

The putting game within the entire game. Total Putts is self-explanatory—the player with the fewest number of putts during the round wins. The game makes a nice side bet for golfers of varying handicaps because it levels the playing field down to the most easily comparable part of the game. Not every player is physically gifted or skillful enough to hit the ball 300 yards off the tee, but everybody can putt.

Bookkeeping for the game is done in two parts: total putts and putt differential. In a friendly game, stakes might be $5 for the fewest putts and another quarter tacked on for margin of victory. If player A took 30 putts and his or her opponent 35, the payout would be $6.25—$5 for the win and another $1.25 for the five-stroke difference in their scores. Remember, a putt is defined as a stroke played from on the green. Using a putter from the fringe, fairway, or even bunker does not count when adding up the final number of putts.

The Way I Play: Putting and Touch

"I cannot tell you much about my putting stroke except to say that it is the one I have had all my life. I developed it as a kid and I use it just the same today. People say I have a wristy stroke; okay, so does Billy Casper and to be compared to him in anything, especially putting, is a great compliment to me.

There is no real wrong way to putt. True, I have an unorthodox golf swing, but to me either everybody or nobody has an unorthodox putting stroke because no two are alike.

I always try to take the putter back nice and smooth and when I bring it back to the ball maybe I give it a little pop with some wrist action. Whatever. It works good for me most of the time. I trust my read, I trust my touch, I make my putt.

I just say to you: beware, because a bad golfer can beat you with good putting and a good golfer can lose a lot with bad putting."

Putting Tournaments

Match play or stroke play, 18 holes or 72, solo or a full field, clockwise or counterclockwise—choose a format, get on the putting clock, and start rolling the rock. Nothing improves a player's touch like an hour or two of competition with the flat stick.

Eighteen-hole, putts-only, match-play games can be played against a friend, by a single player using two balls, or against Mr. Par using two strokes a hole as the target score. Once you've finished the initial game, turn yourself around and play "the course" backward so that you practice putts breaking in the opposite direction.

A stroke-play tournament can consist of everything from 9 holes to a full, four-round, 72-hole competition. You may get dizzy going around the green in circles, but when everything stops spinning, you'll have a much better putting stroke.

Play against friends or drop an extra ball, two, or three, and pretend you're taking on Chi Chi, Tiger, and Jack. All holes in putting games should be played as par 2s, for an 18-hole total of 36. Use the number as a barometer of your game on the greens whether it's practice or during a round. The goal should be to never take more than 36 putts. If you can consistently keep your total putts to 30 or less, your putting game is serving you quite well.

To add spice to putting practice, add some cash to the equation. "You should treat the putting game just as you would the course," says Chi Chi. "Always play for something. Money is as good a something as anything. Although putting isn't the strongest part of my game, nobody on the Tour underestimates me. I have earned quite a few dollars on the practice green over the years."

Around the World

The challenge in Around the World is to sink seven balls (one for each continent—cute huh?) from seven different angles in seven putts. Place seven balls in a circle around the hole, or use one ball and move it to seven different spots, and then make them all.

Start with two-footers, and when you've gone a perfect seven for seven, move back a foot or two and make another world tour. Another option is to keep track of how many strokes it takes to hole all seven balls and attempt to improve on that overall score each trip around the world.

Finally, for the really serious putting student, make a first-class trip around the world. For short putts, go back to the beginning and start over after every miss. For medium-length putts (10 to 15 feet), go back one spot after every miss, another spot after a second miss, and all the way back to the beginning after a third miss. And for long putts (more than 15 feet), a bit of a break—go back one spot after a miss, but remain at that spot until you sink the putt again, and then continue on your journey.

The goal in Around the World is not only to improve the putting stroke but also to get a good look at the hole from different angles to help get a feel for different reads and breaks. Becoming a world-class putter starts with this game.

Ladder

In cartography terms, Around the World is a globe and Ladder is an atlas, putting in a circle as opposed to a straight line. Putt three balls from three feet, and if you sink them all, move back to five feet and putt again. Drain all three of those, move back to seven feet. If you miss one of the three putts, move a foot closer for the next series of three. If you miss two, go back two feet closer. Miss all three, and return all the way back to the starting point at three feet.

Although reading the break is a crucial element of putting, Ladder is a game that is better used for developing a feel for speed. "Never up, never in," says Chi Chi, "is only half right. Hitting a ball too hard doesn't do any good, either, although a putt that goes by the hole *does* have some chance to go in, while a putt left short has no chance. When putting, you must learn to make the ball stop at the hole, better yet, in the hole. After you develop a knack for speed that is second nature, you can spend more time studying the line of a putt."

Make It, Take It

Make It, Take It is a multiplayer putting game that rewards a good putt with another and, hopefully, another and another and another. Think of it as a selfish way to a better stroke. Points in the game are awarded based on the length of each putt made—each foot is worth one point. The goal is to become the first putter to sink 100 feet worth of putts. In the absence of a tape measure (and hopefully you are 'cause who brings a tape measure to a golf course?), simply pace off the distance. A man's stride is usually equal to about three feet.

After flipping for honors, the first player putts from any distance he chooses, the minimum required distance being three feet. If he makes the putt, he receives the points and the option to either putt again or freeze. Freezing protects a player's point total and passes the turn to the next golfer. Any player may elect to continue putting and accumulating points as long as he chooses, provided he continues to sink the putts. Missing a putt drops the player's total back to zero or the last frozen total.

How confident are you? If you make 10 straight 5-footers, are you willing to risk 50 points on an 11th, or is it better to freeze and pick up where you left off? If you're down 95-80 and have just run off 30 or 40 straight points, are you bold enough to roll one from 20 feet for the win? Make It, Take It requires guts, strategy, and a few bucks. Put $20 on a game, and see how shaky your knees are when you start closing in on the century mark.

Fill'r Up

Looking to kill time with your foursome before teeing off? Need a little action to help get the bones and billfold oiled up? Split up and fill'r up. Two-person teams putt at the same hole from 10 feet away. Partners alternate putting, with the first team to sink 20 putts winning the bet. The idea is to have a quick-paced game that will help develop a natural rhythm to the putting stroke.

The game can be played at shorter or longer distances, but putting from inside of 10 feet makes the game a tad too easy, and from distances of greater than 10 feet the game is too slow. The game needs to move to be effective. And, believe it or not, it's possible to drop 20 putts in less than three minutes if your team is on its game.

Lag-nificent

The first thing a player should do on a putting green before a round is hit a half dozen or dozen lag putts to get a feel for the speed of the green. Making them is great, but concentrate more on the speed of the putt and getting the ball to stop hole high.

"On longer putts," says Chi Chi, "I open up my stance a little bit, stand a little farther from the ball, and loosen my grip on the club a little bit. These little changes can make a big difference because on a lag putt what you want is to free the arms and shoulders up to swing back farther and come through harder and give the ball a good strong rap without pulling it off line. A good tip for reading long putts is to go halfway between your ball and the hole, and look both ways. You should be able to see the slope, if there is any, clearly from that spot."

An old and excellent guide for lag puts is to try to hit them into a washtub instead of the hole. Aiming at the bigger target will ensure no more than a two- or three-foot second putt; if the ball does go in the hole—bonus. Do try, though, to make at least one no-brainer before heading to the tee because no sensation (not to mention confidence boost) quite matches the Lag-nificent feeling of canning an unlikely long putt.

The Longest Yard

"I have made putts from less than one inch to over 100 feet. I have made putts for 2s and for 10s and for eagles and everything else. I cannot recall all of them, but I remember the two greatest putts I ever made. In 1963 I made a three-foot putt to win the Denver Open, my first win on Tour. The second putt I sank was also a three-footer, this one to win the 1986 Senior Players Championship, my first win on the Senior Tour. Like most golfers, I don't fear death as much as I fear three-footers. Whether it's a 600-yard par-5 or a 100-yard par-3, the longest yard is the last one—the dreaded three-footer.

"My best advice is to, first, be determined to make it. Think only about the ball going in, not the consequences of missing. Second, make a good, firm stroke right to the hole. Too many amateurs, on short putts, see breaks that aren't really there or try to baby the ball into the cup. Worry less about the break and more about a bold putt going into the back of the cup. Three-footers should *never* be left short. Pick your line and then hit your best putt. Treat it as the million putts you've hit before, not as if there's a million dollars on it. Sometimes the best putting lesson is simply to miss a few and lose some money. And the difference between making three-footers and missing three-footers is the difference between vacationing in Bermuda and vacationing in the Bermuda Triangle."

That Sinking Feeling

The last thing a player should do on a practice green before a round is hear the rattle of a putt hitting the bottom of the cup. Psychologically, it's a sound that resonates throughout a good round of golf. After you've spent time lagging the ball to get the speed of the greens, move in close to the hole and knock 15 to 20 easy putts. The shortest route to self-assurance is to make 'em go in the hole. In putting, you want to have that sinking feeling.

"Missing short putts," says Chi Chi, "does more damage to the golfer's brain than anything, more than bad drives, shanks, anything. Short putts aren't as much about confidence as about self-assurance, the comfort of knowing you can make them every time. On short putts, I stand a little closer to the ball and grip the club a little tighter. I don't want any excess movement on a short putt. Don't take the club too far back. Make a good, short, compact stroke, and move the putter head through the ball. Also, on short putts, don't watch them. Keep your head down and listen for the sound of the ball going in the hole. To me, the sound of a ball hitting the bottom of the cup makes the same sound as a cash register."

Horse II

Golf balls or basketballs, cups or hoops—doesn't matter. The object of the game is exactly the same—get . . . ball . . . in . . . hole.

Horse II (we're giving the short-game version of "Horse" distinction, on the simple basis of its position in the previous chapter) can be played by one golfer with two balls or as many players as you can fit on the practice green.

Establish an order, any order. Don't waste too much time on it 'cause the game gets around to everybody eventually. First player in the rotation picks out a putt; if he or she makes it, the player following him or her must also make it or receive a letter. If the second player is able to match, then the third player in line must make the putt or get a letter. It's a simple cycle of makes and misses. A player is out of the game when his or her misses spell out "horse." Last player standing gets to ride off into the sunset with everybody else's money.

When a putt is missed, the next player in line is off the hook and gets to pick a new putt. Players are saddled with a letter *only* if they miss a putt that's been sunk previously. First-putt misses, like makes, merely advance the game to the next player. And they're off. . . .

50/50

Somewhere between the gimme and the gargantuan lies the game of 50/50, putts that are neither easy nor impossible. The goal is to score at least 50 points on 50 putts, varying in range from 5 to 50 feet. Points are awarded as follows:

One putt = 2 points

Two putts = 1 point

Three putts = –3 points

Four or more putts = –5 points

A perfect score is 100. Score half that, and you're not a half-bad player. The key is to challenge yourself. Putt from a wide variety of distances just as you would during an actual round. Simulating actual game conditions is a must.

"Developing a good stroke on the greens is a must," says Chi Chi, "because a golfer can recover from any bad shot except for a bad putt." Lag the ball lousy, and you set yourself up to waste a stroke three-putting. Miss a short one, and you can never get the stroke back; it's gone forever.

"The opposite of that," says Chi Chi, "is that a good putt can wipe out any bad shot that came before it. One-putt greens will erase bad drives, bad approaches, bad thinking, and bad breaks. That is why, after getting into trouble off the tee, an amateur should make a smart shot and just get the ball back in play. Getting the ball on the green in three is okay. It is much easier to recover and save a hole with a 25-foot putt on the green than risk a long iron from 185 yards out in the rough."

50 points in 50 putts. Do you have the stroke for it? You need to.

Think Small

The best way to make the hole look big is to practice aiming at something little. "I had very big dreams as a boy," says Chi Chi, "and I achieved many of them because, when it comes to putting, I think small. If you stick a tee or a divot fixer in the ground and hit some putts at that, pretty soon the hole will start looking like a paint can." Start from very near the hole, and then gradually move out until you are practically putting the ball on the tee from 25 feet away. Think small to help yield big results.

Square Face

"The difference between a smile and a frown," says Chi Chi, "is a square face. If the head of a putter doesn't impact the ball square with the target line, you'll be putting again." Square Face is a putting game that does away with the backswing completely in an effort to greatly improve aim and follow-through.

Address a putt as you normally would, and then, without taking the club back at all, just sweep the ball forward to the hole. If the ball goes in, then the line and stroke were correct. If it misses, the putt was either misread or the putter face not square at impact.

Hit a series of 10 balls from 10 feet, and if there's a problem with either aim or impact, it will quickly become apparent. The drill can be used from any distance inside of about 15 feet. Beyond that, and the gentle sweeping action of the putt becomes too much of a push and can be detrimental to your stroke.

Spot Check

If aiming becomes a persistent bugaboo to your game on the green, try spot putting. Only two kinds of players exist—hole putters and spot putters. Hole putters make all their aiming references to the cup. No doubt you've heard them and their terminology: left edge, two balls outside the right edge, 18 inches to the left.

Spot putters aim at something other than the hole, and Chi Chi swears by it. "On putts outside 8 or 10 feet, I pick a spot on the green between myself and the hole," says Chi Chi, "and aim for that. I want to roll my ball right over the spot. It might be a tiny brown spot two feet in front of the ball. It might be just inside another player's ball mark. Think of it as a bowler would. He doesn't have his eyes on the pins while he is throwing the ball. He aims for one of the arrows or boards about a third of the way up the lane." Make a spot check of your putting on occasion. Curiously, it may be a target other than the hole you need to aim at.

Blind Luck

For every golfer who's ever angrily muttered, "I could putt better with my eyes closed," here is your game! In Blind Luck, take a couple of smooth practice strokes, then address your ball as normal, and just before starting the club back close your eyes. Make the best stroke you can, and once the ball is on its way to the cup, open your eyes again and watch, with horror or great joy, the results.

The benefits of the game are twofold: It will help develop the desired pendulum motion by, essentially, taking the ball out of play. It's hard to worry about what you can't see, which makes it easier to concentrate on a smooth stroke. And it also helps put the feel of distance in your hands. Because golfers can't depend on their eyes, they have to rely on their touch. Hit a series of five blind-luck putts, from distances of 3 up to 60 feet, and soon you'll find that without even looking you're getting the ball closer and closer to the hole—and that's not luck.

Fringe Benefits

The USGA has no rule on where a golfer can or cannot use his or her putter. One of the fringe benefits of that lack of legislation is that a putter can be an effective tool for getting the ball close to the hole from off the green. Another fringe benefit of practicing from off the green is an improved sense of touch.

The golfing adage "a bad putt is always better than a bad chip" didn't get to be an adage by accident. It's true. "In most instances," says Chi Chi, "an amateur is better off using a putter from the fringe or off a low-cut fairway in front of the green than a chip or pitch shot. It may not be the best play for a pro, but it's probably the best percentage play for an amateur."

To improve your game from just off the green, set up an Around the World game from the fringe. Be sure to pay particular attention to the speed of the putts. Hitting it through the fringe takes a little more oomph, and the difference between leaving a ball short of the hole, getting it to the hole, and blowing it by the hole and across the green is strictly a matter of touch.

Highlights of Chi Chi's Senior Tour Career

- Twenty-two victories
- Eight straight years with a victory from 1986 to 1993
- Major winner in 1986 Senior Tournament Players Championship
- Major winner in 1987 PGA Seniors Championship
- First to win same event three consecutive years in the Digital Senior Classic
- First to win half a million dollars in one season to lead money list
- More than $6.5 million in career earnings
- Record eight straight birdies (holes 6–13) in Silver Pages Classic
- Four holes in one, with the last at 1996 Raley's Gold Rush Classic
- In 1990, 9 top-3 finishes; in 1992, 17 top-10 finishes

Lucky Seven

Getting a putt in the hole isn't lucky. Getting to seven points in this game can be. Ideally, Lucky Seven is played with four but, depending on the number of people available, it works fine with groups of anywhere from 2 to 12. Two golfers make the game easier, 12 considerably more difficult. The goal is to accumulate seven points under the following scoring system:

- Closest to the hole after first putt = 1 point
- *Only* player to sink a first putt = 2 points
- Fewest total putts on hole = 1 point
- One or more players tie hole = 0 points
- Three or more putts = –3 points (regardless of ties)

Now for the lucky part. Players are not allowed to mark their balls! Blocking out opponents is not only legal but also encouraged in an effort to make the game more interesting. If you don't sink that first putt, do your best to at least get it close to block the cup. Lose out on the closest-to-the-hole point, then maybe try to lay a stymie (block) and force a three putt, perhaps, stealing points away from another player. Good strategy can be just as critical as a good stroke in this game.

Given the no-mark provision in the game, order of play in Lucky Seven is extremely important, with honors being doubly important: Not only does the first player up get to choose the putt, he or she also gets first crack at a wide-open hole. The game is best played from medium to long range. Putts that are too short make it too hard to score. Medium-length and longer putts promote a more wide-open game, both in scoring and stymies. First player to seven points wins, and losers pay off anything between $.10 and $10, or play for a long-neck bottle of beer per point.

Dozen

It's only the dirty dozen if you're on the losing end. Dozen is very similar to Lucky Seven but is a two-person game played with two balls apiece. The goal, obviously, is to be the first player to collect 12 points.

Honors, again, are strictly observed, with players hitting both their balls in succession. In Dozen, however, as opposed to Lucky Seven, the balls are marked before the second player putts. Honors are decided by a coin flip before the first hole and, subsequently, by whomever accumulates the most points on a hole. The scoring permutations and combinations are many and as follows:

- Closest to the hole = 1 point
- Both of a player's balls are inside his or her opponent's = 2 points
- A one putt = 3 points
- Opponent follows a one putt with his or her own one putt = 6 points
- Two one putts to an opponent's no putts = 6 points
- Two one putts to an opponent's single one putt = 3 points
- A one putt followed by an opponent's two one putts = 9 points
- Two one putts followed by an opponent's two one putts = 12 points

The first player to a dozen points earns the victory and a payout based on point differential. In the event one player jumps out to a 7–0 lead, the game is then a skunking and the loser pays double. Though perhaps a little complicated, Dozen and other money putting games are a good exercise for improving both a golfer's stroke and his or her competitive character.

"Anybody can make a putt when there is no pressure," declares Chi Chi, "and some people will choke for nothing, but putting for money will help sharpen your focus and steady your nerves through repetition. Putt for a few dollars on a game often enough, and you become comfortable with having money on the line. Putting games are not just about improving your stroke; they're also about learning to love competition and thriving on it."

21

The names and numbers change, but the ultimate goal does not—sink enough putts to reach the magic point mark first. In this case, the target total is 21. As in Dozen, 21 is a game where the first putt is the only one that matters. You have no second, third, or other putts. Bold, get-it-to-the-hole putting strokes are encouraged in 21. Leaving a ball short of the cup is the cardinal sin of 21 and is penalized accordingly. Points are earned in one of four ways:

- Closest to the hole = 3 points
- Made putt = 6 points
- Any putt left short = –3 points
- Putt left short, but still closest = 1 point

This is a popular game on the putting clock of both PGA and Senior Tour events, with the winnings usually paid out in dinner or bar tabs instead of cash. Many golfers will keep a season-long total of 21 and collect at the end of the year. If you choose to play a run-on version of the game, add some extra drama to the competition by allowing the golfer who is down in the race to press the game. Winning wipes out the debt; a loss doubles it. Keep track of 21 over the course of a summer or golf season, and you'll hear some knees knocking late in the year, and it won't be because of the cold weather rolling in. It'll be because the putts aren't rolling in the cup.

1 Ball, 100 Putts

A true pro's game, 1 Ball, 100 Putts is a true test of skill, single-mindedness, and stamina. Mark off a distance of three feet, and then make 100 putts in a row from that spot. Miss a putt, and start all over again from zero. Not only does it take a solid putting stroke, but also, with the pressure building after every make, the concentration required in 1 Ball, 100 Putts strengthens the mind.

Players who finish the game without much difficulty may graduate themselves to greater distances, putting from four feet out and then five. On the other hand, if the game becomes too much of a struggle or too time consuming, try making either 50 straight putts or 100 putts overall. The key is to keep the game beneficial, not have it lead to burnout. If 100 putts in a row is out of reach, begin from a lower total and work up to the century mark. The aim should be to improve, not embarrass.

"Some pros will spend all afternoon, day after day, on the putting green," says Chi Chi, "but not me. I putt only enough to feel good about my stroke and the speed of the greens. I am not saying 'do not practice.' I'm saying don't spend so much time at it that it becomes a chore. I do not put in a lot of time on the practice green because to me, as I always tell amateurs, putting is 90 percent mental. If I feel good about my stroke, then that is good enough. Billy Casper is the same way. Nobody made more putts in tournaments than Billy. He was the best putter on the Tour, but you very rarely saw him spending hours on the practice green. Billy knew his stroke was solid, and when his head and his hands felt good, he went to the course or went home."

The Sword Dance

"I started fighting the bull because Joe Dye, the PGA Tour commissioner, asked me to quit fighting with bullfrogs. It all goes back to one time when I was a small boy sneaking onto the course in Puerto Rico playing for nickels. I made a putt, but there was a frog in the hole. And the ball fell on top of him, and he jumped up and knocked my ball out of the hole, and I lost out on a nickel. After that, just in case a frog might be in there again, I started throwing my hat over the hole, so birdies wouldn't fly away.

"When I joined the Tour, the fans loved it, but some pros complained I was damaging the hole with my hat. How can I damage the hole? I never got that. But after talking with Arnold Palmer after our first round together at Augusta and at the suggestion of Joe, who asked me to do something else, I came up with the idea of fighting the bull with the sword.

"Now the hole is the bull, and when I make a birdie putt, I draw my sword from the scabbard and I stop the bull, wipe off the blood, and put it back in my scabbard. A dance and a tip of the cap, it is all about making fans laugh and enjoy themselves. There are too many serious pros these days. One or two, especially if they are the caliber of Tiger Woods or Ben Hogan, is fine; that is box office. One hundred fifty of them placing first to last in a tournament is watching grass grow."

Head Games: Putting Pace

"A key part of becoming a good putter is finding your best putting pace. I believe in putting very fast. Jack Nicklaus is a very slow putter. Jack takes so much time over the golf ball I can grow a mustache before he hits. But styles work because they fit our personalities and because they are the same every time. My speed helped me become one of the best players in the world, and nobody, nobody made more big-time putts than Jack Nicklaus.

"On all my putts, I read the break, decide on the correct line, and then step up to the ball. I check the line, take one look at the hole, look at the ball, and hit it. Even though I take very little time putting, the whole time, from the moment I mark my ball until I stroke it, I am thinking about making a smooth, rhythmic stroke. If I take a practice stroke, it is only on a very long putt when distance and speed are very critical.

"I think most amateurs take too long to putt. They take three or four practice strokes and then stand over the ball and wait and wait and check and recheck the hole, the line, the ball, the hole, the line, the ball. Spending too much time over a putt leads to tension in the muscles, indecision in the mind, and nervousness throughout the body. Nervous putters are pigeons. Commit to the putt and then stroke it."

chapter 12

Range

Great golf shots do not happen by accident. Yes, on occasion, the mistresses Luck and Chance conspire to guide a poor shot to a good result, but a truly great shot needs no such help. It requires no special bounces or favors from the golf gods, merely the law of gravity to return it safely to earth next to its intended target.

Great golf shots are born out of solid basics and raised on a repetition of practice, the final product of dedication and desire. Great golf shots are, simply, a reflection of all the great work that's gone into them before impact.

No player gets more out of the game than he or she is willing to put into it. Golfers don't fall out of bed and shoot 70 or even break 100, for that matter; they practice and play their way down (up?) from rookie to respectable to first rate. Everybody. Chi Chi Rodriguez included.

"Because of people like Ed Dudley, Pete Cooper—my teachers at Dorado Beach—and Laurance Rockefeller, who taught me about the world, I got a chance to live out my dream as a pro golfer," says Chi Chi. "But opportunity is not entitlement. You have to do something with your opportunity. Everything I have I've earned through my own hard work and sweat."

Golf on the range is definitely perspiration. It's working on a particular club, a troublesome shot, or a persistent problem. What it's not is beating a bucket of balls as hard and fast as possible. "I used to tell all my students, and now I tell my amateur partners, practice with a specific purpose," says Chi Chi. "In my prime, when I was not on Tour, I practiced four and five hours a day because that was my job. Most people, however, do not have that much time to devote to their game. They are lucky if they have three hours in a week to practice, so I stress to them to make their practice sessions accomplish something. Have a game or a goal, and concentrate hard the entire time. Twenty-five balls hit with 100 percent focus are a lot better than 50 balls hit with a sloppy swing."

If you find your game going from bad to worse on the range or if you can't seem to make a shot on the pages of this book come to life, talk to a pro or take a lesson. Don't waste three months practicing without success when a PGA professional can point out the problem in three minutes. "You cannot fix," says Chi Chi, "what you don't know is wrong. For the price of the dozen balls an amateur hits into the woods, they can get some good instruction. Go ahead and ask questions, too. Don't just take advice without really knowing what you're hearing."

Practice and instruction are essential, but don't make a career out of it. The game of golf is out on the course. When 30 minutes at lunch or two hours at dusk is all you can spare, then practice, and practice well. But if you have five hours or an entire afternoon, take your game to the course. Practice players hit perfect shots on the range; golfers hit perfect shots during a round.

Work Up

It's a driving range in name only. It's okay to hit all the other clubs in your golf bag, too. When warming up or going through a general practice session, work up through the bag. Start with the wedge and finish with the driver. Hit each club with the same frequency you would on the course—that means more wedges than woods and more 9 irons than 3 irons. Add a little more power with each swing. Start at about 50 percent and work up until you're hitting at 80 or 85 percent. No need to push it further than that; always keep a little power in reserve.

Take your time and think about each shot before you hit it. Because golfers don't have to walk to their ball on the range, they have a tendency to get moving a little too fast; the extra speed will eventually show up in the swing. If you hit four or five good balls in a row and then start to regress a little, try backing off and slowing down to restore your rhythm.

Also, change targets every so often, and hit in different directions. Most practice facilities have multiple pins or yardage markers to aim at, making this quite easy to accomplish. The range isn't just for practicing the swing; it's for practicing the stance and the setup, as well.

Finally, if possible, always try to practice against the wind. A breeze in your face will produce a truer ball flight. Hooks and slices will be accentuated so that you can work to improve them. Practicing with the wind at your back will hide flaws that may reveal themselves at a bad time on the course. If a player concentrates and doesn't get careless, he or she can dip a lot of improvement out of the golf well with a bucket of balls.

Weakness

What most amateurs call the "driving range," the pros call the "practice tee"—it's a not-so-subtle distinction that goes to the heart of the game. Professionals hit balls to improve their weaknesses; too many amateurs hit balls from their strength. Remember the three Ws—workout, weakness, win.

King of the Clinics

Perhaps no other golfer has spent more time on the practice range than Chi Chi Rodriguez. He just hasn't been practicing the whole time. No, most often, when Chi Chi is on the range, he's showing off—dazzling an audience with trick shots, cracking them up with dead-on impressions of his golfing peers, slaying them with one-liners and well-worn jokes.

No other player is more popular at clinics, more accessible for exhibitions, more in demand for outings than Chi Chi. "Golf is what I do for a livelihood," he says, "and I love it. It's so much fun. And bringing golf to the people is the best of all." And those people are a most diverse audience—everything from kids to corporate bigwigs, senior citizens to sales reps.

To see Chi Chi perform is to see a man drive a ball 250 yards from his knees and make wedges soar 50 feet straight up and land in his pocket. It's to see a spot-on Jack Nicklaus swing or a perfect imitation of the 30-handicapper slowing down play at your club. It's to hear corny jokes—"My family was so poor that when I was born I was stamped 'Made in Taiwan'"—and laugh out loud. It's to get good advice without even realizing it—"Gary Player says I have the only kind of amnesia a golfer should have. I forget all the bad swings and bad holes." The King of the Clinics is an apt title for the people's pro, for to see Chi Chi perform is to watch the master at work. "I try to provide two things at my clinics," says Chi Chi, "happiness and something you can try and take to the course to become a better player."

1 Club, 14 Ways

One club, one swing, 14 ways to get better. In 1 Club, 14 Ways, that security blanket you call a 7 iron, or whatever your favorite club may be, serves as an anchor to improving the rest of the bag. As Chi Chi explained earlier, a good golf swing varies little from club to club; cycling through the bag in a systematic practice session based on your best club can yield excellent all-around results. "If an amateur can learn to hit one club really, really well," says Chi Chi, "there's no reason he can't learn to be pretty good with all of them. And once he becomes comfortable with all the clubs in the bag, then there is no shot on the course that can scare him."

For explanation purposes, we'll use a 7 iron as the favorite club. Begin by hitting three 7 irons, and follow it with three 6-iron shots. Go back and hit three more 7s, then move up and take three swings with a 5 iron. Continue the cycle until you've hit all your irons, and then work back down. A complete schedule looks like this:

3 × 7 iron, 3 × 6 iron
3 × 7 iron, 3 × 5 iron
3 × 7 iron, 3 × 4 iron
3 × 7 iron, 3 × 3 iron
3 × 7 iron, 3 × 3 iron
3 × 7 iron, 3 × 4 iron
3 × 7 iron, 3 × 5 iron
3 × 7 iron, 3 × 6 iron
3 × 7 iron

In 51 balls, a player can work through all the middle and long irons, making only small adjustments in stance, ball position, and length of backswing. These gradual changes will help increase muscle memory and develop a critical feel for the basic golf swing that controls all clubs. Use the same system for the woods or short irons, as well, starting with a 7 iron and working down through the wedges and then back up to the 7.

One Shot

One Shot is not a one-shot deal. It's the same shot until you get it right. Does fading the ball give you grief? Can't hit an 8-iron punch shot? Better dead than draw a long iron? There's one way to learn it—practice it.

Whatever shot troubles you, make a quick study of the fundamentals needed to execute the shot, and then begin working on the problem. You might not get it right away, but with determination, any shot can be solved or corrected. Remember, four of the fundamentals can be reviewed and improved before ever moving the club. Get those right first, then concentrate on one element of the swing at a time. For a draw, think about bringing the club back a little more inside or hitting the ball from seven to two on the clock face.

Once you begin seeing results, start scoring your progress. Twenty-five balls, two points for hitting the shot properly, subtract one point if you fail to execute the shot. Reach double figures in points, and you can take it to the course. Twenty points, and you can give it a try if the risk isn't too great. Thirty points, and you've got a shot you can use under any condition.

Routine Practice

Don't just practice hitting the ball at the range; practice your entire preshot routine. "Simply hitting golf balls on the practice range," warns Chi Chi, "is not practice. Hitting the golf ball as you would on the golf course is practice. And when you are on the golf course, you have a certain preshot routine that you perform every time. So, why wouldn't you perform it when you are practicing? To me the golf swing begins when you pick the club out of the bag and ends when the ball stops. Practice it the same way."

You have nobody pushing from behind and no group to keep up with ahead when you practice; take advantage of that pace of play to work on your routine. Don't make a trip to the range a race to get back to the car. The creature of habit in all of us is comforted by doing the same thing over and over again. Developing a good, consistent preshot routine serves to both reassure and reduce stress before a swing.

Routine Practice? Yes. Practice that is just routine? No.

Aim High

"When I was struggling with my swing," says Chi Chi, "I would do one of two things: go see Sam Snead or concentrate on hitting the ball very high with my long irons. If you can hit a 3 iron high and straight, then, boy, you can hit all the rest of the shots you need to." Hitting a good, crisp, long-iron shot works as a cure for a lot of swing evils. It means your grip is correct, the ball position is good, the swing tempo is right, the swing plane and angle into the ball are excellent, the club face is square, and the follow-through fine. Get the swing grooved with a long iron, and all of those qualities will trickle down through the rest of your clubs.

Work hard at sweeping the ball away; do not hoe or scoop at it to try to get the ball in the air. A good tip: Place a tee or a coin a foot in front of the ball, and focus on staying down and following through the ball all the way to the tee. This will help promote a fundamentally sound downswing and follow-through, while taking your mind off of trying to help the ball up. Swing sound and let the club face worry about the ball flight.

As for Sam? "He could fix my swing in five minutes," says Chi Chi. "Sam would take a look, give me a tip or two, and I'd be cured in minutes. One time, he gave me a quick lesson, and I said, Sam, if this works I'm going to give you 10 percent. I finished very high in the tournament and wrote him a check for $5,000 before I left the locker room."

Half and Half

Half the balls hit with half swings. Often times, the best way to fix a problem, learn a new stroke, or fine-tune an old one is to start small. Taking only half a swing cuts down the chances of something going wrong during the swing. The longer the backswing, the more margin for error. Hit a good number of controlled half shots to groove the bottom half of the swing where acceleration, a square club face at impact, and a complete follow-through are so crucial.

"I also start my practice session hitting half shots," says Chi Chi. "Then when I feel that my swing path is good—sometimes that's after 3 balls, sometimes after 15—I add a little length to my backswing each time until I am hitting full shots. The half shots are key to building muscle memory in the golf swing. They also help you judge distances with shorter clubs when only a half or three-quarter swing is needed to get the ball on the green."

Play Practice

A driving-range drama acted out in 18 separate scenes. "When I am at home practicing for an upcoming tournament," Chi Chi says, "often I will play the course on the practice tee. Since I have played most of the Tour courses so many times, I know them by heart, and I know exactly which shots I will need to play. If I was going to Augusta, I would work on hitting my driver right to left and my iron shots as high as possible because that is what is called for at Augusta National."

It's a pretty good bet most of us won't get a tee time at Augusta, but we can still practice the course that we plan to play. Picture the layout in your head, and simulate as many of the shots as you can.

If the first hole is a straight-away, 380-yard par-4 with no trouble, hit a driver; and then, depending on how far you estimated the first shot traveled, hit the appropriate approach shot, maybe a smooth 8 iron if your drive covered 250 yards. Follow the same routine around the entire course. Drawing the ball when called for, fading it if you have a dogleg right. Hitting a high shot into the green if it's fronted by a bunker or water, hitting a low chaser if there's an opening to the putting surface. If you're unfamiliar with the course, grab a scorecard from the pro shop before heading to the range and study up.

Not only will play practice help sharpen your swing, it will also focus your mind on the upcoming round so that you can hit the course confident and with a sound game plan, without any surprises. Play well enough, and you'll be back for encore after encore.

Play What You Have

Amateurs need to remember that the range has two different uses. The first is for reviewing fundamentals and warming up before a round. The other is for practice. Do not confuse the two.

When you are loosening up before a round, get the feel of your game for that day. It is important to play what you have that day. Don't try to make a lot of changes and fix things just before a round; that will only lead to confusion on the golf course. If your swing is producing a little bit of a fade that you don't normally have, go ahead and play it, don't fight it. Chances are most things will work themselves out during the round. Save the fixing and problem solving for practice sessions when you have more time and aren't under the gun to get to the first tee.

Bucket

"When I go to the practice tee, I always gently knock the bucket of balls over with my club instead of my foot," says Chi Chi. "This is very important to me because I never want to 'kick the bucket.' [Rim shot, please!] I plan to be playing golf until I am 150 years old." Regardless of the method you use to spill balls out of a range bucket, the goal in this game is to use them to pile up points. Bucket is a betting game that, ideally, leads to better golf. The game is best for two players but works fine with three, provided you can line up enough spots in a row on the range.

Points are awarded based on the club a golfer hits—the longer the club, the higher its point total. A player chooses his or her club and then announces to his or her opponent the intended target. If the shot is successful, the player banks the points. With an unsuccessful shot, the available points are subtracted from the player's total. The first player to reach 100 points wins and collects on the point differential from his or her rivals. The scoring and success in Bucket is as follows:

Driver = 14 points—20 yards either side of target
3 Wood = 13 points—15 yards either side of target
1 Iron = 13 points—15 yards either side of target
5 Wood = 12 points—15-yard radius of target
2 Iron = 12 points—15-yard radius of target
3 Iron = 11 points—15-yard radius of target
4 Iron = 10 points—15-yard radius of target
5 Iron = 9 points—15-yard radius of target
6 Iron = 8 points—10-yard radius of target
7 Iron = 7 points—10-yard radius of target
8 Iron = 6 points—10-yard radius of target
9 Iron = 5 points—10-yard radius of target
Pitching wedge = 4 points—5-yard radius of target
Sand wedge = 3 points—5-yard radius of target
Lob wedge = 2 points—5-yard radius of target

Accuracy figures are rough estimates, and players may adjust them to fit their game: tougher standards for better players, easier ones for novice players. Bucket is a practice game that, as an added benefit, carries some of the qualities of match play. A golfer must not only worry about his or her swing but also keep an eye on his or her opponent and the score in determining strategy during the course of play.

To limit losses, Bucket comes with a mercy rule: The game ends automatically if a player falls behind by more than 50 points. The rule can be waved if players have the wallet to pay the debt and the self-confidence to suffer the humiliation. If 100 points proves to be too big a challenge, play a best-of-three series up to 50.

Bad Weather

Don't let some more-often-wrong-than-right weatherperson keep you from practice. In fact, make it a point to get out in the elements once in a while, and see what effect they have on your game. "The golf ball acts in many different ways," says Chi Chi, "depending on the weather. When it is very hot, it will travel much farther. When it is cold, you need to add an extra club. In the rain, you need to pick the ball a little cleaner and work hard at staying dry. In a crosswind, instead of just letting the ball ride the breeze and hoping to get lucky, I always keep the ball low and shape a shot back into the wind, so the wind will hold it on line. Some of the straightest shots I hit are when the wind is blowing across the fairway."

Weather is the one aspect of golf that cannot be simulated—it must be experienced. Heated, covered driving ranges are a wonderful convenience, but they aren't always the best training grounds. Get wet and try to stay dry. Get windblown and try to keep your swing straight. Bundle up and work to stay warm. And don't just hit a couple balls. Hit 50 to 100 shots. Challenging elements take their toll on the mind more than the body, and you need to be outside wrestling with the weather for an extended time to effectively train your brain to grind it out under adverse conditions.

When your spouse says you're crazy to play on a day like this, tell her or him you'd be crazy not to—really good bad days don't come along very often.

Hit at Stuff

Because you and a friend can only play closest to the pin for a dollar so many times during a practice session, occasionally take aim at something a little more exotic. First player to bounce it off a yardage marker wins. Ricocheting one off the beat-up vehicle picking up range balls should pay, at least, double. Perhaps, a bet that your well-aimed 6 iron can throw a scare into an unsuspecting squirrel can liven up the game.

"One time, at an exhibition for some U.S. and Canadian service personnel, a Canadian officer asked me if I could hit a cat that was about 185 yards off in the distance. I told him that since I had served in the U.S. military and had also been made an honorary two-star general in the Air Force, I would need permission to hit the cat. So General McPeak (Retired General Merrill A. McPeak, former Chief of Staff, U.S. Air Force) asked, 'General Rodriguez, can you hit that cat?' I said, 'Yes, Sir, I can hit it.' Well, he says then, 'Go ahead and hit it.' Now, I wold never hurt an animal—ever—but the cat was far enough away that I knew I couldn't injure it in any way. I took out a 5 iron, and sure enough I rolled the ball up and I hit that cat right in the stomach. It gave a little meow and just walked off. They had never seen anything like that with a 5 iron. A perfect bull's-eye.

"In Texas, Ben Crenshaw bet me I couldn't hit a deer standing about 270 yards away at the end of the range by this farm. I hit it right between the deer's legs, and he just kept on eating grass as if nothing had happened. One time in Las Vegas, at the Badlands—a course Johnny Miller and I codesigned—I would show off by hitting shots from 250 yards out into the back of dump trucks as they were moving dirt. It's the only time I tried to hit my ball into the sand on purpose. Hit at stuff like that, and landing a ball on the green near the pin is nothing."

Roundup

Any golfer can get practice balls out of a bucket; the really good ones can fill the bucket back up . . . from 100, 150, or 200 yards away. Count out 25 balls, pick a target, and see how many balls you can round up inside a 10-yard radius. Twenty-five balls makes it easy to keep track of what percentage of shots you make or miss; simply multiply your total by four.

Play by yourself and try to improve with every series of balls. Play with a friend, and wager $5 on the match and kick in a quarter a ball for the difference in scores, to sweeten the pot. Play with different clubs to keep the game fresh or with different radiuses around the target to make the game more or less challenging.

Doctor Divot

Whenever possible, practice your game on grass, not driving-range mats. This may not always be a convenient or accessible option. Golf ranges, literally, take a beating, and mats are much more cost effective than turf. But when you can, get on the grass to do it.

"There is no substitute for grass," says Chi Chi. "*The game is in the grass.* I never saw a golf course with plastic grass on it in my life. So why would you practice on it? Basketball players work out on the same kind of court they play on for games. They don't practice on turf, then go inside on the wood. I don't like baseball or anything on artificial turf. You must be able to feel your spikes in the ground and club, hitting earth."

Practicing on grass also allows you to study your divots. Their depth and direction reveal much about the golf swing. Watch a pro, and he or she will skillfully cut out a perfect square or rectangle with his or her divots, one after another side by side, studying each for clues about the swing that produced it. Although you may not be able to carve a cameo into the ground, you, too, can learn a lot about your game from the holes you leave behind.

"Divots should be small, thin rectangles," says Chi Chi, "leaving behind a same-size cut in the turf pointed straight at the target. If they are too deep, the angle of your swing coming into the ball is too deep. Too big, and you are putting too much of your power into the ground and not into the ball. Take a divot behind the ball, and your ball position is incorrect, your head moved, or any number of bad things happened on the downswing. A divot pointing left means your swing is coming outside in; if it points to the right the swing is inside out. Divots deeper on one side than on the other could mean the lie of your clubs is wrong. Watch your divots or have a pro look at them. Divots are golf's version of footprints—track them and you will know what animal you are up against."

Matted Down

If you must hit on mats, focus on accelerating through the ball. The mats do not give, and if you slow the club head down at all, the rubber will grab it and force a bad shot. You also want to make sure you hit the ball first, even pick it a tad, so that the club doesn't bounce on the mat and then into the ball, resulting in a kind of false ball flight. Where a ball hit fat on grass might go only 20 to 55 yards on a mat, the club can bounce into the ball and hit it four or five times farther. "But mats aren't all bad," says Chi Chi. "That's all I hit off of when I was in the army."

Mats do give a golfer the benefit of a good lie every time, provided they're not allowed to wear down, which can help with a beginner's confidence. Putting a high handicapper on a grass driving range that's bare down to the dirt can be detrimental.

Whiffle Ball

They're inexpensive and they're not that heavy; still Whiffle balls have gone out of style a bit in recent years. The growth of golf has led to a building boom of both courses and practice ranges, leaving lots of those hollow and hole-filled little balls on the shelves of sporting goods stores everywhere. . . . Buy some.

Whiffle Ball is a game you can make up on your own and play at home. Design a golf course around the house. Trees make excellent pins. Driveways, sidewalks, or any other asphalt surface make a fine substitute for water hazards. The flower beds are almost always considered OB. Be inventive.

On after-dinner walks, take a Whiffle ball and club, and see how many swings it takes to get to the end of the street and back. Because the balls won't break anything, work on various ball trajectories by trying to hit at first-floor or second-floor windows. Lob one onto the roof if you have the loft. Whiffle balls are excellent training aids because of their light weight. Any slice or hook spin will show itself immediately. Hit a Whiffle ball straight and the real ones will fly just as true. Best of all, you have no drive time to the course, no bite to the wallet, and no real physical exertion to retrieve them.

Head Games: Eliminating Intimidation

One of the most nerve-racking parts of golf is getting grouped with a better player than yourself. Golfers can have their day ruined before the first ball is struck out of fear of embarrassment or dread about not being able to keep up.

Fear not. Generally, you will find golfers with a higher skill level sympathetic; after all, they were beginners at some point, too, and endured the same struggles. Pay attention and you can learn a lot by watching how good players swing and manage their way around a course. Quiz them on their thoughts about a particular shot that gives you trouble. Listen to a tip or two, but be careful not to try 73 suggestions at one time on one hole.

Instead of being intimidated by a good player, think of it as Chi Chi Rodriguez did when he was first starting out on the pro golf circuit—a golden opportunity. "Until Tiger Woods came along, Sam Snead was the best player I ever saw. Sam won more than 100 tournaments, even though he only gets credit for 81.

"When I first started out on tour, I tried to play with Mr. Snead as often as possible. A great man, Sam Snead, and he always took my game. We would play a five-dollar Nassau four ways. Five on the front, five on the back, and a five doubled on the 18, for a total of 20 bucks.

"I used to lose almost every time. Every time! Guys would say, 'Chi Chi, how come you let Sam hustle you every week?' Hustle? How much does it cost for a lesson—$50 or $100? The lesson lasts what, for a half hour or an hour? I got to play and learn from Sam Snead, the greatest golfer I know, for four hours almost every week, and it only cost me $20. Who got hustled?"

Epilogue

Eighteen holes. Eighteen dollars.

Spend an entire day with Chi Chi Rodriguez, speak with him at length on the phone, or make an extensive study of his life—all of which I have done over the past 10 months—and you learn that the motivation and the method for his career success, the bedrock and slab forming the foundation for his philosophy on life, can be reduced simply to 18 holes and 18 dollars.

Eighteen holes, a round of golf, for Chi Chi Rodriguez it's a day at the office, for the gallery following him it's an afternoon of fun and laughs, four hours of splendid shots and a shag-bag full of one-liners. "Golf, to me," says Chi Chi, "is show business. You're on a beautiful outdoor stage—give people a show. So many people work hard but don't enjoy their work. I try to give them something to smile about when they come to watch us play. I like making people laugh."

When Chi Chi first arrived on Tour the fans were laughing, but not all of his fellow pros found the clowning as funny. His antics and animation earned him the nickname

Four Stroke Penalty from the other pros who believed their scores soared by four with Chi Chi as a partner. "I was different," recalls Chi Chi, "but it's not a sin to be yourself. That is why the criticism hurt, because I was just being Chi Chi Rodriguez. I wasn't trying to bother the other guys. When I made a good shot or sank a birdie putt I was happy and I liked to show it. I still do. Listen, without the galleries there wouldn't even be a Tour, right? That's why I always want to give the gallery something for their money."

Not to worry. The paying crowd never complains when Chi Chi's game is the main attraction. What separates Chi Chi from most other pros is that while he's entertaining he's also making an excellent living at the same time. His 30 combined wins and 30 plus years on the regular and Senior PGA Tours have been worth more than $8.5 million in prize money. His endorsement deals, popular clinics, and speaking engagements have netted him millions more. There are homes for himself and his family, a private jet, and, most importantly, even more money to give to others in need.

"I would rather live rich and die poor," Chi Chi says without the slightest hint of greed, "than die rich and live poor. You have to give. Takers eat well. Givers sleep well. I get in bed, say my prayer, close my eyes, and I am out.

"When you enjoy life, share with others, and have peace of mind, you have everything. I was a mental millionaire long before my bank account caught up."

It's a life that exceeds even the biggest dreams of the small barefoot boy who pushed a plow through a sugar cane field under the hot Puerto Rican sun for $1 a day. The fortune, however, has not made Chi Chi forget his humble, poverty-stricken beginnings; on the contrary, it's only served to remind him of how far he's come. "A poor man doesn't have anything to prove," Chi Chi explains. "A rich man has to prove himself all the time. I want to prove I'm worthy of what I am worth in the bank. Remembering the hard times of my childhood does that. Those hard times also have helped me in ways that are hard to describe. I always knew that what other people had—material things—I could eventually get. And what I had—hunger and desire born of true hardship—they could never get. I didn't think of being poor as a disadvantage; I thought it was lucky because it made me a stronger person."

It is why, no matter the amount in his checkbook, Chi Chi has never been greedy or forgotten the value of $18.

The modest sum of $18 represents the most money Chi Chi's father ever earned in a week. It was from his father, a man he admired and longed to impress, that Chi Chi learned, among other things, respect and benevolence.

"My father worked very, very hard, 12 or 14 exhausting hours a day. At one time in his life," says Chi Chi, "he had a heart attack and got fired from his job. Still, as poor as we were, he did his best to always provide. If he did not have enough food for the entire family, he made sure to feed all of us children first and swallowed the hunger himself.

"And no matter how hungry he was, he always shared with people poorer than ourselves. If my father saw any starving kid, he'd give him his food too. He would tell us, 'He needs it more than me.'

"One time my father caught a man out back of where we lived (a tin-roofed shack) who claimed he was hiding to get out of the rain. Well, there were only stars in the sky and my father said to this man, 'Give me your machete.' He then went into the banana grove for a few minutes and returned with a large bunch of bananas and gave them to the man and said to him, 'Next time you need food, you come through the front door and ask.' "

It is from these small snapshots of childhood that Chi Chi grew to learn life's larger picture. "You see, back then," says Chi Chi, "it was an honorable thing to steal for your children. But the way my father handled that man was one of the biggest influences in my life. He taught me how to give; even when you had next to nothing you could always share. Like the golf swing, giving is in my genes. And though he was an adult my father always had his eyes open to the child."

When it comes to helping children and giving, Chi Chi Rodriguez inherited his father's gift.

"I think I love kids so much because I was never a kid myself. When you are very poor and have to go to work so early in life to help your family, it's hard to really have a childhood. And it's a lot harder to be a kid these days, period.

"Most politicians don't do anything for kids because the kids can't vote. It's sad, they always say they are worried about the future generation. So using my name, we started a foundation to help troubled kids, using golf to get them going in a positive direction."

The Chi Chi Rodriguez Youth Foundation was founded in Clearwater, Florida, in 1979. An organization that began as an autograph request by former pro Bill Hayes, who was working as an assistant warden at a detention center, turned into a full-fledged free golf clinic the following day and over dinner that evening turned into a plan for a foundation.

Chi Chi, not as well heeled at the time, gave Hayes $1,000 seed money, then called on his friends and corporate contacts to help put the foundation on firm financial footing. Since that time Chi Chi's contributed and helped raise millions of dollars for a program that now helps upward of 650 troubled or abused kids a year.

"They learn through golf and affection," says Chi Chi. "Math in the pro shop. Agronomy from the greenskeeper. It's all golf related. We teach through the best traditions of the game: honor, respect, and dignity. What we don't do is talk to them like a drill sergeant. I was in the army and that is fine for the army. Kids you need to talk to like kids and when they speak you have to be a kid, too. For a lot of students, this is the first time anyone has even treated them decent or shown them they care."

Not content merely to give his money and lend his name to the project, Chi Chi makes several visits to the Foundation's public school every year: meeting the kids, checking their progress, encouraging them to stay on task with school, even getting phone numbers so he can check up on them while he is on the road. Chi Chi always manages to find time in his hectic weekly schedule to talk some of his students. Kids are also given adult golfers to play with and talk to after their rounds in an effort to build relationships with quality role models. "The goal isn't to simply teach them to make money," Chi Chi explains. "The goal is to teach them to make something out of themselves and their lives. When I was a kid the biggest present I ever got was a marble and I want to give kids so much more than that."

The result has been a model program that has helped turn a lot of lives in the right direction. "And when we started," says Chi Chi, "I was thinking it would be great if we could just help a few.

"All the trophies I won in golf helped feed my ego, but these kids, they feed my heart. They call me Uncle Chi Chi. All of them, black, white, hispanic, younger kids, and the teenagers. Uncle Chi Chi, that is what they call me.

"When money, wisdom, and compassion are used as tools instead of weapons," says Chi Chi, "wonderful things can be built and lives can be changed."

Isn't it amazing the amount of inspiration you can buy for $18?

Isn't it fantastic the amount of impact a man can make over 18 holes?

Donations to the The Chi Chi Rodriguez Youth Foundation may be made by writing or calling:

The Chi Chi Rodriguez Youth Foundation
3030 North McMullen Booth Road
Clearwater, FL 33761
Phone 727-726-8829; Fax 727-726-8553
Email: info@chichi.org

Index

About the Authors

One of the most popular players in the history of golf, **Chi Chi Rodriguez** has more than 40 years of experience as a professional golfer. He has 30 official career victories on the PGA and Senior PGA Tours and has won countless games against all competition.

Known best for his charm as an entertainer, Rodriguez is a member of the Senior PGA Tour and is a World Golf Hall of Fame inductee. Rodriguez is also the founder and chairman of the Chi Chi Rodriguez Youth Foundation in Clearwater, Florida. The Foundation uses golf to encourage inner-city youths to succeed in life.

Through his golf career and his humanitarian work, Rodriguez has amassed countless awards including the Ambassador of Golf Award from the Akron Golf Charities, the Salvation Army Gold Crest Award, the Hispanic Achievement Award, the Civilian Meritorious Service Medal, and an honorary doctor of human letters degree from Georgetown College. Rodriguez lives in Dorado, Puerto Rico.

John Anderson serves as co-anchor of ESPN SportsCenter. He joined ESPN in June 1999 as an ESPNEWS anchor after spending nine years as a sports anchor for local stations in Tulsa and Phoenix.

Anderson won the Outstanding Sports Feature Reporting Award in 1994 and 1995 presented by the Oklahoma chapter of the Society of Professional Journalists. In 1997, he received the Associated Press television award in Arizona for outstanding performance in broadcast journalism.

Anderson earned his journalism degree from the University of Missouri. He lives in Southington, Connecticut.